If The Shoe Fits

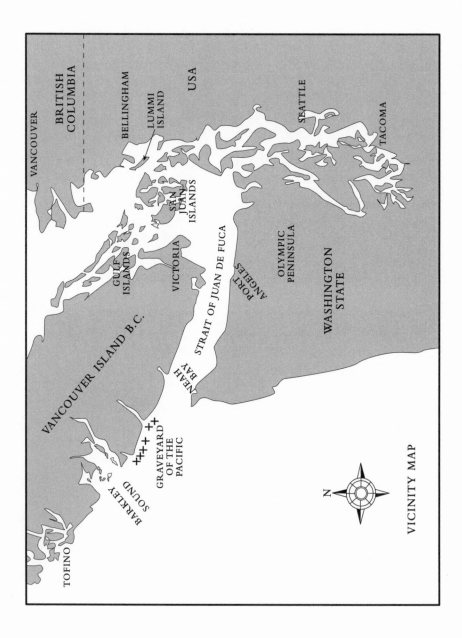

VICINITY MAP

If The Shoe Fits

The Adventures of a
Reluctant Boatfrau

RAE ELLEN LEE

SHERIDAN HOUSE

First published 2001 by
Sheridan House Inc.
145 Palisade Street
Dobbs Ferry, NY 10522

Library of Congress Cataloging-in-Publication Data

Lee, Rae Ellen
   If the shoe fits: the adventures of a reluctant boatfrau/
   Rae Ellen Lee.
     p. cm.
   ISBN 1-57409-118-2 (alk.paper)
   1. Lee, Rae Ellen. 2. Women sailors—United States—
   Biography. 3. Boats and boating. I. Title.

   GV810.92.L44 A3 2001
   797.1'24'092—dc21
   [B]   00-053346

Edited by Janine Simon
Designed by Jeremiah B. Lighter

Printed in the United States of America

ISBN 1-57409-118-2

This book is dedicated to Tom Lee, who said to me, "I'll feed you and give you something to write about," and kept his promise.

ACKNOWLEDGMENTS

I am indebted to fellow writing group members Kit Axelson (and John), Ann Barcomb, Scott Brown, Susan Davis Brown, Cary Deringer, Sue Erickson, Joan Kraft, Paul Miranda, Sally Siliasson, Colleen Schwartz, Lou Vanderwoude, and Denyse Wilson for all their helpful critiques. Robin Holbert and Jan Willing carefully reviewed the entire manuscript and made suggestions that saved me from considerable embarrassment. Sarah Naomi Lee, my teenaged reader, offered especially astute advice. Thanks to Carol Hasse of Port Townsend Sails for the encouragement and the chapter title As THE SHOE Sails. My Priest River contingent indulged me with love, support and fresh raspberries—thank you, always, Sherry Gohr, Penny Bews, and Kathryn Hamshar. I'm especially grateful to Lisa White for sharing tears and laughter and the chapter title, I Only Cuss When I'm Sailing, and to Mark White and Jeff Hubbard for their humor and for being there. Special thanks to Wes Koenig, sailboat broker and human extraordinaire, and to Roger Van Dyken, Mr. San Juan Sailing, for stories and inspiration. Thanks to Canadian writers Nancy Lee and Kevin Patterson for sound advice and to Wyoming writer, Ron Franscell, for his mentoring about getting published. Niki Stilwell, my South African friend, thank you for cheering me on and for the stimulating talks about sailing and life. I'm grateful to Linda Rae Ridihalgh, editor at Living Aboard Magazine, for providing the title If THE SHOE Fits and for putting wind in my sails by publishing several of my stories. A special thank to Jon Lopez for his expert photography.

And Tom, thanks from the bottom of my heart for the Terror of the High Seas Writing Grant, for the technical support that saved me from killing my computer, and for providing the ballast that kept me afloat.

CONTENTS

1

SIGHTINGS—A PROLOGUE

Sometimes you only see what you're looking for when you're lost or in the dark, or you see one thing and think it is something else entirely.

I'm now 53, and I've been single most of my adult life. Illusive sightings have been all too frequent; being endowed with a phenomenon called *adaptive optics*, I often saw desirable traits in potential mates—traits that couldn't be found upon closer inspection.

During my single years I desperately wanted to be happily married, victim as I was of a childhood in the fifties where *Father Knows Best* represented the ultimate in marriage and family. I would be in a family like that some day, as soon as I found my very own husband. When scouting for a mate, I had just a few criteria: the man had to dance, have a sense of humor, like books, and enjoy the outdoors. Oh, and he had to make eye contact. In fact, if a guy made eye contact with me I considered us engaged. At these times, when I believed with all my heart that I'd tracked down a likely candidate, he'd disappear in a flash—just like the mountain lion I thought I saw one day in the woods. If I did actually succeed in catching a man, I'd usually discover he wasn't a keeper.

Married men pretended to be single. One married man, much older than I was (elderly is more like it), kept offering me new fifty dollar bills in hopes of getting at least an occasional feel. I finally took one, a fifty that is, giving the man a wink as I walked away. Then I drove to a hardware store, bought two gallons of paint, went home and painted my living room while listening to the Beatles' song, *Can't Buy Me Love*. Other bottom feeders accosted me as well. Don't mis-

understand. I'm quite average looking. I blend in with my environment much like a moth whose markings resemble the bark of her favorite tree.

I began to think Mom was right when she said, "Men! They fool
you by walking upright."

Then there were those two brief marriages, after which I re-
claimed my birth name. Dozens of failed relationships followed,
some with men I hardly knew. I finally gave up the idea that I was
marriage material and decided never to remarry. In my late thirties I
put myself through college. When I graduated, the U.S. Forest Service hired me as a landscape architect. Now, if you're interested in
geezers, the Forest Service is an agency of unusual species richness.
Some of them, especially those in the earlier stages of achieving
geezer status, can be quite charming. I did have several wonderful
female friends, most of them single and all of them characters of the
independent, outspoken variety. We hiked, skied, talked about good
books, went to art galleries, and, yes, talked a lot about men.

After all that, after I'd concluded that I simply wasn't marriage
material—here I am, married.

I first spotted Tom one evening in December 1992, at a country
and western dance class in Helena, Montana. I'd been going to the
class with a man whose girlfriend kept showing up and making a
scene, so I told him he should take dance lessons with her. A few
weeks later, after I'd worked up enough courage to go back to the
class, I went alone. The first hour of class was line dancing—something you do solo—but for the second part of the lesson you needed
to be half of a couple.

Mary, a woman who had thought to bring a partner, said, "You
should go over and ask Tom Lee to dance. He's a good dancer, and
he's real nice."

I glanced over at him—tall, handsome, silver haired, distinguished looking, and obviously brilliant. I shook my head. Quite
frankly, I'm more comfortable with short, nerdy guys. "Handsome
men are nothing but trouble," Mom had also said. But I love to

dance, and the music was beginning . . . *some girls don't like boys like me, aw . . . but some girls do* . . . A nice slow swing.

"Go ahead," Mary said, giving me a push.

So I trotted across the dance floor, stood panting like a puppy in front of this gorgeous man, and said, "Will you dance with me?"

"Well, sure." Smiling, he took my hand, led me onto the dance floor, made good eye contact with his Big Sky eyes, and said, "I'm Tom. What's your name?"

I was a goner. We laughed and tripped through the lesson. When I couldn't get a swing step right he accused me of being afraid to bump into his chest, so just to disprove his comment I hugged him goodbye. Since he lived in Bigfork, three-and-a-half hours north of Helena, I didn't expect to see him again. Then he said, "If you ski, come on up and I'll show you around Big Mountain." Just a few weeks later, my truck, Streak, and I were on the road for Bigfork.

If you believe with all your heart that you have seen something, does it qualify as a sighting?

During our courtship, Tom and I took many hikes in the woods. Tom longed to see wolves, so I arranged an April weekend at a cabin along the North Fork of the Flathead River, home of the North Fork wolf pack. The Forest Service rental cabin faced east, overlooking the Flathead River and miles of meadow. Beyond, above a dark blue line of conifers, the white peaks of Glacier National Park glowed in the late afternoon light. As we left the cabin with our binoculars for a hike, the hard, crusty snow crunched under our boots. We saw a few deer and birds, but the wolves must have heard us coming and cleared out.

Down in the meadow the snow was wet and my light hiking boots quickly became soaked. My cold feet ached. If my toes didn't get warm soon I'd surely lose them, but I didn't want to complain or cut short our hike. We ambled slowly back up the hill and returned to the cabin. When Tom discovered how cold my feet were, he removed my wet boots and socks and held my icy feet on his bare chest, warm as a wood stove. At exactly that moment I decided to marry him.

One day several years ago, my truck, Streak, and I became hopelessly lost on a muddy ridge-top logging road somewhere west of Priest Lake, Idaho. While driving through an old clear-cut I became enveloped in a cloud of Monarch butterflies, fluttering all around me. All I could see was a swirl of orange effervescence. I could hardly see the road, or maybe I wasn't even on a road. Maybe I had driven over the edge and entered heaven in an orange halo. The butterflies escorted me for several minutes before I found myself on the other side of their magic, on a muddy road in a clear-cut.

Much of my courtship with Tom was like driving while under the influence of butterflies. This sensitive, warm, affectionate man seemed interested in many of my favorite things. He talked and, even better, he listened. Oh, we had our differences. The word Republican immediately conjured a stop sign in my head—but, during his two terms as a legislator, Tom had introduced a statewide land planning bill, music to the ears of any landscape architect. He liked books but only read non-fiction, and instead of movies he watched documentaries. Our biggest difference, however, proved to be that he was deeply religious while I was much more of a naturalist with a Unitarian view of things—be considerate of others and remember to recycle.

A justice of the peace named Wally married us on September 1, 1993. Wally, an acquaintance of Tom during his years in politics, asked us one at a time if we agreed to conduct ourselves in specific, positive ways throughout our marriage. We each eagerly said, "Yes." My son, Jeff, 23 at the time, served as witness, best man and ring bearer at this lovely, straightforward ceremony. After Tom, Jeff and I ate lunch at The Windbag Saloon on Helena's Last Chance Gulch, Tom and I headed south to the Jarbidge Wilderness of Northern Nevada for a backpacking honeymoon.

I'm a careful person. For years I would not go hiking in grizzly country. When I'd see a bright red sign at a trailhead that blared, *You are entering grizzly country*, I usually turned around and ran back to my truck. The Jarbidge Wilderness had no grizzlies, but after our honeymoon, after we returned home to reality, Tom and I found that it was grizzly country at our house. Even the butterflies were gone. The courtship and honeymoon had been one thing; life on a daily basis was something else entirely. If we discovered an area of our marriage where a problem didn't already exist, we'd invent one. Had we, as a couple, been only an optical illusion? Would this marriage, too, become a catch-and-release statistic?

Although we decided to take the road less traveled and stay married, we could never have imagined the schemes we'd devise and the curious plots and places in which we'd find ourselves, during our search for those missing butterflies.

2

A NOVEL IDEA

"Well, where is she, anyway?" Tom asked, glancing into yet another hospital room. "She's supposed to be in Room 215."

Tom's mother, Alta, a high-spirited lady approaching 80, was healthy, except she needed a new heart valve.

"She probably met some old duffer in the waiting room and ran off with him to a Caribbean island," I suggested.

"Yeah, probably with a geezer whose big dream in life was to fix up an old sailboat and sail it around the world. Might have been his last chance," Tom added.

"Maybe Alta wanted to try snorkeling while she still could," I said, imposing a long-submerged dream of mine into the plot.

Tom and I finally found Alta waiting in a room to see the anesthesiologist. The next day she sailed through her surgery and became the proud new owner of a pig valve. Sometimes we said "oink, oink" to her instead of "hi" or "hello." For fifty-somethings, we don't always act too mature.

But where had this sailboat idea come from? Tom was a person who loved to backpack and take close-up photos of two bugs *doing it* on some alpine floral wonder up on a mountain top. You sure don't get to know a man until you marry him. Tom had only once mentioned sailing a scow when he was a kid in Minnesota. And I'd only ever seen sailboats off in the distance. One August in the early 1980s, my son, Jeff, and I drove 500 miles to the San Juan Islands with our bicycles hanging off my VW beetle. When we arrived at Lopez Island, Jeff, age 10 at the time, said disgustedly, "There's hills here." So we put the bikes back on the car, drove around the island and headed back home. It was on this outing that I caught a glimpse of a few sailboats. Until then, sailboats existed in my brain cells at about the same level of knowing as, say, seagulls.

After Tom and I returned home from the hospital in Missoula, the story we'd invented about the two senior citizens who run off to the Caribbean took on a life of its own and wouldn't leave us alone. Ideas for the novel popped up at odd times. Tom would stop what he was doing and say, "How about this? The old guy's a retired cherry orchardist from Bigfork, a widower in his late sixties who spends his spare time watching sailboats on Flathead Lake wondering if this is all there is to life. Maybe he has a near death experience of some sort in the hospital and it scares him enough to *do* something with his life."

"Ethel has terrible migraines," I said, cutting up carrots for stew. "And she was at the hospital for tests (by now we had changed Alta's name to protect her innocence). Let's say she's a widow from Trout Creek. The only reason she has enough nerve to run off with this guy, why not call him Hollis, is because she'd attended a *Wild Woman* discussion group."

Driving home from the hardware store one Saturday, Tom said, "They go to the U.S. Virgin Islands, where they don't need passports."

"Hollis knows he could kick the bucket any minute," I said, "so at the hospital he tells Ethel he has a Visa card just burning a hole in his wallet, and says, 'Let's go, woman.'"

Story ideas flew back and forth. We talked about the characters as if they were real, as if they were our friends. We called our story idea, *Hollis and the Wild Woman*.

So, now I'll tell you about our *own* story—the one we were actually living when we conceived the idea for our novel. Tom and I didn't live together except on weekends. He worked in Kalispell as a precision machinist and lived in Bigfork during the week. I lived in Rimini, an old mining town near the Continental Divide, and worked in Helena as a landscape architect for the U.S. Forest Service. Tom is very smart and can do many kinds of work, but it was easier to find a tropical beach in Helena than it was for him to find a good job. His political science degree and years of experience as a commercial pilot, DEA agent, farmer, seminary student, furniture builder, machinist, and legislator didn't seem to qualify him for any job in Helena, not even the new dog catcher position that opened up. So every weekend he commuted about 180 miles and nearly four hours each direction on the Swan Highway, so named because it follows along the west side of the Swan Range. The highway is narrow and scenic and has a high accident rate. Every Friday evening Tom arrived at the renovation project I called home—an old brothel in Rimini.

The year before I met Tom, I'd bought the place for the price of a used car and then paid a lot of money to a local carpenter who saved the old two-story building from collapsing by installing the following items: new rafters, new roof, new second floor joists and floor, new foundation, and new first floor joists and floor. Since it wasn't possible for me to take out a construction loan on a pile of weathered boards, on a piece of land with no title insurance, I had to take out numerous signature loans. These loans dried up my cash flow to the extent that I could no longer keep my apartment in Helena. In June 1993, a few months before Tom and I married, I moved into the brothel. By that time the carpenter had made the building structurally sound, but the interior was unfinished. Tom and I never called the place a house—always *the brothel*.

It's probably just as well that Tom and I didn't live together, because for all the fun we sometimes had hiking and skiing, we sure didn't get along very well on weekends. We spent a lot of time with a marriage counselor we called *Bedrock*, because that's where he took us, back to the core where our little inner children fought together on the playground we now called our marriage. The prognosis was that our dysfunctions were incompatible; however, with hard work and a lot of humor, which we had, we just might make it. So we talked and cried and laughed when we could as we cut, sanded and nailed boards in an effort to finish the brothel. Maybe we made up the story of *Hollis and the Wild Woman* for some relief from the relentless discussions about *us* and our problems.

The brothel and the two other log buildings on the land were served by an outhouse. In fact, we had no plumbing at all. Tom and I drove about ten miles to get water from a spring next to Highway 12 at MacDonald Pass. In summer, after filling our gallon jugs at the spring, we hiked nearby on the Continental Divide National Scenic Trail. When we made a water run in winter we took along our cross-country skis. At least with no running water at the brothel, we didn't have to worry about the pipes freezing.

It was cold in Rimini. In fact, it was a lot like Siberia. In the evenings we sometimes read aloud from the lively, funny book, *Tent Life in Siberia*, written by George Kennan about his 1860's effort to find a telegraph route between America and Europe via Siberia. George and his team met many Koraks, both settled and nomadic inhabitants of Siberia, and stayed with them in their tents and yurts during their travels across the tundra. We began to call ourselves Korak Construction Company, just for grins, using the term Korak to mean people like us who lived in crudely built, spartan, sometimes untidy surroundings.

This lifestyle was not new to me, having grown up on a stump ranch. Whenever I brag about this aspect of my childhood, people always ask, "What in the world is a stump ranch?" Well, it's a piece of land that's been clear-cut. After the slash is burned, the stumps turn black, the grass grows back a bright green, and the land is sold for a cheap price. This practice still occurs in North Idaho. We owned 80 acres but lived in the valley where most of the stumps grazed—if you blurred your eyes they resembled a herd of black angus cattle. Our particular valley had once been an ancient oxbow of the Priest River. Conifer-covered hills, the former river banks, protected us from wind on three sides. Pockets of river clay in the hillsides gave my sisters and me hours of play, shaping and drying clay items. In early spring, ponds formed in the lowest areas of the valley and produced polliwogs to play with, and in early summer the entire valley was carpeted with wild strawberries. For years we tracked clay and dirt onto the plywood floors of the house my dad built. And it's because of this stump ranch heritage that I wore the Korak tribute so easily. Tom, on the other hand, was new to this rustic barn board and plywood culture.

While the real Koraks in *Tent Life* had their dogs to keep them company around the fire, I had my cats. When I'd don my hides and furs to trek to the outhouse, my old cat, Fatty, followed me, opened the door with his big paw, jumped up onto the adjacent seat, walked onto my lap and talked to me. He made funny little meows that sounded almost like words. When I'd say something back to him, like "You be careful when you jump up here or you might fall into the hole," he'd tilt his head and meow in such a way that I knew, without question, that he thought I was the most interesting conversationalist he'd ever heard, and he wanted to hear more. Fatty was more fun to talk with than many humans I knew, and I'm not the only one who noticed his outstanding personality. Several friends mentioned it, and Tom, although he's allergic to cats, reported having some very intelligent discussions with Fatty in the outhouse.

During the week, when Tom was in Bigfork, both Fatty and my crippled cat, Spook, stayed indoors with me at night in the brothel. The three of us sat around the wood stove together in the evenings, shooting the breeze. Spook listened attentively as Fatty and I conversed. When it came time for me to go upstairs to bed the cats hopped up the stairs behind me, watched as I crawled under the down comforter, then climbed on the bed and curled up next to me. As we drifted off to sleep, we lay in the dark listening to the neighbor's dogs bark and the slabs of snow calving off the new metal roof.

During the time I lived in the brothel, I had many strange dreams. In one dream, two men were shooting it out in my backyard by the creek as I watched from the upstairs window. On a walk one evening shortly after this dream, I saw the carpenter who did most of the basic structural work on my building. As a hobby he had researched the history of Rimini, and he told me my place had been one of the seventeen brothels in the Rimini mining district. When I mentioned my dream his eyes got real big and he said, "A murder like that really happened here at the turn of the century."

While Tom and I worked weekends to finish the old place, we continued to kick around the story of *Hollis and the Wild Woman.* We finally put down the saws and hammers, cleaned the sawdust off the computer and began to write out a story line. After numerous error messages, like *abort, retry, fail,* which at the time reminded us too much of our lives, we completed an outline and character descriptions. We did this based on instructions in a used book on how to write a novel. When I read the story line to my writing group they loved it, but one woman said, "Well! You can't write about the Virgin Islands if you haven't even been there." She, of course, had been there, and she was right. We would just have to take a research trip to the islands.

3

TWO KORAKS IN PARADISE

Historic buildings on Ten Mile Creek in Rimini, Montana. Pre-1900 log cabin and shop plus turn-of-the century brothel, recently reno-vated for rustic living. Must see. Only $60,000.

Shortly after we list the brothel with a realtor I dream that Robert Redford buys it, and that I continue to live in the building as a ghost. In my dream he has a dog like Benji, and he takes the dog everywhere he goes in his four-wheel-drive vehicle.

Instead of Robert Redford, a middle-aged bachelor from Arkansas spots the *For Sale* sign and visits the brothel. He returns several times, each time with different friends and always with a tape measure.

"Have to make sure my trophy elk head will fit in here," he says, measuring the doorways and ceiling height. "Looks like it'll squeeze through the door. Do you mind if I bring it over to make sure?"

He returns with a friend and together they muscle the creature through the front door and hang it on the wall. The antlers nearly touch both the floor and the ceiling, and the head projects about five feet into the room. Our potential buyer smiles and signs the buy-sell agreement. But complications often surround titles to mining claim properties. In our case the title search reveals that since 1904 a guy named John H. Murphy has owned one-quarter of the land under the brothel, as well as land belonging to several neighbors. We have to carry the contract with our buyer while an attorney prepares a quiet title action for us and half the residents of Rimini. What if an heir of Mr. Murphy's steps forward to claim his percentage? You might think it impossible, since Mr. Murphy had never paid taxes on the lots. But stranger things have happened in Rimini. This stressful little title transaction takes eight months.

In the meantime Tom and I buy a house in Helena. In early June 1996, exactly three years after I moved into the brothel, we transport all our belongings to Helena in 27 trips with pickup trucks and U-haul trailers. Our new home has running water and indoor plumbing. Things are looking up.

After we settle in our new abode, we resume discussion of our novel, and decide it's time to celebrate our move with a book research trip to the U.S. Virgin Islands. We sell an antique wood cookstove, find a Visa card with some room left on it, and make reservations for a Thanksgiving visit to St. John—one that coincides with a full moon.

The morning we board the Delta flight for Salt Lake City it is minus 10° F. Since we've arranged to camp at Cinnamon Bay on St. John we max out our luggage quota with all our camping gear. We could stay in a cottage on the beach for what our huge new tent cost, but you know Koraks—we don't like to be too comfortable. That evening when we land in St. Thomas it's 80° F, and moist as a sauna. We spend a buggy night in a motel with no air conditioning and the next morning catch a ferry to Cruz Bay on St. John. There we climb into an open-air taxi—a pickup truck with a canopy, bench seats, and calypso tunes blasting out of the cab. A few minutes later, after a hair-raising ride mostly on the left side of a narrow, steep, winding road we arrive at Cinnamon Bay, loosen our grips on the roll bar, haul ourselves and our bags out of the taxi, and find our campsite near the beach.

For ten days we stare, awestruck, at the turquoise water. The dark forms of magnificent frigate birds, once used by Polynesians as homing pigeons, flit overhead as we lounge on the beach in deep white sand.

One cloudy, 70° morning we see a ghost crab, or think we do. When we look a second time, it's gone. As Tom approaches the ocean, where we saw the movement, sure enough a ghost crab races out of the water toward his feet. When it spots him it frantically digs itself straight down into the moist sand, leaving only its black-tipped eye stalks visible. We watch the antics of the ghost crab for hours. The tiny white creature runs headlong into the surf and gets tumbled ashore, end over end. A few minutes later it runs like lightning a few yards up the beach, then buries itself again. Each new species we learn about, including this ghost crab, becomes our friend.

Every night, under the full moon, we're serenaded to sleep by breaking waves and odd jungle noises. A rain shower the second day adds new night sounds to the symphony—one like a rusty gate hinge, another like percussion with small, hardwood blocks. On a Caribbean island we had expected monkeys and parrots. At a naturalist's talk in the campground pavilion one evening, Tom asks, "What can you tell us about the night life?"

"You can find some reggae bars over in Cruz Bay," she replies.

"No, I mean the night sounds in the trees here," Tom says. Everyone laughs.

"Nearly all the night music is from tree frogs—very tiny ones, and an occasional insect."

In the middle of the night when one of us has to make a trek to the toilet, we wake up the other person and go to the bathhouse together. We then walk the short sandy distance through sea grapes to the edge of the ocean, where the beach, the sky and miles of water are illuminated by the full moon. We stand together, absorbing the magic, longing to carry it with us always. Afterwards, as we return along the path to our tent, we walk around a palm leaf shadow pattern cast by the moon onto the trail. It's a matter of respect. I can still close my eyes and see the image of that palm leaf.

Small lizards dart everywhere. The longest we see is about six inches. Near our campsite they crawl on every tree trunk and on an aloe vera plant, so large it seems jurassic, that arches over our picnic table. Sometimes, when a lizard on one of the aloe vera stems suddenly finds itself only inches away from one of us, it will pooch its neck way out to warn us away. They're perfectly harmless and quite charming, really, but we keep our tent zipped so they can't crawl around on us in the night.

Inland and across the main paved island road from the campground, we find Cinnamon Bay Trail, a shady history and nature loop trail that passes through an old sugar factory site. We explore the trail many times, and each time we step off the pavement into the clearing it's like we travel back in time a couple of centuries. Two crumbling stone walls, made with pieces of coral and stones of many colors, draw us into factory-sized rooms. The rooms are open to the sky, with steps leading nowhere and concrete vats filled with rain water. Leafy shadows and streaks of dark gray stains add to the lively patterns on the walls. Some walls have numerous lizards darting around on them and we wonder if they ever run into each other. We sit and sketch and swat mosquitoes.

Moist, rocky Cinnamon Bay Trail leads into a dense thicket of sansevieria, like the common house plant only more robust, and under a deeply shaded tangle of guava trees, turpentine trees with breast-like knobs on their trunks, strangler fig and mango trees. Some say the mango is the most delicious fruit in the world; unfortunately, the fruit is out of season now. Our favorite tree on the trail is the bayberry or myrtle tree, whose shiny, leathery leaves hold an aromatic oil once used in the production of bay rum for cologne. A common name for this special tree is wild cinnamon. When we crush a leaf it gives off a startling warm, tropical fragrance that I want in my life forever—along with the tree frogs, teal blue water, white coral beaches, calypso music, the tropical sun. I'm tired of being cold for six months every year. How lovely it would be to feel warm from the inside out, all year long. And I like how the humid air makes me feel full, moist, voluptuous—and just the right size.

Termites have built nests, huge as brown bears, up in the trees along the trail. We've read about these nests and their inhabitants. The termites build tube-like tunnels for themselves on the tree trunks and ground, and they never go outside these tunnels. If the termites want to go to a new place they simply build another tunnel, and if anything happens to a tunnel they immediately fix it. These termites never let themselves out into the world. That's what our life in Montana has felt like. We each have our own tunnels. I travel in my tunnels back and forth to work, the hardware store, and the health club. Tom follows his tunnels back and forth on weekends between Bigfork and Rimini, and between Bigfork and Kalispell, where he works during the week.

We rent snorkel gear at the campground and catch an open-air taxi to Salt Pond Bay, a protected cove on the east end of St. John. After Tom shows me how to put on the mask and snorkel tube, we kick our fins along a reef. In the underwater gardens below us we see corals that look like brains, others in the shape of pipes; plants that resemble whips and fans; black, thorny, round creatures; bright blue, flat-as-a-pancake fish; fish that bring to mind trumpets; and dozens of other bizarre shapes, movements and shadows. I feel an overwhelming need to point things out to Tom and to talk about what I'm seeing. This is impossible through the mouthpiece, but it doesn't stop me from grunting unintelligibly and pointing. Sublimely happy while suspended in the warm turquoise water, I watch the changing show beneath me and, listening to my breathing in and out the snorkel tube, I feel wondrously, vibrantly alive.

On a guided day-hike along the Reef Bay Trail we meet a wonderful local woman in her seventies, Miss Lily, and decide she, or someone like her, will be a character in our novel.

We meet a young couple, Don and Kim, who live on a 30-foot Alberg sailboat anchored in Coral Bay. They invite us aboard for a swordfish dinner. Don picks us up from shore at Coral Bay in an old Boston Whaler dinghy, the chewed-up survivor of five hurricanes. As the relic's tiny motor propels us toward their boat, the gunwales are only a couple of inches above the waterline. Don points out a beautiful sailboat that washed into the mangrove swamp during the most recent hurricane. Tom and I joke that Korak Construction Company should rescue it and give it a new life. At least at the time we both think it's a joke.

After reviewing the outline of our novel and the character sketches with Don and Kim, Don says, "Yes, a story like that could happen here on St. John, but you guys need to learn more about sailing."

All too soon it's time to say goodbye to our discoveries on St. John. We leave a clean camp at Cinnamon Bay and return to the island of St. Thomas. We cry on the ferry. One time at a movie theater I not only cried out loud, but actually howled. It was terribly embarrassing, and that's what happens to me on the ferry. Some people look away; others nod their understanding. Why haven't we been to the Caribbean before? And why do we have to leave now?

Between the time our flight leaves St. Thomas and stops in Atlanta, we make our decision. We're going to break out of our tunnels for good and rescue that sailboat in the mangrove swamp. We'll fix it up, and live at Coral Bay on St. John. We're not sure how, but we're going to do it.

When I was a first-year landscape architecture student at the University of Idaho in the late 1970s my first assignment was to design an island, then build a model of it using clay, pebbles, dried plants and paint. Knowing nothing at all about islands I spent days at the library researching these mysterious pieces of land surrounded by water. As an older student and a single parent, I was referred to as a non-traditional student. Jeff, 8 at the time, joined in the fun and built an island, too. We spent several evenings together at the design studio, and when we received our grades Jeff got an A and I got a B. During my island research I recorded an enchanting piece of text about islands (source unknown):

On an island you want mystery and romance, and strange animal noises in the night. You want to walk along, beside, and maybe cross over, that line that separates you from voodoo, the super-natural, the things you do not understand. You want the island to take control of your life in ways the mainland never could.

And that is exactly what the island of St. John does to us. It wrecks us like a hurricane. Back in Montana we completely lose interest in our jobs. While I have a good position with the Helena National Forest and enjoy my fellow employees, I've never been all that interested in designing clear-cuts, and I long to follow creative interests. To make things worse, the Forest Service, like other federal agencies, is undergoing serious financial problems. In an effort to save money I've already been zoned with a neighboring forest. I'm now trying to champion scenery management on two national forests totaling three million acres. The supervisor has developed a surplus list of employees and holds several family meetings about the need to reduce the workforce. Morale drops to an all-time low. During these meetings I hear many phrases I'll never forget, like "down-budgeting," and "recent accounting adjustments will be charged back to our office, causing an anti-deficiency." But my all time favorite is this, "We'll want to watch out what we do now or it might rear up and bite us in the future." It's a good time to think about leaving.

Tom fires our shrink. Not that our relationship is so harmonious after we return home, but he decides it's time for us to figure things out for ourselves. How will we manage without a referee?

Next Tom phones our new friends at Coral Bay and discovers that the sailboat we want to rescue from the mangrove swamp is mired in a messy divorce. No one can buy the boat. We toy with buying a classic old T.H. Butler wooden sailboat that *is* available on St. John, but after Tom asks around about the repairs needed to make the boat whole, we decide the cost in time and money, at least for us, would be too high.

With renewed determination Tom begins to call sailboat brokers in the Seattle area, where we *can* buy a sailboat. By his way of thinking, we'll simply sail ourselves back down to the Caribbean. In order for us to gain a little sailing experience Tom arranges a one-day charter in March with a company in Bellingham, Washington, two hours north of Seattle. I can't believe it. All my life I've heard about the gray, windy, rainy winter weather on the coast. And that is where I'll have my first sailing experience? I'm being hijacked by the characters we dreamed up for a novel. I long to talk to old Bedrock, but Tom's mind is made up.

"A shrink can't help us. We need to live together, preferably on a sailboat in the Caribbean. If Hollis and that wild woman, Ethel, can do it, so can we."

"Well," I sigh, "I just hope it doesn't rear up and bite us in the future."

4

GOING WITH THE FLOW

"A sailboat is often on *a tack*," Tom says. "Tacking. That's how you get to your destination if you're going into the wind. You can't just sail in a straight line."

"Oh!" Would this make more sense if I were fully awake? It's early, and Tom and I are sitting in bed drinking coffee. He's leafing through a book on sailing, trying to prepare me for our upcoming charter.

"For instance, say we decided to sail from our house to the Myrna Loy theater and the wind was coming toward us from the direction of the closet over there. We'd aim the bow of the boat toward Tom and Sandy's house across the street. When we got there we'd turn and aim the bow toward the purple mansion over on Broadway, turn again toward the Red Meadow bar, then back toward the theater. We'd tie up to a mooring buoy at the Myrna Loy theater and see what was playing."

"Got it. Sounds like a lot of work."

"And when we're going to the lee direction we're *falling off*."

"This doesn't mean *man overboard*, does it?"

The sailing lessons continue as we drive west a week later on Interstate 90 toward our appointment with a sailboat in Bellingham. I read from a how-to book about sailing: *A boat has no ropes—only sheets, lines, rodes, and halyards, as in haul the yard, or mainsail.*

We stop at Priest River, Idaho, to stay overnight with friends Sherry and Sam, who live north of town on a terrace of land overlooking the river. That evening, Tom and I walk with our friends the half mile to the Priest just as stars begin to appear above fir trees and field. We amble down the hill along a trace of road past an old orchard and an abandoned barn, down another bank to former pasture land, through the dusk and the distant honking of Canada geese. At the edge of the river we watch the flowing water, swollen with snow melt, then turn and walk back to the middle of the field with a purpose. There it is in the northwest sky—the Hale-Bopp comet—and to the east the beginnings of a total eclipse of the moon. As if this isn't enough, Mars is also showing off. We each take a turn eyeing the celestial phenomena through binoculars, isolating one miracle at a time, enlarging its brilliance. When we put aside the technology, the entire scene of sky and landscape speaks more powerfully than any one piece of it close up.

Tom and I leave our friends early the next morning. I continue to read aloud from the how-to book so we can discuss sailing terms, and I'll know what to expect. It still feels crazy to be going sailing this time of year, but Tom insists that we have to act on our sailboat idea immediately. "If we wait for everything to be perfect, we'll never do it." But March, and this my maiden voyage, the one to determine if I will like sailing? Certainly a first time in the Virgin Islands would have been preferable. But of course when we were there in November we didn't know how the trip would change our lives.

Keep Washington green signs dot the sides of the freeway as we drive across Eastern Washington's flat, dry, channeled scablands. I learned in college about how this oddly carved terrain was created. The term channeled scablands aptly describes the aftermath of a glacial lake breaking loose, near what is now Missoula, during one of the ice ages and splashing across this landscape. Besides dry channels, the flood caused depressions called potholes, and another sign says *Potholes State Park*. One joke is that Montana's potholes get dumped here after a highway repair job.

The studded snow tires on our four-wheel-drive Bronco click along in the sunny, 70° day. Maybe the weather will be nice for sailing after all.

That afternoon in Bellingham we roll past blooming rhododendrons and azaleas to the metallic tune of our snow tires, the hubs still locked in from the drive over slushy Snoqualmie Pass. The city has rows of bumps built into the streets to keep cars in their own lanes and Tom drives along on them for blocks without even noticing.

"Did we take a wrong turn and end up on the Oregon Trail?" I ask, glancing up from my map.

"Don't know. Feels like I'm back in Montana, driving the Swan Highway."

We find bookstores, coffee shops and libraries amid the green grass and flowering shrubs. The smell of buds and moist bark in the air holds a certain magic for us, with spring in Montana still two months away. Friendly people and brochures tell of free concerts, book readings, parks, and bicycle paths. The rain stops and starts so often I feel like a broccoli at the supermarket, frequently misted to stay fresh. But we're both smiling, our anticipation and hope for this new adventure escalating as we drive toward the harbor.

Using a map the charter company had sent, we find the harbor easily. Since navigation is such an important duty of a good first mate I've developed a special GPS, a Grunt and Point System. At the San Juan Sailing offices we pick up the key to our floating rental home and meet Wes, a sailboat broker Tom had talked with on the phone. Wes is an easy-going, friendly man our age, and even though he's originally from Billings, Montana, he knows all about sailboats and cruising. Tom has read numerous books on how to buy the right sailboat—a seaworthy, sea kindly boat. I listen patiently as they talk.

"My family, four of us, lived on a 35-foot boat," Wes says in his slow, easy way. "You'd probably want one around that size. Get one too big and you'll be working on it all the time. Cuts down on your sailing."

"From all my reading I've pretty well decided I want a full keel fiberglass boat with traditional lines," Tom says.

"Sounds good. But you know," Wes says, his head tilted to one side, "there's no perfect boat. It's a matter of tradeoffs. You need to look at a lot of different boats. It usually takes people 18 months to find the right boat. That's the industry average."

"We don't want it to take that long," Tom says.

"Well, here's the key to a boat we just listed. It's a low-maintenance, full keel aluminum boat. They're nearly indestructible. A good entry level boat that'll take you wherever you want to go, and it's junk-rigged. Raising and lowering the sails is a breeze. You'll find it three boats down from the boat you're staying on, across the dock. It's distinctive looking. You can't miss it."

Tom and I hold hands as we walk through the rain down the dock toward our chartered boat, each of us wearing an Army surplus rain jacket. Every time we wear these jackets the Velcro on Tom's sleeve gets stuck to the Velcro on my sleeve. It's another good system. For instance, if a car hits one of us crossing a street or one of us falls off this dock, the other one can break away easily.

We walk past the boat Wes wants us to check out. It's painted tan, and it is neither sleek nor beautiful.

"Looks utilitarian," I say, the emphasis evenly distributed on each syllable.

"U-til-*i-tar-i*-an. That's how you say it."

"I don't care. Looks like a tin can boat to me. And it's junk-rigged. We wouldn't have to sell all our stuff, just pull it along behind us on a barge. Now that's utilitarian." I love to have the last word, especially with someone who thinks he's so smart. Just the other day I got him on the word *archipelago*. He'd never even heard of it, and it's an important word to know if you're planning to sail in the Caribbean.

We climb aboard the 35-foot boat that will be our home for the next three nights and two days (we've arranged to stay on the boat the night before and the night after the charter). Tom unlocks the companionway hatch, removes the panels, and we descend into the cabin down three ladder-like steps.

"Wes said this boat has one of those modern fin keels. Wish we could have had a boat with a full keel," Tom says.

"It's nice in here. I like this boat," I say. The interior is modern, wide and roomy like a large camper-trailer, only this one moves just a little all the time. The motion is slight, but I feel that if I'm not prepared to maintain my balance I might topple over. I hang onto the overhead grab rails as I move about the cabin, my knees slightly flexed, like when I rode the transit buses in Washington, D.C. a long time ago.

"It's moving because of the tidal current," Tom says.

We unroll our sleeping bags on the V-berth at the front of the boat. Then Tom turns on the propane cook stove and I warm up our dinner, which we brought in a cooler. Since it's off-season, the boat's refrigerator isn't hooked up yet. Even so, it feels a lot like luxury camping.

After dinner we walk over to check out the tin can boat. Tom is already excited about it, thinks maybe it's the one for us. The boat is interesting looking, and the low maintenance and ease of handling the sails sounds good. Carrying our flashlight, we climb through the companionway and down into the all-aluminum boat.

"It smells dank, and the floor isn't level in places," I say. "And look, there's not one comfortable place to sit. Besides, it costs too much." In just a few seconds I've dashed all Tom's hopes. He's quiet, disappointed. I'm disappointed, too. It would have been fun to say we owned a junk-rigged, tin-can boat.

"I'm afraid if you don't like this boat you won't like any boat," he says.

We continue strolling up and down the docks, holding hands, ogling boats. The marina has hundreds of them at several different gates. On the outermost dock we see one of the biggest sailboats in the marina, WILD THING. Its mast is higher than all the others and it has a toilet seat welded onto the railing in back. Wes has said the boat wins races and the owner tells great stories about his sailing experiences. We return to our own boat to turn in early. Tomorrow is the big day.

The next morning after breakfast I read aloud from the how-to-sail book: *Sails are cut and sewed on the bias of soft, strong fabric, with an air foil shape and just a little give.*

"Oh, like beginner bras, like mine," I add. It's just a joke.

"I love you just the way you are," Tom says, putting his arm around me.

"I know you do, Mister Rogers."

Nathan, our charter captain, knocks on the boat about 10:00 a.m. "Hi. Ready to go sailing?"

It's cloudy, rainy and windy, and our skipper is too young. I could be his mother. He should have gray hair and a beard and wear a captain's hat, but, for better or worse, we'll be spending at least twenty-four hours with Nathan on this boat. He will be the captain and Tom says we have to do what he tells us. Nathan tosses his gear in the corner of a berth in our cabin.

"Wind is from the west," Nathan says. He turns on a radio to listen to the marine weather forecast and, even though the volume is up, I can't understand a word I'm hearing. It's like a foreign language. Not one of the romance languages, either, but maybe Russian or Serbo-Croatian. I do, however, hear three unsettling words: *small craft advisory*. "Well, looks like we won't be putting up the spinnaker today," Nathan says, then unrolls a map. "I'll quickly figure our course, in case we get into some fog and have to use the Loran and radar."

Fog? I hadn't thought of fog. Tom watches everything Nathan does, asks questions, then follows him up on deck to help remove blue canvas covers that are fastened to various pieces of equipment. Then our skipper starts the engine. The diesel fumes stink, but I hear no sputtering, no strange sounds. So far so good.

When we are unleashed from the slip, Nathan backs the boat out just like it's a car, then aims us in the direction of the harbor entrance past the rock jetty.

"See the red buoy to port, on your left side, and the green buoy on the right?" Nathan says to me. "We have to stay between those two markers. The rule is *red right returning*. Remember that." Okay, I think. I can handle it, whatever it means.

"Here, you take the helm while Tom and I put up the mainsail," Nathan says.

"What should I do?" I ask, gripping the huge wheel.

"Steer into the wind."

"Which direction?"

"Well, do you feel the wind on your face? That's one way to tell."

"But it feels like the wind is coming from everywhere."

"You can also look up at the arrow on top of the mast," he yells over the wind, as he steps onto the deck and strolls toward the mast. Tom is already up there, eagerly awaiting his instructions.

"Okay," I yell to Nathan's back as I crane my neck to see the top of the mast, fifty feet up. But the bill of my hat blocks my view. This isn't going well. I'm steering while they're both up on the deck, the boat bobbing like a cork. I don't like this one bit.

After raising the mainsail, Nathan returns to the cockpit and pulls a rope (oh, yes, a line or sheet) at the back of the boat in the cockpit and unfurls a sail called a jib at the front of the boat. Now we have two huge sails up. We're going along at five knots, according to the knotmeter. Seems a little fast but I hang onto the wheel with my hands at 10 o'clock and 2 o'clock, like I learned in defensive driving.

Now the crew is hungry, even though I'm not. Tom takes the helm while I go below to get the sandwiches I prepared earlier.

Soon Nathan and Tom are sitting casually against the sides of the cockpit eating their sandwiches, talking about sailing. Since I'm not hungry, I'm at the helm trying to steer a straight line. We're tipped sideways slightly, but it isn't too bad.

"I've read that cutter-rigged boats are the best way to go," Tom says.

How does he know all of this stuff?

Suddenly a gust of wind tips us way over sideways, until the railing is nearly in the water. "We're going over," I scream, abandoning the wheel to cringe in the uphill corner of the cockpit. I moan, whimper and hyperventilate all at the same time. Just like that. Nathan's expression is one of disbelief. He stops chewing and his mouth hangs open.

"It's okay, Baby," Tom says, jumping up to take the helm.

"Don't ever call me Baby again," I sob.

For the next five hours we curtsy and bow in the gusty wind while I sit in the corner of the cockpit, barely breathing, glaring out at the cold, bleak world, thinking it would be a lot more fun to have another baby or even to be attending one of those family meetings back at work. Why am I so scared? Why do I think I'm going to die? Why am I the only person who sees how dangerous this is? I don't know, but I hate it out here, and I'm incredulous that anyone thinks sailing is fun. Nathan's disbelief at my reaction only makes it worse. He doesn't like me, I can tell. Anyway, I'll have to hate him for seeing me act like this. I'll hunt him down if he tells anyone. At least Tom is enjoying himself. They talk some more about which boats are best, what it's like here in Bellingham, which sailing books contain the most information.

As we approach Sucia Island, everything changes. The wind dies down and the sun slants through the late afternoon sky. I awake from my glaring stupor and see that we've sailed right into a dream.

"We're in a rain shadow here because of the Olympic Mountains," Nathan says. "I thought you'd like it."

Maybe Nathan's okay after all. The air is almost balmy here. The wet moss and trees on the island sparkle as we approach the mouth of a long, narrow cove. Fossil Bay extends its arms to draw us in and embrace us. Nathan motors slowly up to a mooring buoy. Using a boat hook, Tom catches a ring on the top of the buoy and together they tie a line from the bow of the boat to this ready-made anchor. The boat becomes gloriously stationary.

"Get me off this boat," I whisper to Tom after he helps Nathan with the mainsail.

We climb into a rubber dinghy that's been tailing us the entire way. Tom rows us to the dock, and when we climb out of the dinghy the ground is unsteady, like quicksand, but it soon feels stable. For over an hour Tom and I hike on a trail under arching madrona trees and Douglas firs, past luminous moss-covered ground and rock outcrops. The trail winds through patches of glacier lilies, shooting stars, and Oregon grape holly, until we come to a rocky point jutting into Georgia Strait.

"We'll do a lot of this kind of exploring when we have our own boat," Tom says. "You'll get used to sailing. The weather wasn't good today, and remember, that boat has a fin keel. Our boat will sail much better. I also think the boat had too much sail up for the conditions. It's set up for summer sailing."

"Well, sailing will have to be a lot more fun than it was today."
Now I'm on land, beautiful land, where it's spring—all moist and hopeful. I feel restored. I love islands. Certainly sailing in the tropical, turquoise Caribbean would be better than sailing here during late winter.

The next day, when we sail back to Bellingham, the conditions are no different from the day before, maybe a little worse, and I'm sure my reaction to it meets or exceeds everyone's expectations. While Tom and Nathan fuss with the sails, I have to take the helm several times. I strain my shoulder muscles trying to keep the boat sailing a straight line in the gusty 25-35 knot winds and rain and cold. The strings of cuss words I mutter drift up and over their heads. Cussing is the only thing that keeps me going. Surely sailing isn't usually like this. No one would do it.

Back at the harbor, when we're safely secured in the slip, I sit in shock in the cabin of the boat, physically and mentally frozen. It wasn't a very good first time. Nathan leaves. I don't say goodbye. Tom is as upset at my reaction to our adventure as I am. What did he expect sailing to be like here in March? After a while we walk up to San Juan Sailing to talk with Wes about our trip.

"I hated it, Wes," I say, as soon as we close the door behind us.

"I heard."

Nathan already told him. I'll get him for that.

"Well, sailing isn't for everyone," Wes says, motioning for us to sit down. "I know one man who spent years building a sailboat in his backyard, then outfitted it for ocean cruising. He finally retired and had the boat trucked over here, then he and his wife sailed west through the Strait of Juan de Fuca, and out into the ocean. But when he saw those first big swells, with no land in sight, he turned tail. Sold the boat. Never went out on the water again. People get divorced over sailing. Some couples can compromise. I've seen situations where the husband and a friend sail the boat to Mexico or the Caribbean. When they get there, the wife flies down and they do some island hopping together."

"Really?" I begin to feel understood, like I'm not a freak. I almost start to cry again. Tom sits frowning. Clearly he doesn't want Wes to say these things.

"When my family and I sailed to Hawaii several years ago we got into 100-knot winds. The wind actually blew the ocean flat. We were knocked down and blown 200 miles off course."

"If you're trying to sell us a boat, why would you tell us that?" I ask.

"Oh, sailing's a great lifestyle, but, again, it isn't for everyone. Stormy seas aren't the norm, either, but they do happen."

"Show us some pictures of boats for sale," Tom says. "Since we're here, we might as well see what's available, besides that aluminum boat."

After looking at several photos we find a 1972, 37-foot Alberg-designed bluewater cruiser at Port Ludlow, over on the Olympic Peninsula southwest of Bellingham. This boat is in our price range, has a full keel and classic lines. Coincidentally, it's the same design as the sailboat we ate dinner on last November at St. John.

The next day, as we drive and ferry toward Port Ludlow to see the boat, I remind Tom of our deal. "As long as you can accommodate whatever happens with me and sailing, we can get a boat."

"I'll do it your way. It's better than nothing. But don't forget that wherever a boat sails, here or in the Caribbean, it heels over depending on the direction the wind is coming from."

"I know, but if we can go to places like Sucia and go ashore to explore, I'll try hard to like sailing."

When we see the Alberg we both like it. Tom is impressed with the boat's clean lines and how well it's been maintained. I like the comfortable cabin, the salesman calls it a saloon, and the compact kitchen (the galley) with its propane cookstove. I figure I can adjust to the recessed icebox, built into the counter. And I'll sew new curtains. We head home, and when we get off the ferry on the mainland Tom calls Wes to make a ridiculously low offer as a starting point.

The day after we return to Montana and our jobs, Wes calls to say our offer was accepted.

"No negotiating?" Tom asks. We're suddenly engaged to this sailboat and we're both surprised. Isn't this supposed to take longer?

We aren't financially organized to buy a boat so soon. But I guess that's what loans are all about. When we apply for a boat loan, however, our bank in Montana wants for collateral a lien on all our assets including our retirement plans and future grandchildren, in exchange for a partial loan with an astronomical interest rate. Tom calls our buddy, Wes, who gives us names of banks on the Washington coast accustomed to making boat loans. This time our loan application is quickly approved for the full amount.

Tom and Wes arrange a mid-April sea trial, haul-out and survey of our betrothed. This is all happening much too fast.

Back to the coast. On the April Saturday of our sea trial we have no wind at all so we motor the entire way from Port Ludlow to Port Townsend for the haul-out and survey, then back to Port Ludlow. Everyone jokes about how well the engine sails. The noise and diesel smell make this sailing experience about as enjoyable as my first one, but at least the boat doesn't tip sideways and I'm not scared, just cold. The owner, a very fine gentleman who is selling the boat for health reasons, spends the day with us, along with Wes and the surveyor. The owner assures us the boat sails very well, and we believe him. We take photos of the boat while it's in a sling out of the water at the boatyard in Port Townsend—16,800 pounds, dripping wet. After poking around inside the boat all day, the surveyor tap-taps every inch of the hull. He identifies some minor problems which need to be fixed, but nothing serious.

The boat will be ours, the paper signing is arranged, the wedding will be in June.

Since we have decided to moor the boat at Bellingham, we spend the next day there job hunting. Tom finds shops that do precision machining, introduces himself and leaves his resume. Several shops are busy crafting pieces for Microsoft billionaire Bill Gates' new house near Seattle.

A week after our return to Helena and our jobs, the owner of a machine shop calls Tom and asks how soon he can start work.

I panic. "What about selling all this junk we have? I can't do everything myself."

"Well, what if I tell them mid-May? That'll give us three weeks.

We'll have a huge moving sale before I leave and I'll take stuff we'll keep in a U-haul to put in storage."

"Okay. Now let's look at the photos we took on St. John. I need to be reminded why we're doing all of this!"

5

COLD FEET

I enjoy adventure and new experiences on a sailboat in the Caribbean.

This is an affirmation I say at least once a day. Montana is a nice place to visit, but because of the climate I don't want to live here any more. For one thing, my feet are always cold. Because my concerns about moving to a sailboat are almost too numerous to mention, I wear affirmations to warm me—like electric socks. While they (the affirmations, not the socks) play with my subconscious and often seem incompatible with reality, they do sometimes help. It's like any religion.

First of all, I'm having trouble getting used to the idea of living on a sailboat. I wish I wanted to, but nowhere in either my psyche or my wildest dreams is there an image of me living on a sailboat. My only sailing experience was mostly miserable. But how is living on a sailboat any stranger than living in an RV? Or, for that matter, in an old brothel? That I'd even consider this unlikely lifestyle probably stems from the fact that I was raised without fences. As a child I wandered through the free, aromatic woods and fields of North Idaho, unrestricted, never lost. If I came upon a fence, I didn't take it personally. Fences were built to stop cows, not people. In my childhood, all my clothes had rips from the barbed wire fences I crawled through as I roamed about the countryside, free as a blue jay.

Follow your bliss.

That's what my hero, Joseph Campbell—scholar, philosopher, writer, and teacher—said to do. When I first heard this intriguing idea I thought, *Yeah, right. That might work for others, but it sure hasn't worked for me.* I'd already tried it and failed.

Long before I knew a thing about following my bliss, I left home. My parents and sisters never sat around the dinner table discussing concepts like bliss. We were busy grunting and pointing. I'm still like that around food. It would take decades of mistakes and counseling for my real self to begin to separate from the mashed potatoes of my youth. The day after graduating from high school I left for Butte, Montana, to attend business college. At the time, of course, I didn't know who I was, what I thought or felt, or why. All I knew was that with office skills I'd have a passport to discovery, or at least I could pay for my own food, clothing and shelter.

At Butte Business College I enrolled in the Nancy Taylor Executive Secretarial Course with Modeling. A family took me in, and I helped around their house in exchange for my room and board. Mom and Daddy wanted to help me find a way to make something of myself. They paid the tuition, even though they couldn't afford it. Years later I learned they'd gone without electricity one spring so they could make the payments to the school. This still completely overwhelms me. I paid them back, of course, but you can never repay a gift of love that big.

When I left Butte I was still as dumb as a box of rocks about life, but I could type real fast and apply eyeliner at the same time. I worked as a secretary in Spokane for a couple of years. Then I remembered reading an article in *The Sandpoint Daily Bee* when I was 16 about a young woman who was a secretary in the Foreign Service, a branch of the State Department. The article showed her riding a camel somewhere in the Mideast. I wrote to the State Department about a job. After reviewing the stack of information they sent, I decided the State Department was a reputable firm and completed an application to join. After a year of clerical tests and a character investigation (I've always wondered what they found), they wrote that a job awaited me in Washington, D.C., where I'd work for a year until I was 21 and old enough to go overseas. The evening news showed riots in our nation's capital. This scared me, but I figured I could always quit and return to Spokane, so I bought a trunk, packed all my belongings into it, and shipped it off to my new destiny. There were no riots anywhere I went in Washington, D.C. though the news continued to show riots, people marching with placards, and bras being burned. Headlines featured free love, drugs, and all kinds of interesting things, but I saw none of it happen. While I've benefited from the passions and activities of those who marched for peace and civil rights, the events of the 1960s sort of came and went without me.

Anyway, I spent a year in Washington, D.C., two years in Switzerland (the closest place to bliss I've ever lived), six months in Yugoslavia, and a month back in Washington, where I worked briefly at the White House before quitting the Foreign Service. Life was so simple when that trunk held all my belongings, but as I traveled I accumulated stuff and, like a snowball rolling downhill, I've ended up in a pile of debris. In it somewhere is my trunk.

Now Tom and I are on a search for bliss. The pursuit of this elusive state, while interesting, feels mostly like a midlife crisis. If that's what it is, we'll have to live to be over a hundred. And why not? But then, what if we do this sailboat thing—sell everything, move to a boat—then change our minds? One previous scheme was to buy a bunch of goats and train them as pack animals so we could go backpacking without feeling like beasts of burden. We'd take other people into the mountains, too, and they'd pay us big money for this unique adventure. Our goats would be big, sturdy Alpines, and we even selected names for them. Then, since we didn't have a place to keep farm animals, we finally gave up the idea of packing with goats. What would we think of next? Each of us is bad enough alone; when we're together it's like a chemistry experiment gone berserk.

One other scheme Tom and I had was this: we invested in ski-touring equipment suitable for back country travel, including skis with metal edges, boots suitable for mountain climbing, and special skins for our skis so we could tromp up steep slopes. We'd learn to do telemark turns, then go to Europe and ski the Haute Route. Turning fifty wasn't going to stop us. We bought the equipment, read up on how to do those tricky little gymnastic turns, and Tom did them, easily, effortlessly and often. But I couldn't do a telemark turn, not even once, without falling. I finally took off my skis, threw them like spears as far as I could, and got a muscle spasm. Either I had to quit trying to do these turns or have a nervous breakdown. But I couldn't quit. My life, my future happiness, depended on it. I went alone to see our counselor, Bedrock. "You don't have to telemark ski," he told me. "You have a right to change your mind." I was so relieved. Old Bedrock really came through that time.

Then there was the brothel renovation project, but that was my fault. In counseling I learned that I have a caretaker personality. Saving things is what I do best. Old buildings and scraps of furniture, pets, even people aren't safe from me. I've long been guilty of taking over other people's responsibilities, literally asking to be taken advantage of, then feeling resentful. I'm trying to leave all that behind. I want to stop being a rescue service.

I am a calm, relaxed, happy and well-adjusted person.

This is not a joke. This is an affirmation—a positive statement that something is already so—and I say it every day. But I've been a counseling junkie for over twenty-five years. I've left some well-traveled shrinks in my wake. Whenever I move and take up with a new one, he or she phones a travel agent right after our first session. You see, I have good health insurance and I'm a steady customer. We'll go along with our sessions for a few weeks, then the counselor will simply disappear. When he or she finally comes back I'll say, "What happened? I was worried about you, and I really needed to talk. I felt like snail ooze."

"Oh, I finally took a trip to Greece. I'd always wanted to go. Now tell me, dear, what's bothering you?"

Just what is bothering me? Could it be the semi-melancholy, peasant Germanic world sadness I carry around like tattered brown luggage that's been a lot of places, most of them not especially scenic? Or, could it be my childhood? Certain family members would hate me if I said too much, but my colorful, interesting early years were filled with loud noises.

People like to say about me, "She's such a nice person, so pleasant, so together." But I'm not. Inside I'm a childish, confused, terribly ambivalent and troubled person who just happens to look and act like someone's grandma.

There won't be any shrinks on the ocean, when we're sailing. Maybe I could just find someone to smile and nod. They wouldn't even need to speak English. No sir, now's a good time to wean myself from all of them. I'll just say affirmations instead and put out an ad for a guardian angel. Of course, she'll have to be a caseworker without any other clients; helping me will be caseload enough for one angel.

What about solitude? How can I possibly live with another person, one almost as troubled as I am, on a sailboat, on an ocean. Every time I think about this it makes me gasp for air. Even when I was a child I'd frequently go off by myself. One summer Mom decided she'd had quite enough walking through chicken shit to get to the outhouse, so we butchered and ate all the chickens. Afterwards, my sisters and I helped scrape and clean the chicken coop, which soon became storage for overflowing boxes of stuff, including old magazines. This old chicken coop became my hideout, where, by reading *True Romance* magazines, I first learned about romantic love.

"Rae, Rae," my sisters would call, over and over. But I wouldn't answer. I'd finally emerge from the chicken coop, sneak over to the path that led down to the creek, crouch low as I made my way through the bracken ferns past our milk goat, then turn around and saunter back up toward the house.

"We called and called you," they said.

"I was at the creek," I lied.

I am exceptionally healthy and I feel good.

Saying this sometimes causes a severe muscle spasm in my upper back. The last time it happened it was like a horse kicked me just above my shoulder blade.

I'm not in too bad a shape, really, except for my shallow, practically non-existent breathing and the fact that my back muscles are out of whack and pull one leg shorter than the other, and, whenever I overdo anything physical or become stressed, my right shoulder goes into spasm. For instance, the other night I got a repetitive stress injury while eating a tub of popcorn at a movie.

Oh, and I suffer severe headaches, too. For years, when the headaches wouldn't quit, or when an attack on my right shoulder kept me from turning my head for days, I'd visit a chiropractor. The one I frequented laughed a lot and called me darlin' and sweetie. At each appointment he'd fix me up and bring me cheer, except when I thought to ask, "Will I ever be normal?" He expressed his amusement loudly, pushed down on the vertebrae between my shoulders, and said, "We'll be together forever, darlin'." But you can't take a chiropractor with you on a sailboat, on the ocean. If you need a fix every week or two just to get along, you might as well marry one and take him with you. But we were both already taken, so I went to my physician with my problem and she lined me up with a physical therapist.

"I think you have fibromyalgia," the physical therapist said. "It's something you learn to manage with exercises, hot packs, and a positive attitude."

"But I am exceptionally healthy and I feel good," I sobbed, then drove home and had another muscle spasm.

I now have a new physical therapist. This one specializes in persons with myo-fascial, spinal-cranial predicaments, like mine. "Yes," he says, "You probably do have fibromyalgia, which means you have a bundle of symptoms, like chronic muscle pain and sensitivity to noise and light. And I'll bet you tire easily."

"I'm a nervous wreck, too."

"That's part of it, but we can make you better. You'll have to work hard, though. Retraining muscles is a big job. And you'll have to learn to breathe; your muscles aren't getting enough air."

Every session lasts nearly two hours and, after two months, I'm down to one session a week. Apparently muscles have memory. Accidents and emotional trauma become locked into muscle tissue. For the first twenty minutes of each session I recline on a massage table with a moist hot pack the full length of my back. I wear gym shorts, a hospital gown, and wool socks. A blanket covers all of me, including my cold feet, and my job is to lie still, practice deep breathing, listen to pleasant music, and relax. Then comes the acupressure, the digging of fingertips into my neck, the pulling on my head. "Keep breathing, just let it go." My neck catches fire, then my tears and grief spill and howl out over the gentle piano music, until the muscles unknot. The fire is out until next time, but it's hard to stop crying. Then the manual traction on my legs, one at a time. He swings out a leg, lifts it up and crosses it over the other one, and pulls for several seconds, until both legs are the same length once again and for a little while. Massage, ice, learn more exercises, get dressed, schedule the next appointment.

The headaches diminished after the first session, but it will take months, possibly years, to retrain my muscles. Between P.T. sessions I do exercises at home and at work, lie on an ice pack morning and night, and work out at a health club on electronic weight machines and a stairmaster. On the weekends, Tom pulls my legs and gives me massages. We call it foreplay. Following instructions, I listen to music by Yanni and dance around doing airplane exercises, holding out one or both arms, sideways or up over my head, and push at the air, not earning frequent flyer miles.

Then there's my teeth. What happens if you're at sea and a filling falls out? They don't last forever. Some of my teeth are on their third round of fillings. I've practiced good dental hygiene ever since I paid about half my first job's earnings to a dentist in Spokane who filled all the cavities. While my roommates bought new clothes, I invested in my teeth and my dentist's new car—a dark blue Le Mans complete with shiny magnesium wheels.

There's also my eyesight. One day I was standing with a guy named Dave from one of the ranger districts, talking about a project. I couldn't focus my eyes on him. The problem had to be my bifocals. When I'd back up so I could get him into focus, he'd step closer. I'd back up again.

"I'm not coming on to you, if that's what you're thinking," he finally said.

Recently I watched an insect flying around the room, my eyes following its flight path. After a while I realized it was a dark speck on the inside of my glasses. What if a wave hits me when we're sailing and washes my glasses overboard? This could be serious if I suddenly need to find some object on the boat right away, like the helm, so I can do something important, like steer.

I find a good home for Fatty. He is loved and cared for always.

One of my most wrenching concerns is what to do with Fatty. I must find a home for him or be strong enough to have him put to sleep. The problem isn't like *Sophie's Choice*, like abandoning a child, but this dilemma is causing me profound anticipatory grief. That's what the pet loss hotline at Washington State University calls it. He's not just a cat, he's my friend, my animal companion. We're very close. I've had Fatty 14 years, since 1983 when Jeff and I moved to West Yellowstone, Montana. Fatty was young and slender then, and his name was Algernon. He spent most of his time with us in the little house we rented, although he liked to go outdoors sometimes, too. One night during the first winter, when it was minus 20° F, he disappeared. We made *Cat Wanted* posters, complete with his picture, and tacked them on telephone poles and taped them in store windows. We walked the snowy streets calling him, but no Algernon. Was he under a pile of snow? After a few days one of Jeff's friends came to our house holding him. "He was sitting under his *Cat Wanted* poster outside the post office," Jeff's friend said.

A few years later, when I moved again and couldn't find a place that took cats, Algernon lived with my parents in North Idaho. For some reason Mom and my cat didn't always get along. She'd chase after him with a broom, then feed him. By the time she gave him back, happily, a year and a half later, he was a different cat. He'd gained ten pounds and his belly dragged on the floor as he slunk around, looking over his shoulder. That's when we began to call him Big Fat Algernon, quickly shortened to Fatty. Also while he lived with Mom, he learned to talk. He'd look right at me and say little meows, then tilt his head so I'd know it was my turn to talk. I told him, "I think she liked you, Fatty. I really do." Fatty would often lie on my chest and study me as he meowed and drooled and purred.

When Tom and I moved from the brothel into Helena, Tom built Fatty and our crippled cat, Spook, an insulated, heated house, which now sits on the other side of the sliding glass doors on the deck. We call it a Rasta shack after the small, rustic places on St. John in which Rastafarians (as well as visitors with little money) live. Because of Tom's allergies, the cats can't come into the new house.

All the carpets would collect their dander. But Fatty wants to come inside. He sits up like a prairie dog on the other side of the sliding glass door, begging to come indoors to be with me. It breaks my heart. Spook and I aren't especially close, although I take good care of her. Both the cats love our fenced double lot with its hillside, bushes and trees.

We sell or give away our belongings to people who will make good use of them.

You can only take about four things with you on a sailboat, so we must get rid of almost everything. Some of my things are too precious to leave behind, however, especially all the materials for projects I've never had time to work on—like the beargrass for making baskets that I collected on the Nezperce National Forest in Idaho. I've moved it eight times. Someone, I think it was E. B. White, said trophies are like leeches. Maybe, but my trophies are all fine items scavenged from the environment—beargrass, a beret and spool of wire to make a Mr. Wirehead sculpture, old project boards. My uncompleted projects have guarded me from my biggest fear, next to spiders and losing my glasses, that I will run out of things to do (at the very same time I've always longed to run out of things to do). Now all these trophies will have to go.

I dance freely and confidently on the tops of ocean waves.

What will it feel like to go from employed to unemployed? I'll be working for love, not money. Pare down, sell out, liquidate. Live cheaply. Tom still has to work at a real job because of former family obligations.

"I'll feed you and give you something to write about," he tells me.

"Oh, you mean a *terror on the high seas* writing grant?"

Yes, that pesky fear of water. On St. John I was surprised when I surrendered so completely to the warm, turquoise water as I fluttered along in my snorkel gear looking at the exquisitely colored fish and coral sculptures. But cold water is different. I've nearly drowned twice because I panicked while trying to swim in cold, dark water.

Part of the problem is simply that water isn't land. Land is familiar and safe.

Tom and I have already agreed that we'll come back to Montana and Idaho every summer during hurricane season in the Caribbean. We can work and visit our friends and families. This makes the idea of living on a sailboat seem more reasonable. Recently, however, Tom has begun to read books written by couples who've sailed around the world, couples who don't go home during the hurricane season.

"We could do that, too," he now says. "We'll just sail outside the hurricane zone."

Maintaining important relationships with family members and close friends *is* a major consideration. Jeff and his wife, Lee, are busy working and building a life together. Right now they aren't far away; we talk every week on the phone and I see them twice a month. If they had children, I'd be a grandma, of course. Would I be able to leave and sail the oceans blue?

Over the years I've befriended several colorful characters, each one absolutely unique and irreplaceable. They're scattered all over. Of course, we'd keep in touch the way we do now—by mail, occasional visits and phone. People can come for brief visits on the boat. Also, Tom says we'll use a ham radio to connect with loved ones by phone patches through local ham radio operators.

Most important of all, Tom and I will finally be able to live together. It's true we're still having some noisy relationship enhancement events, many of them not in the bedroom, and it's true we'll be going from a weekend marriage to living together every day in a very small space, but that's probably as good a test as any for a marriage.

6

ITEMS TOO NUMEROUS
TO MENTION

*Moving to a sailboat. Everything goes. Household goods, antiques,
art and craft materials, skis, books.*

Saturday, May 10, 8-4

Although the lilacs are blooming, hugely and fragrantly, as they
have since this elegant old house was built eighty years ago, I am
tearful—a river at flood stage during spring runoff. There's no stopping the flow.

It's hard to go to work where I'm not who I really *am*, when I
need to stay home to sort through my life and assign value to items
that represent who I *was*, before now. The boat deal is signed, sealed.
The house we've lived in less than a year is sold. My life is rushing,
leaping forward out of control.

Isn't this a cleansing, an opportunity to wean myself from un-
needed items and activities? Yes. Now is the time to extricate myself
from the clutter of a gummed up life and never again let it get so
complicated.

What few items should I take with me on the boat? What should
I put in storage? What are my things worth or, rather, what will someone pay for them? What should I give away? It's one thing to talk
about selling all your things and moving to a very small space, like a
sailboat. It's another thing to actually do it. As everyone at work likes
to say, this is *where the rubber meets the road.*

We post notices of items for sale at grocery stores and Laundro-
mats. I run ads in *The Adit*, an advertising weekly. Tom's chainsaw

sells right away, complete with extra chains, chaps, and a helmet for eye and ear protection.

"I kept the family warm for years with that," he says. "It hurts."

My full-sized bed with the pink floral pillow-puff top, mattress cover, and box springs goes for $75 to some kids who pick it up in a dirty, belching pickup truck. As they begin to toss the mattress onto some greasy tools and tires in the truck, I yell, "Wait! I'll give you an old blue blanket to put down first." They accept it, load the mattress on the blanket, then pull out of the driveway with the bed bouncing around unsecured, their old truck leaving behind a puddle of black oil the size of a bathroom throw rug.

Next the wicker set on the porch sells for $50. Moving to a sailboat provides a wonderful opportunity to be generous.

Jeff and Lee buy some of our best items for a song—the stereo, a table saw, and the vacuum cleaner that does everything except the dishes. We present them with boxes of other belongings, too, like the mounted deer antlers my dad gave me, my heirloom rocking chair, a VCR, a jar of garnets Jeff and I dug together years ago that I tumbled glossy in a polishing machine, and a basket of postcards from my three years in Europe, so long ago. I force other items on them. "You'll need these things some day, you'll see."

They take my old sheepskin slippers for their two dogs to chew on, instead of Lee's shoes. Unfortunately, they can't take Fatty and Spook.

"We have so many dogs and cats already we have to borrow a horse trailer when we take them to the vet," Jeff says. Two large dogs and three cats *are* probably enough. Besides, my cats don't like dogs.

I pray for a natural disaster—a tornado, a flood, a lightning strike followed by a fire storm—that will clean out everything in the house, and especially the garage. But it looks like I'll have to engineer my own losses. We're going from being settled Koraks to the wandering kind, and they only pull with them the essentials for living an interesting life on the move.

We're kissing goodbye to our wind chimes, bump jumpers (those cool wood sleds with just a small seat and a runner), cowboy boots, a restored baby buggy and a big rag doll, guns, more wicker, nine pairs of skis, project materials for baskets and odd garden sculptures, pieces of barnboard and fancy old hinges, unused canning jars, and thousands of other non-nautical items too numerous to mention.

At the office, talk of downsizing the workforce continues.

"I'm leaving August 15, if that helps any," I announce to my boss.

"We'll miss you," he replies. "You've done a good job."

"But will you replace me?"

"No, we can't afford to do that."

"But you would have kept me on if I weren't leaving?"

"Yes."

At home my own downsizing program progresses—the sorting and pricing of things I would keep if I weren't leaving.

More ads: *100-year old, 1-inch thick rough-sawn lumber from interior of old mining town brothel. Square nails removed and available. Planes beautifully to make distinctive cabinets and furniture pieces.*

I'm practically giving away these priceless boards, yet no one responds to the ad. But then old boards aren't hard to come by in Montana.

I sort through a box of loose photos, the ones that never made it into albums: a black and white photo, 1948, of me sitting in a little wagon, probably red; 1965, all five sisters in a row at the place on Riley Creek; a Polaroid of me, a skinny bottle blond, taken in 1966 with friends in Washington, D.C.; 1971, Jeff at age one, holding a play telephone; 1986, the landscape of Lazyman Hill on top of the Gravelly Range near Ennis, Montana, complete with a sheepherder's wagon; 1988, Jeff's high school graduation in which he wore a bright red gown, the day I noticed how tall he'd grown; 1995, Tom and me on Skyline Ridge in which my hair is blown sideways in the jetstream.

Tom arrives from Bigfork the Thursday evening before the first moving sale, pulling behind him his two motorcycles and the rest of his belongings. This was his last trip down the Swan Highway. He'd spent the week packing and seeing his kids, which made it harder for him to leave. To commiserate, we go out to dinner. We remind each other why we're doing this. He brought with him a stunning find—a painting of a schooner sailing the high seas—a picture he now remembers staring at for hours in the house where he grew up. It had been packed in a box for decades, much like this sailboat idea had been packed away in his subconscious.

The next day I head off to work while Tom does errands. He sells one of his motorcycles, a prearranged deal. He then delivers Spook to the humane society, where we hope she'll be adopted. All morning at work I know this is happening, and all I can think of is "poor, dumb Spook." Fat and crippled as she is, her chances for adoption are slim. It will take a special person. At my desk I go quietly to pieces in a flood of tears and leave. I return home where I can cry and sort through items at the same time.

The amount of junk we've accumulated, separately and together, seems endless.

"You had quite a federally-funded, debris-recruitment program," Tom says, with reference to the source of my income from the U.S. Forest Service.

His debris, on the other hand, consists of boxes of mystery stuff: rusted tools and other strange items in toolboxes whose lids no longer function.

"I've got some excellent instruments, here," he says.

"Well, let's see them."

He breaks into one of the rusted toolboxes and explains. "Elastrator bands for castrating sheep, hoof trimmers, and these are syringes to inoculate animals. Used these when we lived on the farm in North Dakota. The hoof trimmers would've come in handy, if we had bought those goats."

In another box are two-quart glass jars filled with a golden liquid. "Bear grease for reloading," Tom says. "I did that at one time. My friend, John, rendered the oil from a bear he shot out of his apple tree."

"Who's going to want that?"

"Oh, lots of guys. Black powder enthusiasts. You'll see."

On the day of the moving sale I give up much of my terrestrial history, trading objects and memories for a new life I'm not all that certain about.

The good weather holds. Antique dealers show up early and offer pitiful amounts for some of my best primitives: old pickets and wood doors, a charming blue garden table, a scythe, coffee cans full of square nails, a rustic white wardrobe closet, and a weathered moose antler I'd found in the Elkhorns. I talk them up in price. It's kind of fun. Even though I'll miss the antler, my artist friend, Jennifer, and I both sketched it next to a bright red amaryllis, that week a few years ago when we painted together and grieved the loss of our fathers. I'll keep the paintings.

A strong breeze wafts lilac smells across the yard as people poke around, pick up things, put them down. Fatty lies sprawled under the clothesline in the back yard watching the invasion, unafraid. He would run and hide if he knew what tomorrow holds for him.

People enter our driveway past a dilapidated dry-sink, a primitive piece of furniture out by the curb. We'd used it for years as is, with every intention of fixing it. Who else would love a piece of junk like that? Late in the morning a woman asks, "Can I have that lovely old piece out by the driveway? It has so much character."

"You just made my day," I say, and hug her.

Another woman buys the old Rimini outhouse seat, a two-holer, scrubbed and bleached. She wants to make a bench-planter-conversation piece with it.

People adopt all my best project materials: red-osier dogwood stems for making twig shutters and lamp shades, beargrass and pine needles for baskets, and a lovely birch branch for use as a drapery rod. A girl buys a huge dog harness for her 4-H sheep.

The young buyers of our house come early and buy the pile of barn boards. As part of the house deal, they're also getting several large antique pieces—furniture items not yet paid for.

The day is fast-paced and fun, but people are cheap. If an item is easily worth $15 or $20 and I've priced it at fifty cents, they say, "Will you take a quarter?" I'm prepared for this. I've done the same thing at yard sales myself, so I usually say yes.

We earn enough money to pay off our furniture and the Visa

card, the balance of which includes several items we practically gave away at the moving sale. Buy high, pay interest, sell low, then pay for the item. You have to start somewhere.

After the sale I'm so exhausted I can hardly walk. Then we load a U-haul trailer with things Tom will pull to Bellingham the next day—mostly tools he might need for the boat. I'll follow him as far as Priest River, Idaho, with items for my sisters and for my friend, Sherry. My sister, Patsy, has agreed to take Fatty so I'll deliver him and his Rasta shack to the home place, where he was born.

After a six-hour drive I arrive at Patsy's. We find a nice location for Fatty's house—up a hill past the small orchard, under a big Ponderosa pine tree next to several outbuildings. Good lion king habitat. Fatty is as motionless as a roadkill in his house as we carry it through tall grass so green it shimmers, past flowering apple trees and singing robins. When we reach the pine tree we carefully set down his house. He does not move when I reach in to pet him and comfort him. He does not move when I bring him fresh water and fill his food dish. And when I check his house the next morning, he is gone. I call him. He does not answer.

Tom leaves early for Bellingham and I head back to Helena, driving through the sunshine and iridescent greenness of May in a downpour of tears—not about the items I've given away or the temporary separation from Tom, but about Fatty. And, since Fatty always met me at the gate, my grieving intensifies as I pull up in front of the house in Helena. And when I walk into the mostly empty house I think I see Fatty at the sliding glass door looking in at me, but when I look again he's gone.

Good news greets me on the answering machine, however. I need a place to stay after I move out of the house. As it turns out, the mother of the young man who bought our house will be spending a few months in New Hampshire with her daughter. I can sublet her fully-furnished place, a small, north-facing apartment with a picture window and views of lawn, trees and birds.

I spend the next day with a work party re-routing a trail and installing signs at a trailhead in the Elkhorn Mountains. This day of physical labor and renewal in the sagebrush foothills is also the last field day for my boss, Jim, who is taking an early retirement to start a consulting business. As a supervisor he has believed in me and understood how hard I worked, and that my job wasn't easy. I give him two hand hewn beams to use at his ranch. He'll hang one over the entrance to his driveway—an honorable life for a century-old piece of Montana.

A music store buys dozens of my CDs. People at work buy dressers, our queen size bed, the couch. I donate stove pipes and fixtures to one of the ranger districts for use at a cabin they are fixing to rent to the public. Of the files of papers and clippings in our four-drawer filing cabinet, I keep only a few, but not the file titled *Home Ideas*—filled with a lifetime of ideas to use in my dream house, the one I never inhabited. Every house I ever lived in proved to be a nightmare of painting and repairs, electrical and plumbing disasters, and yard maintenance—a financial and emotional black hole that left little time or money for play. If there's one thing I know for certain now, it's that I am not a house person. A small apartment, maybe. A sailboat? I hope so.

Tom calls me a couple of days after he arrives in Bellingham. He's staying temporarily at the National Guard Armory, and says his new job is stressful but it's all right. He says he hangs out evenings at Squalicum Harbor meeting people, watching boats come and go, visiting with Wes at San Juan Sailing.

"The seagulls are mating," he says. "I wish you were here."

"I know."

"It's a little dangerous on the docks, though. I was walking along under a light post yesterday evening and a seagull crapped on my head."

"That's too bad," I say, stifling my laughter as I change the subject. "I'm having another yard sale Memorial Weekend."

"I wish I could be there to help you."

"Me too. But I can handle it. I'm fine," I lie.

The second moving sale is surprisingly successful. I unload almost all the stuff that didn't sell the first time. Because the weather prediction was lousy, people canceled their out-of-town plans, but when the weather perks up Saturday morning, shoppers are out in their cars with time and money to spend. More people come to this sale than the first one. Since I'm alone I wear a nail apron so I can carry around all my loot and make change easily.

After the sale, I donate leftovers to the Salvation Army. Jeff and Lee help me move my few remaining items to a storage unit. I'm less burdened by stuff now, although I did keep the trunk that was once big enough to hold all my belongings—before I began my debris-recruitment program.

7

THE SWEET SMELL OF CLOVER

"Three in one day when I'd never seen one before," I tell Tom. "Woodcocks—first one, then two more, sitting on fence posts. And you should have seen the wildflowers, the birds, the light, and the clouds. We *will* be spending some time on land, I hope, and not just on the boat."

Tom is back from Bellingham for two weeks to teach at the Army National Guard Academy. We're in my cozy little apartment, eating dinner.

"Well, I like land, too," he says, taking a bite of salad.

"But now you seem to be only interested in the boat," I say. "That worries me."

"You'll just have to trust me," he says, looking hurt or frustrated or both. "Exploring all those islands is one of the main reasons we're getting the boat."

"I know. I guess over winter I forgot how incredible it is outdoors this time of year. Or maybe I'm paying more attention now that it's field season and soon I'll be leaving all this land behind."

"It almost sounds as if you'd rather stay here, like maybe you want to forget about moving to the boat."

"Funny you should say that," I reply. "When I got in such a goofy rapture about the landscape today one of the guys I was working with said, 'You sure you want to live on a boat, Rae Ellen?' The problem is, I feel free and easy and comfortable on land. I need to feel the ground under my feet."

"Sure, and you will. Here, let me show you the nautical charts and the course Isaac and I will take when we bring the boat from

Port Ludlow to Bellingham," he says, unrolling two large maps. "We'll leave early and sail into the harbor at Bellingham about dark."

In about ten days, Tom's 18-year-old son, Isaac, will be coming down to Helena from Bigfork. He'll drive back to Bellingham with his father to spend a few days on the water.

The next evening at dinner I report, "Today I saw mule's ear daisies and cinquefoil in every meadow, and yellow violets and lady slippers in the woods. This year is one of those big clover years, too. It's along all the roads. It smells so good when I drive past with the windows down. The whole outdoors just shimmered today—green and alive like it was dancing and singing. And that's not all. Near Nevada Creek I saw a huge, cinnamon-colored bear. Then, as we drove into the edge of the Helmville Valley, three great blue herons and a golden eagle flew right over the truck."

"Don't worry," Tom says. "We'll see lots of herons and eagles when we're sailing."

What have I done, agreeing to move to a sailboat? I guess I didn't realize the strength of my connection to land. And even though I loved snorkeling in the warm, turquoise sea at Salt Pond Bay on St. John, I'm still afraid of water. During my childhood Mom warned us repeatedly to stay away from bodies of water. When my family fished together from the shore of the slough at Priest River, I could hardly get close enough to the bank to cast a line and catch a fish.

One evening while Tom is playing war games with the National Guard, a new friend, Eleanor, and I drive on a muddy back road to a trailhead near the Missouri River. Not far from the route Lewis and Clark followed on their way west, we begin our hike up the Missouri Canyon Trail in a rain shower. We don't care; we're wearing rain gear. Besides, the landscape smells better when it rains. The evening sun reappears as we hike through aspen groves and across steep hillsides of wet heartleaf arnica, through the pungent aroma of sagebrush. Later, as we traverse our way back down to the car, a small herd of elk watches us from the ridge line—a perfect end to the hike. We drive away from the trailhead at dusk in Eleanor's car on the narrow dirt road, now flooded with water in the low places. As she shifts down and eases the car into the ponds of water across the road she tells me a secret, with great excitement and animation.

"I get so depressed I often think about suicide," she says, her eyes focused on me and not on the road.

"Eleanor, your car is so low! We'll get stuck. The water will come right up through the floor," I say, lifting my feet. If I'd been driving alone from the Missouri Canyon trailhead, I would have spent the night on the other side of the first big mudpuddle. To my way of thinking, it's downright suicidal to drive through bodies of water that size.

"We're just fine. Don't worry," she said, her voice now a calm, even tone.

As we drive into and out of yet another small lake, Eleanor talks about the bleakness of depression. "I think a person has the right to commit suicide if she wants to, without feeling guilty about it."

"Is there something you really want to do in life?" I finally ask, not knowing what to say to her. "Maybe you should do it."

For me, the incredible wonders of our evening hike, the wild-flowers, the smell of wet sagebrush, the sight of elk on the ridgeline, are reason enough to keep going. Most of my life I've pretty much lived the way I thought others wanted me to, even when I felt de-pressed. The idea of suicide is too big to contemplate. Someone might miss me, and I sure wouldn't want to cause another person any discomfort.

I think of my own mother and her battles with demons, one of them a fear of mudpuddles. On several occasions when I was a child, Mom drove us miles out of our way to avoid going through a low pond of water across the road. In the narrow panhandle of North Idaho, such a detour could have easily slid us over into Washington or Montana, but the risk was worth it to my mother. "If we sink into that hole, we'll never be seen again," she'd say, throwing the car into reverse and cranking the steering wheel. "Goddamn muddy roads," she'd add as my sisters and I tumbled about in the back seat. When spring came to North Idaho, so did the mud. In an effort to lay a solid subgrade, one neighbor dropped an old wringer washer and some busted farm implements into the muddy lane that led to their place.

By my mother's way of thinking, if a household appliance as big as a cow could disappear into the mud, so could we. And I believed her.

Every few evenings I call my sister's place in Idaho to see how Fatty is doing. One evening I ask Tom to call her, since I always cry when I call. They tell him what they always tell me. They feed him but don't see him, even though they think they hear him meow. Poor Fatty. To be abandoned by his human so casually, to be tossed away without knowing why. I cannot bear the loss. I want to drive back to Priest River to bring him home. Except we've sold our home.

On a Monday morning in the middle of June, Tom and Isaac leave for Bellingham, a twelve-hour drive west from Helena. I leave for a field assignment at King's Hill on the Lewis and Clark National Forest, about three hours east and north of Helena. To save the government two night's lodging costs I decide to stay in a cabin near Showdown Ski Area on the Continental Divide.

The first evening at the cabin, flies as big as bumblebees buzz around me. The electricity is out. Filigree curtains, sagging on their slender rods over filthy windows, offer no privacy. Duct tape holds together several broken window panes. I can find no newspaper for starting a fire in the wood stove, and I am cold. Glacier lilies are still blooming next to the back door by a pile of snow. As for the outhouse, the vent pipe is missing from the roof and rain has spilled through the hole onto the toilet seat. A few miles north of here is Bob's Bar and Motel, but staying there would be so ordinary. This cabin is a challenge I can handle.

Summer has not yet arrived at this elevation of 8009 feet, and I shiver much of the first night in my old down sleeping bag. In the middle of the night I use a yogurt container as a chamber pot instead of dashing a hundred yards through the cold darkness to the wet toilet seat. In the morning I manage to start a fire with some glossy paper I find in a drawer, along with some wood chips from the woodshed. I pour water into a pan over the sink so I can heat it on the stove and make drip coffee. When I spill some in the sink it runs all over the wood floor. I investigate under the sink and can see no drain pipe, not even a bucket.

As I drink my coffee and huddle near the wood stove I think

about Tom and Isaac sailing the boat from Port Ludlow to Bellingham today. Tom has never before sailed a boat as long as 37 feet. Isaac has never even been on a sailboat. What will the weather be like for their voyage? Will Tom like living on the boat? Will I like living on it with him after I move there the end of August?

Over the next couple days I drive to the ranger station and various sites to do field work for the Kings Hill Scenic Byway Interpretive Plan. I'm also working on a scenery analysis for the Little Belts Landscape Assessment. Soon I'll be quitting this job. Soon I'll have time to write something other than environmental assessments. My longing to write books again is another reason for making all these lifestyle changes. Writing, and thoughts of writing, keep me going. In the meantime, the importance of scenery cannot be underestimated. I'll do my best to document and preserve it. For now, it's my job.

At the end of the day when I arrive back at the cabin, I have electricity. After I reported the outage at the ranger station a power company lineman discovered that a squirrel had fried itself on an electrical wire on the utility pole and blown the fuse. The receptionist at the station told me the lineman said, "What was left of that squirrel looked like shoe leather."

At the appointed time—10 p.m. in Montana, 9 p.m. in Washington—I make my phone call from a pay phone at Bob's Bar. The phone is indoors next to an enormous moose head hanging on the wall. Tom is waiting for my call at a pay phone on the dock at Squalicum Harbor.

"We had a wonderful trip," he says, after our initial hellos. "The weather wasn't very good, and Isaac didn't know how to do anything I asked him to do. We did have some frantic moments, but it was still great."

"Did Isaac like sailing?"

"Oh, yeah. We had a good time, except when we got to Bellingham Bay we sailed right into the middle of a sailboat race. Missed every one of them, but Isaac dropped a bumper in the water and we circled it four times before he snagged it with the boat hook. We got a lot of attention. From where I'm standing I can still see the sailboats sailing around out there."

I've never heard so much excitement in his voice.

"How was your landing? Was it easy to park the boat in the slip?"

"It was just fine. Didn't wreck a thing."

"I'm so relieved that you made it safely to Bellingham."

"We're headed for Sucia Island in the morning. We'll stay overnight."

"You're kidding," I say. I'm stunned. They survive the day, manage to put the boat safely in the slip, and the fools are going right back out again tomorrow?

"No. I'm not kidding. We're going to Fossil Bay, where we went on our one-day charter. Remember?"

"Oh, yes. How could I forget? It's Sucia's fault that I agreed to get the sailboat," I say, smiling in the direction of the moose head. Its big brown eye, the one on my side of his head, is about the size and shine of the knob on a sea kelp.

At the end of my third field day I drive back to Helena. As I leave the Smith River Valley northwest of White Sulphur Springs I begin to crave something sweet. Stopping in Townsend, I buy a dozen donuts in a carton, get back into the van, and eat five donuts in 12 miles going 65 miles an hour. Then I feel sad and desolate, like the morning after my only one-night stand a long time ago. I feel desperately tired. When will I not feel so tired? My neck and right shoulder both hurt and I can't turn my head to the right. But at least I'm not hungry.

That weekend, on Saturday, I drive west over the Continental Divide, then drop down into the Helmville Valley, a wide valley of ranches and cattle. The old TV show, *Bonanza*, could have been filmed here. I sit in the hot sun among tall grasses for over an hour sketching an old log shed, a pole corral, and black angus cows eating the luminous grass in the dipping, rolling valley. My sketch isn't very successful but it doesn't matter. I am restored, no longer tired.

On my way back to Helena I stop in Elliston, on the west side of the Continental Divide, to see Jeff and Lee. While Lee cooks dinner, Jeff and I deliver their trash in the back of his truck, to the Dumpsters on the edge of town. As we bounce along the gravel road near the Little Blackfoot River, Jeff points out the open window and says, "See that big rock? That's where Lee's parents met."

I've always loved going to the dump and what it represents—cleaning up a place and getting organized, after which life will surely be better. As a child, going to the dump with my dad in his old truck was nearly as much fun as hiking with him in the woods every Thanksgiving Day. Jeff and I had also hauled truckloads of debris from the brothel renovation project in Rimini to the sanitary landfill north of Helena, before they closed it down and landscaped it.

As we drive home from the dump, my only child, who walks so much like my father did when he was alive, says, "I love you, Mom."

"I love you, too, Jeff." I glance out the open window at the river as we drive back past the rock where Lee's parents met. "You've never been far away. Now I'm leaving." Jeff doesn't like it when I cry and I decide not to do it, not now. "You and Lee will have to come over to Bellingham to spend some time with us on the boat."

Back at the apartment in Helena that night, I talk with Tom on the phone.

"The baby seagulls have hatched," he reports. "Those matings I witnessed in late May paid off. The babies are like fluffy grapefruits with bird feet."

"They sound cute," I say. "Right now I'm sitting on the bed looking out the picture window at some little gray birds flitting around the spruce tree."

Today I work in the office, and feel exhausted. In the morning I go to the library to do some historical research on the King's Hill area. Another woman goes along to do some work on another project.

"You sure look slender these days," she says.

"Thank you," I say. But I don't believe it.

After work I take myself to dinner at Uncle Ron's (Home of the Plateful). I really only wanted the salad bar, but I go weak in the knees when I see the twelve different kinds of meat in the buffet and I order that instead. After eating way too much, I haul myself home to bed.

If Fatty were here he'd be lying on my chest, meowing, purring and drooling as I drift off to sleep. For fourteen years Fatty served as glue to hold my shaky life together. In return I fed him good food, too often. Feeding a cat, after all, is cheaper than buying alcohol. Without Fatty I feel less certain of who I am.

"I think he's gone," Patsy says when I call. "We haven't heard a meow in days."

There's one last hope. Maybe he's found a home with Patsy's neighbors, a fine couple who lives across the road and up the hill. When I call them, the woman has bad news. Not only has she not seen a cat meeting Fatty's description but her own three cats have recently disappeared. She saw a mountain lion in a nearby field and is convinced it got her cats and probably Fatty, too. We cry together on the phone and agree that our cats died quickly, without much suffering. So, Fatty is dead. If only I'd been strong enough to have him put to sleep. Instead he became part of the food chain, nothing more than a furry snack for a mountain lion.

I work near Lincoln again, this time in the campgrounds, where over-mature trees have grown brittle. Crews have cut down several trees before they could fall on campers. The trouble is, no young trees are growing underneath the old trees to replace them. At my favorite site, a campground on the Blackfoot River, we hear the songs of thrushes, finches, nuthatches, and the splashing of water in the nearby river. But we can find no young cottonwood trees growing underneath the old, dying giants. Our small team—a recreation forester, a silviculturist (who writes prescriptions for managing stands of trees), and I—eat lunch at this campground. After lunch I fold in on myself with tiredness.

On Sunday night I call Tom at the appointed time. He tells me he's been up to the top of the mast of our boat in the bosun's chair, with the assistance of a man who lives down the dock. Saturday he sailed alone to Lummi Island, where he tied up to a mooring buoy at Riel Harbor.

"I didn't go ashore," he says. "There was a whole flock of sea kayakers there. I just wanted to tinker with the boat."

I knew it. He's given up land completely. I'll probably end up imprisoned on the boat, never to set foot on land again.

One day I work at Nevada Creek Cabin, located in a stand of lodgepole pine near the creek in the mountains between the Helmville Valley and Lincoln. I meet a small crew from the ranger station. My job description doesn't include roofing but I want to help install a new roof on this old miner's cabin so the ranger can rent it to the public. I'll rent this cabin myself sometime when I return to Montana.

As soon as the crew places the ladder against the cabin, I climb up to the peak of the roof to sit and listen while my three co-workers discuss how to deal with the crooked, out-of-square roof.

"Just so the bottom edge of the roof is even," I interject several times, until I get my way. This will mean trimming the metal roofing panels along one side as well as along the peak. A clean, even edge seems important to the finished appearance. After all, am I not still the Queen of Aesthetics for the Helena National Forest? I sit tall on the crumbling, green asphalt roof. Gravity slowly lures my body down the slope of the roof; however, my underwear and jeans stay in place—up around my ears. I'm glad when the work begins. With power from a portable generator the project progresses quickly. I help move pieces of new corrugated brown metal roofing into place so they can be screwed down. We roof the north side of the cabin first.

After we install the shiny roof panels on the first side, I discover that I'm too big a chicken to climb down off the roof. The metal is slippery. I decide to go down the unroofed, south side because it still has the old, textured roofing on it, a surface with better traction. Unfortunately, that side of the roof is steeper. When I take in the sight of the men on the ground looking up at me, I feel dizzy. They're all aware of my dilemma.

"So, do we still have to trim the roof and make the bottom even?" one of them yells up at me.

After a little encouragement from the crew boss, who says, "Come on down. We'll hold the ladder for you," I gather enough wherewithal to lie flat on my stomach. Grabbing onto the edge of the roof I inch my way sideways down the old asphalt roofing while, once again, the crotch of my jeans creeps upward. When I reach the top of the ladder I hesitate then swing a foot over and onto the top step, and climb down slowly. The second my feet hit the ground I scurry off to the outhouse to rearrange my jeans. After that I work inside the cabin where it's cool, cleaning dirt and dead flies off the windows before measuring them for curtains.

The crew finishes the roof, locks up the cabin and waves goodbye to me. I decide to explore the trail east of the cabin toward the Continental Divide before heading back to Helena. A few weeks earlier I had seen a bear along Nevada Creek, and I've heard reports of a mountain lion stalking one of the trail crew to the north on the Divide. To be honest, I'd like to get my hands on a mountain lion right now, because of what one of them did to Fatty. Invincible, I stroll down an old road through the silence and the warm, spicy aroma of lodgepole pine resin. At the bottom of a hill I splash, without second thought, across shallow, icy Nevada Creek and step into a clearing filled with clover, lupine, cinquefoil and thistle. When I come to a bog I turn and drop down to rest in a patch of sweet smelling clover. I want to drink the gentle perfume, absorb the fragrance, hold it in my lungs forever. Two dragonflies dart past. I watch as a Monarch butterfly lands on the head of a nearby thistle, its long body a sleek sailboat, its vertical wings fluttering like two sails above a lavender sea. At this moment I feel, with complete certainty, that everything will be all right—that this summer of change and loss will someday be worth it.

8

PACK IT IN—PACK IT OUT

People at work suddenly adore me, now that I'm leaving. Everyone is friendly, encouraging and happy for me. I'm on display. It's kind of fun. But the dark cloud of downsizing talk hovers overhead—I'm the only one who feels safe from it.

"It's like the Titanic around here," someone says. "I wish I were brave enough to leave and do something exciting, like you."

It's important to leave a clean camp. As I drop files of e-mail messages and reports for environmental assessments into the recycling bin, bureaucratic phrases and slogans swirl around in my head: visual quality objective, partial retention, sensitivity level, seen area, cable logging, the Elkhorns Landscape Assessment, Oil and Gas EIS, the Poorman Project (unofficially called the Unabomber Timber Sale because of its location next to the Unabomber's cabin). And I recall the words of one logging engineer: "The trees have reached their culmination of mean annual increment. If they're not cut soon, they'll just stand there and rot." I smile and reach for my college diploma, certificates of merit, and the credo list for landscape architects everywhere (so idealistic, so right). I'll take them with me, even though I know there won't be room for them in my new life.

Officially, I'm taking a one-year leave of absence so I can retain my status until I'm certain of this move to a sailboat, to such an unlikely lifestyle. But I have no intention of working as a landscape architect again. Those closest to me know I won't be back. Friends treat me to dinners and lunches. Farewell messages beep onto my computer from employees at the three ranger district offices, the supervisor's office here in Helena where I work and the regional office in Missoula.

Tom and I talk twice a week on the phone, Wednesday evenings and again on Sunday evenings. On Wednesday nights his voice is flat. During the week, he says, his long hours at work feel like the horse latitudes—uneventful and dull. On Sunday evenings his voice is filled with talk of sailing to one island or the other, seeing harbor seals and otters, fixing things on the boat.

"On Saturday I single-handedly sailed to Spencer Spit at Lopez Island, under power most of the way, of course, since we're becalmed over here under a high pressure system. I use the starter on the engine more than the sails," he says. "I'm wearing it out.

"Then, at Spencer Spit, I was among about 40 boats, all anchored fairly close together. When I got up at sunrise on Sunday morning and went out to the cockpit, the water in the bay was perfectly calm—flat and glassy like a mirror. The bow of every boat was pointed the same direction except for one sailboat at the far end of the bay. Its bow was pointed toward the rest of us. Brought to mind a minister delivering a sermon to his congregation. Then a flock of Canada geese flew past me, low on the water, honking as if they were discussing something."

"Oh, like geezers flying in formation to the nearest coffee shop?" I say.

"Or like sinners skipping the sermon," Tom replies.

We laugh together. I do love that man's sense of humor.

Tom continues his story. "Later when I tried to leave the bay, a breeze had kicked up so I decided to hoist the mainsail, raise the anchor and sail away like a pro. But the anchor was stuck so I cranked on the windlass to pull the anchor free, then everything happened at once. The anchor broke loose and the boat took off toward shore, while I watched from the bow. Luckily it stalled out just before hitting the one-fathom mark and the beach." He pauses, then groans. "Tomorrow it's back to work. I wish you were here. I really miss you."

"I miss you, too," I say. But I don't, really. The truth is I need more time here, alone in this little nest of an apartment where I'm safely surrounded by land, trees and little gray birds outside my window. I'm in no hurry to start my new, floating lifestyle.

I tell everyone at work I don't want a big going-away party. They arrange a happy-hour in my honor at a nearby sports bar, to be held one evening during my last week of work. Between forty and fifty people show up to drink beer and wish me luck. They give me books about the San Juan Islands. The other landscape architects in the region present me with money collected among themselves so I can buy some saltwater fishing gear. They figure I'll need to catch some food since I'll be without income. I get hugged half to death, and hear several endearing comments like, "Many days you made it worth coming to work."

On my last day of work I finish a final report. After turning in my keys I say goodbye to my drafting table and sneak out the back door. On my way home I have second thoughts: maybe I'll leave and come back so I can leave all over again; or maybe I'll change my mind and not leave at all, because if I'd known how much people cared, maybe I never would have decided to leave in the first place. Then it hits me. It's the work I have a problem with. The people are great.

"I just saw a great blue heron perched on top of a mast, standing on one leg," Tom tells me on the phone Sunday evening. "And the weekend was wonderful. Matt, from work, and his wife, Christina, went sailing with me. We left Friday evening. No wind, of course, so we motored to Inati Bay. They brought two crab pots, and some fish heads and turkey legs for bait. When we got anchored we dropped the pots overboard. Next morning we had five keepers. Matt dropped them live into boiling water for five minutes. It's quite a deal, removing the shell of the main carapace, draining out the yellow fluid, then pulling off their legs and digging out the meat. We each took one apart, ate it and tossed the shells overboard."

"Did you like the taste?" I ask, noticing the darkness creeping across the yard out the window.

"It was good, but I thought I heard the crabs squeal when they hit the hot water. I felt sorry for them. And I'm not so sure about eating them after they're cooked in their own guts and all."

"Let's not catch crabs," I say. "I've lived this long without eating them."

"Sure. I don't need to do it again. But there's more to tell you. In Hale Passage a seal surfaced in the middle of the channel with a huge salmon still wiggling in its mouth. Then, as we approached Sucia Island we saw a pod of orca whales heading east. They're so beautiful. I wish you could have seen them."

"Me too. I'd really like to see some whales."

"Then we anchored in Snoring Bay at Sucia," he says, "and in the middle of the night the boat began to roll from side to side, first gently, then wildly. We all woke up. But with no wind or waves we couldn't tell what was causing it. I counter-rocked the boat, and it stopped. I think it was some kind of scientific phenomenon related to rolling moment and inertia. Waves have a circular motion. The boat must have been perpendicular to the moment, or something like that."

"Really," I say. I feel like I am inertia in the wake of a rolling moment, and Tom seems light years away, like maybe he's Einstein.

Monday evening I enjoy my last hike on Mount Helena, a city park on the edge of town that's been a convenient, steadfast friend since 1990 when I first arrived here. Often, when I felt badly about something or just needed some fresh air, I'd stop off at Mount Helena to explore the trails. In late winter and early spring I'd slip rubber straps with studs onto my boots and make my way over the icy trails. In late spring and early summer I'd come up here to see what wildflowers were playing. This time I hike the entire loop, up one side of the mountain and down the other. As darkness approaches I sit near the trail and watch the lights twinkle below in Helena, Queen City of the Rockies. On the horizon to the east, basking in the glow of a tangerine sunset, stretch the Big Belt Mountains, the mountains I once scanned from my office window.

Soon I'll be going from traveling up and down mountains to traveling horizontally on the water. But I realize the world is much larger than the view from a Montana mountain top, and a boat *is* a good way to get places—like back to the Caribbean.

9

IF *THE SHOE* FITS

It's raining lightly and I have cold feet as I carry my suitcase down the ramp and onto the dock. Is this the first day of the rest of my life or some terrible mistake? Seagulls fly back and forth overhead. One of them swoops in dangerously low. I duck, just as a splat hits the concrete dock in front of me. The bird squawks off. Sounds like it's saying, "Welcome to the neighborhood."

"Moving to a sailboat will solve a lot of problems," Tom had said many times. "And we can live together, for a change. They say married people do that."

One thing for certain, this will be a lifestyle of the poor and confused.

What will Tom look like, after spending so much of the summer in cramped quarters with only about six feet of headroom? Will he still be 6' 4" or a hunched over, silver-haired guy with a crab-like gait? Will we get along? And what about all this water? I'm skilled at stepping on boulders to cross streams and I've jumped to the other side of hundreds of creeks, but here we have an ocean.

The dock is as wide as a logging road and as long as an airport runway. I walk past cabin cruisers bigger than many of the places I've lived in Montana, with names like EGG US ON, Y-ARK, TRUE GRIT. A woman approaches pushing a two-wheeled cart stacked with duffel bags and a cooler, and on top of it all a happy, black Scottie dog with his ears blowing back in the breeze. Sailboats with names like LIONESS, HONKER, MERLIN'S MAGIC, STRESSLESS, THE WIND rock gently in their slips. Tom told me on the phone that I'd find our boat on the second dock from the end, west side. The water in the harbor is the color of day-old coffee with not quite enough cream in it, and a ghostly fish head as big as a basketball with teeth floats near our dock. Nothing whatsoever in Montana resembles this place. The closest visual reference would be to compare the masts here with the telephone poles there. After a right turn I meet a tall, middle-aged guy with a pony tail walking an orange kitten on a leash.

I take the long step up onto our boat, grab the handle sewn into the dodger, hoist the other half of myself up, and step into the cockpit. This is really the boat's back porch, although I'm not supposed to call it that. I push back the horizontal panel over the entryway, remove two vertical panels, turn, climb backwards down a ladder and step into a sink full of dirty dishes. Whoops! Tom had swung a step back to access the sink, and left it in that position. But once safely standing on the floor I can see that my new home is just the same as it was during a brief visit at the end of June—cold, damp and cluttered, with one of Tom's shower thongs stuck under the hatch cover to allow ventilation. I step over the puddle of rain water on the floor under the hatch cover and sit down. My first thought is, *so much for the idea of feng shui.*

I climb back up into the cockpit to sit under the dodger and wait. Soon Tom arrives on our dock and strides toward the boat, very tall, tanned, erect and happy to see me, looking forward as he is to a permanent honeymoon in our new home. It's wonderful to see him. Yes, I'm glad to finally be here.

When we bought the boat in the spring, the spec sheet told us the boat slept seven. This may be true, but only if they're toddlers and leave their diaper bags and moms at home. Sleeping options include several bunks, or berths—one in the rear of the boat behind the navigation station; a "pilot" berth, elevated on one side of the boat; a settee below that which doubles as a single bed; and the settee on the opposite side, shaped like an L, that makes into a 3/4-size bed. A V-berth in the front of the boat is configured like a pool ball rack. That first night we sleep well on the 3/4-size bed. Tom doesn't snore, but in Montana he breathed like a 747 when he slept, which kept me awake and made me cranky. Here he breathes quietly, which we attribute to the moist air. The air you breathe in Montana is so dry that, as you exhale, all the moisture is sucked out of your lungs to keep the sagebrush alive.

Alternative housing always makes odd noises in bad weather. My new home is no exception. As the wind howls through the harbor, rigging slaps against masts. The fenders hanging down between our boat and the dock groan and make strange rubbing noises as the water pops and sloshes against the hull. Thanks to my ear plugs, I finally drift off to sleep.

Living on a sailboat, I soon discover, requires that I be excruciatingly organized. This is a desirable way to live, of course, but it takes some getting used to. During the next few days I walk several miles back and forth between the boat and my little truck doing errands, going to the storage unit, trying to get organized. I wash Tom's clothes—our sailboat is white, our sails are white, and now Tom's underwear is white. Then I remove everything from the storage lockers, most of which are only 6" high and vary from 6" to 3 feet deep. I have to get on my hands and knees with a flashlight to see into the lockers. Instead of finding missing items like gloves, socks, library books, and overdue bills—I find mold.

"Let's rename the boat THE MOLD GARDEN," I say when Tom comes home from work. He's offended.

Instead, I've decided to call our sailboat THE SHOE because, quite frankly, I feel like Mother Hubbard. The particular shoe we live in is a very large sneaker, but one not nearly large enough, and it smells—like mold in some corners, and like a poodle lifted its leg in others. Tom tells me the boat has a soul. It's important not to say anything to cause harm to its little inner sneaker, for if I can learn to like sailing this boat will take us to the Caribbean.

With features so close together on the boat it's only natural to bump your head, back, hips, knees, legs, and elbows several times a day. Since Tom is taller than the six-foot headroom we have on the boat, he often looks like a car crash victim. Sometimes we even bang our heads together. We're thinking about applying for one of those handicapped parking stickers. Maybe we can get a wider space in which to park THE SHOE.

One of the biggest sensory differences between here and Montana is the sound of seagulls instead of barking dogs. It isn't an occasional squawk you hear, but a cacophony of whining and shrieking, as if the wings of all the seagulls are broken and they're dying from the pain. Other times they sound like pigs mating or prehistoric chickens laying eggs that are way too big. But I'd much rather hear seagulls squawking than dogs barking. Many other noises compete with the seagulls and other birds. On occasion, and sometimes all at once, I can hear: the battery charger, which is in the way and sounds like a squirrel running in a cage; the water pressure pump, which goes on and off at random and makes a deep growl under the settee where I like to sit; and a foghorn that honks loudly nearby every few seconds when fog slips into Bellingham Bay. But my favorite sounds are made by the toilet pump handle. When I pull it up, it makes a loud slurping noise. When I push it down, it snorts. Using the toilet requires that I do this repeatedly—slurp...snort...slurp...snort—until I get toilet pump elbow. Then I can quit.

Tom gets up about 4:30 a.m. weekdays, while I try to sleep in for another hour. This morning while I doze, the wind is howling and Tom is walking around making the floor panels go *creak, creak, creak*; shaving with his electric shaver; and brushing his teeth, after which he sucks the toothbrush loudly.

In these early morning hours when Tom walks around the boat, the floor creaks like the floor of the Riley Creek place of my childhood, where we lived after leaving the stump ranch. That house had a sagging, linoleum-covered floor my mom painted gray on her hands and knees. Then, using the end of a sponge, she stippled it yellow, red and blue. The floor was rotten underneath the linoleum. It sagged and creaked most where the huge wood cookstove sat and where my hefty mother often stood. While we knew that a fall through the floor wouldn't be too bad (it was less than a foot off the ground), the story would be a different if Mom and the cookstove fell in together. I was a worried child.

The early morning noises on the boat are annoying but tolerable, because I'm in the nice warm bed in the V-berth while Tom is getting ready to meet *zero tolerance* at his job machining pieces for Bill Gates' new house. It strikes me as odd that a person who lives in a shoe makes architectural pieces for a house the size of a hospital.

Later in the day I'll do my job, which is to write down scraps of thought about life here among the seagulls and sailboats, search for lost items, figure out what to cook for dinner, run errands and generally serve as boatfrau to a Viking sea captain.

Tom wakes me every morning about 5:45 a.m. I have asked him to do this before he leaves so I'll get up before noon. The first time he calls me he says "SweetHEART?" with the last syllable raised an octave, something like a robin's call. I think, *Yeah, okay, in a minute.* The second time, a few minutes later, he calls a little louder, "SWEETheart!" with the first syllable raised, more like the call of a phoebe bird. I finally crawl out of bed. But he's been up for over an hour, walking the 12 square feet of floor thinking about all kinds of things to replace or fix on the boat. He feels the need to tell me about these ideas as soon as I can sit upright, when my eyes won't focus and I feel like a sunken vessel.

"Honey, can you please write these things down on some endless list, like maybe toilet paper?"

"SWEETheart!" It's the call of the phoebe bird.

During my first week on the boat Tom introduces me to a young couple, Mark and Lisa, also novice sailors. Lisa, who has been to Bible school two years, says that she, too, only cusses when she's sailing. I meet another young couple, Carl and Christy, who are preparing their boat for departure to California and on to Mexico.

"When are you leaving?" I ask.

"Next Wednesday," Carl says, confidently.

Since both their first and last names begin with a C, I call them C^2. Over the next few days, I pull a cart back and forth past their boat, URSA MAJOR. While I attempt to assemble my new life, they frantically work on their boat so they can leave before weather conditions turn unfriendly out on the ocean.

C^2 are building additional features on their boat, replacing things and buying spare parts. Because I have a handy little truck and they have only bicycles, I take Christy to pick up 400 feet of 3/8" anchor chain out of their storage unit and bring it down to the boat in three pieces: 1 of 100 feet and 2 of 150 feet. We load it all into the back of my truck, Streak. After 237,000 miles my truck performs with brave determination, grace and style, even though the tail end drags pretty close to the pavement all the way back to the harbor.

Tom and I help them step their mast, which they'd taken down to paint. We motor with them over to a different dock where a hoist provides the assistance we need to get the mast vertical again and seated in its proper position. It's a hot, nearly tropical day and I love all the activity.

"We'll leave next Saturday," Carl announces, after the mast event. "Too much to do to leave Wednesday."

But I'm growing fond of them. In the last month I've said enough goodbyes to last for years. I'm not looking forward to another one.

That same weekend my friend, Sherry, arrives from Priest River to visit, along with her partner, Sam, her son, Mike, and his girlfriend, Kim. It's always wonderful to see her. Sherry is of a generous size and spirit, and when she squeezes between the narrow passageway from the saloon to the head, she yells, "Where's the Wesson oil?"

None of them has ever been on a sailboat before today. Tom, as Colonel of the Urinal, advises our guests of the toilet rules: everyone must sit down when they use the head. These are good-sized people; Mike, for instance, is 6' 6" tall. After each visitor peeks into the tiny cubicle that serves as our toilet, they all agree that anything they might have to do can simply wait.

Soon we back THE SHOE out of the slip without incident and enjoy a perfect Sunday afternoon sail across Bellingham Bay to Inati Bay on Lummi Island. Everyone loves it. I exhibit my usual fears when the boat heels even slightly and Sherry, who is sitting to one side of the bow in hopes of catching some spray or spotting a seal, yells, "Don't worry, honey. I'll just move to the other side of the boat and level it out for you." This is why I love her and why she'll always be my friend. Besides that, she thinks I'm funny. It's a fine day on the water.

With such interesting new pals and the blessings of favorite old friends, surely Tom and I will have a happy life together aboard THE SHOE.

10

WILD NIGHT AT ECHO BAY

"We have to sail in all kinds of weather! It's the only way to prepare for ocean sailing," Tom yells over the howling wind.

Our first challenge is to back our boat out of the slip in one piece. This will be tricky. We'll have to back south, into a southeast wind, and once the dock lines are loose the wind can blast THE SHOE against our neighbor's boat. Tom decides it would be best if he handles the lines this time while I take the helm and steer the boat.

"This is how it'll work," Tom says. "I'll walk backwards along the dock holding the line as I pull our boat away from the other boat. Then I'll get on. Your job is to put the engine in reverse, give it a burst of acceleration, then stop."

With lines in hand, Tom stands on the dock while I do exactly as instructed. But things go wrong, just like I knew they would. The wind is too strong, my burst isn't big enough, and a walloping gust kicks the toe of THE SHOE against the heel of the neighboring boat.

"Don't forget to climb on!" I yell over the shrieking wind. "I don't know how to drive this thing!"

At this reminder, Tom leaps at the side of the boat across the four-foot distance from the dock, clinging to the shrouds while he holds his feet up out of the water. He just hangs there, like the cat on those *hang in there* posters. Is he unconscious? Slowly he brings first one knee up onto the toerail, then the other. Like a crab, he scrambles on his hands and knees to the bow, pushes THE SHOE away from the other boat, then runs back to grab the helm. Gunning the engine in reverse we back up fast toward the rock jetty, clear that obstacle, and continue to scoot backward toward our next target—a red fishing boat the size of a small cruise ship. Just in time, Tom turns us around and we motor forward out the harbor entrance into the monster waves and gusting winds in Bellingham Bay.

My next job is to steer the boat into the wind toward Fairhaven and the black and white Alaska-bound ferry. I do this for hours, it seems, while Tom is raising the mainsail on deck. He's raising only part of the sail, trying to tie the unraised part onto the boom with reefing lines. While he does this he hangs onto the boom, which plays back and forth three or four feet in each direction as we buck into the waves. I worry that Tom might fly off the boat while I'm barreling down on Fairhaven and the Alaska ferry. This situation makes me terribly anxious and I issue a steady stream of my favorite cuss words.

Finally Tom yells, "Fall off!" The first time I ever heard this I yelled back, "Don't you dare fall off!" But he means we are ready to sail, to turn slightly away from the direction of the wind; however, I don't know which way to fall off. It seems like I should turn to the right (oh, all right, starboard), toward our usual Friday evening stopover, Inati Bay, but you never know with sailing. Depending on the wind and current, you might sail back and forth for hours, just to go a mile. We've done it. I believe we've even sailed backwards, but I'm sure Tom would disagree.

After Tom tells me which direction to fall off, the boat doesn't sail so hot with only the reefed mainsail, and he decides to unfurl the jib, the sail up at the front, or bow, of the boat.

"Now don't let out all the sail. We don't need much up, in all this wind," I recommend loudly.

"Of course not! But we'll sail much better with some jib up."

I've heard this is true, yet he accidentally lets out too much jib and we heel way over. I'd honestly rather have a root canal. And since I'm at the helm I feel in some way responsible for this mess. My string of mantras intensifies. I hyperventilate. Tom can't say anything to make me stop and I won't let him touch me. Panting, I look up through my tears and fear to the top of the mast. The wind vane will tell me when I'm steering too close to the direction of the wind (the tail of the arrow on the wind vane cannot appear to be touching either of the two little squares). Otherwise, we'd sail directly *into* the wind and lightning will strike us dead. At a minimum the sails will luff their heads off, and the boat will completely stop sailing. As I understand it this is almost as bad as leaving the bumpers hanging off the boat a minute longer than necessary after we leave the harbor.

Tom reduces the jib and immediately the boat sails in a more upright manner, like a nice boat should. Now it's more like getting a tooth filled instead of having a root canal. I want some of that gas they give you at the dentist's office, and some New Age music, too.

I go below deck to wipe off the tears, snot and rain so I can start over. When I crawl back up to the cockpit we encounter even larger waves, five or six feet high, and THE SHOE treats them like mere no-see-ums. One of the waves leaps up and sprays Tom, which I enjoy immensely from my safe corner under the dodger, except that this Viking oaf I'm married to actually enjoys it, like a little kid running into a sprinkler on a hot day.

We finally approach Inati Bay. Furling the jib is an easy task, requiring me to pull on a rope (the furling line) to roll the sail up on itself like twine on a spool. Tom drops the mainsail, which he loosely ties to the boom so that it looks like a pile of laundry.

We anchor without incident. The boat rocks and rolls in the wind as we climb into the V-berth. I sleep well enough, exhausted from all the adrenaline activity, until I get up to use the head. When I crawl back into bed I lie awake and think about my fear of sailing. When I become bored with that I think about how we're swinging around in circles on the anchor, just inches from the rock cliffs and the other two boats anchored nearby. I hate my fear.

On Saturday morning, Tom cooks a breakfast of scrambled eggs with cheese, tomato, and turkey bacon. His interest in cooking breakfast is one reason I married him four years ago. Another, of course, is that he lets me put my ice cold feet on his warm, bare chest. Now I eat breakfast with my beautiful husband while watching the scenery of trees and cliffs change through the portholes, as we swing in slow circles at anchor. This is better than TV.

When Tom pulls up the anchor at Inati Bay I'm at the helm

ready to salute the captain. I'm supposed to drive forward, go into neutral, and then I forget what. The minute I touch the helm, I'm scared. I think I was born scared. I want my mother. I wish I'd asked her more questions.

To minimize yelling when Tom is at the bow and I am at the helm, he has devised some arm and hand signals. If he points up I'm to go forward; down is reverse; palm down, wig-wag, is neutral. The others are easier: if he points right, guess where I go? It's the same for left. If he pats the air like those construction workers with the orange vests, that means slow down.

It's now after lunch and we're sailing along the southern end of Georgia Strait toward Sucia Island. Six knots, jib unfurled, mainsail still reefed. It's cloudy-bright and not too cold. We're heeled over only a few degrees. This isn't too bad. Maybe last night I outgrew my *sniveling nautical behavior* as Tom calls it, but only when it's safe to make a joke.

"We're on a beam reach," he says, "going 6 1/2 knots."

The boat seems happy and Tom is ecstatic. He's determined to return to the Caribbean. So am I, which is why I signed up for this improbable lifestyle. Today isn't soon enough to be in Caribbean waters, but Sucia Islands State Park will have to do. Like every other boater in the region, we love Sucia.

We're now entering Echo Bay on Sucia Island, sailing slowly and silently past dozens of fat, lounging harbor seals sunning themselves on the warm side of South Finger Island. Through the binoculars I watch them lazily roll over on each other, moaning and bawling like cows. Their cream, tan, and brown bratwurst bodies blend so perfectly with the sandstone rocks that I might not have seen these shapely creatures but for their movements catching my eye.

Winds will be coming from the west-southwest, according to the marine weather report. Tom drops the anchor where we'll be shielded from the predicted winds, bringing us to rest about 75 feet from a sandstone cliff with rock formations that resemble the tails of orca whales. We'll have a quiet night.

Before we go to bed Tom checks the anchor line and makes a sobering discovery. He had somehow failed to cleat off the nylon anchor rode (line). The rode could have unraveled until we crashed to a stop against the cliff, but instead it had become caught in the windlass, the device that assists in letting down or pulling up the anchor, and it had held. It's a lucky thing he checked, for just after midnight we're awakened by extreme pitching and rolling, as if we're riding a bull at a rodeo. The winds roar into Echo Bay from the southeast, not from the predicted westerly direction. Tom gets up and puts out more anchor line to minimize the chance of the anchor pulling loose. I know that if the anchor pulls free we'll smash into several other boats anchored and moored behind us or, if the wind changes direction, which it obviously sometimes does, we'll become one with the whales' tails in the rock cliff. All this to worry about and right in the middle of the worst of it, Tom goes back to sleep. It's now 3:00 a.m. and I'm becoming more and more motion sick. Every few minutes I look out the portholes. Someone has to. But by 4:00 a.m. I'm so sleepy, disgusted and bored with it all that I put my earplugs in and go back to sleep myself. I'm too tired to stay awake for the payoff—to be able to say, "I told you so. I told you it wasn't safe to go to sleep."

In the morning the weather is gray, drippy, and only slightly windy. My morning-after seasickness feels like the flu. Tom brings me a warm, wet washcloth to put on my swollen face. He desperately wants me to like sailing, so when we're anchored out in the San Juan Islands he waits on me. He used to take care of me like this when we backpacked in Montana, but now I know I'll never again lure him up above timberline, or maybe never even above sea level.

Tom gives me a pep talk. "Sailing is a little like backpacking. Getting there can be a struggle, and even scary, if you do it in grizzly country. Then it rains the whole time you're out or the mosquitoes are as thick as fog. But when you reach the top and see all those alpine flowers and mountain goats, it's worth it."

"Well, now that I think about it maybe backpacking isn't so hot, either. Would you please bring me some more coffee?"

Blue skies are on the way. We eat another great breakfast prepared by Chef Thomas. Then he shows me how to look up the tides and currents in some booklets so we can plan our departure. The optimum time to leave is 3:00 p.m. With so much to think about when you sail, not to mention surviving those takeoffs and landings and the sailing itself, it's no wonder so few sailboats ever leave the harbor—and when they do, many of their owners just motor them from island to island. Maybe it's like so many things in life—the *idea* of sailing is better than the reality of it. Right now all I want is to be motionless. Let's hope the sail back will be pleasant and calm; I've had about all the anxiety I can stand for one weekend.

A steady wind pushes us back down the Strait of Georgia. Six knots and heeled over, but I don't care. We're going home to our slip where I can climb off this bucket and stand still. I'm at the helm, and since I can't see through the top of the dodger I stand with one foot on each side lazarette—storage lockers as big as caskets that also serve as cockpit seats. In order to be ready for anything I flex my knees and stand with a slight sumo squat. I'm holding the helm with my left hand and the main sheet in my right hand. You'd think a sheet would be a sail but, no, it's a rope you can use to let out the mainsail if the boat heels over too far. When you loosen the rope some wind spills out of the sail and the boat sits up. I know Tom has me hold this sheet so I'll think I have some control, and I'll admit that I enjoy the momentary feeling of power and authority over the boat, and over my fear. I am Ben Hur riding my chariot home.

11

A SIBILANT SYMPHONY

"Ah! Wind, the sibilant symphony," Tom says as a gust of wind tips us over sideways to 20 degrees.

"Sibilant?" I ask, bracing my legs against the opposite cockpit seat. I'm all too familiar with the *halyard chorus* that sings through the harbor during a howling wind, when hundreds of halyards clang against their masts—but now *a sibilant symphony*?

"Yes, it means having or making a hissing sound," he announces.

"Oh," I say, wondering why I've never heard of the word *sibilant* before. Where have I been? Obviously not in the wind. What am I doing out here sailing during a small craft advisory, wearing four layers of wool and my rain gear? I don't even like drafts. I'm glad my mother will never know about this.

On this same outing—a long, cold evening passage across Bellingham Bay—I tell Tom, "You know, I've got to start cooking beans from scratch. They're a cheap source of protein and they store well on passages even longer than this one."

"What kind of beans?"

"Oh, lentils, split peas, garbanzos, black beans. They come in all colors. I'll just paint us a meal or two with some beans and we'll see how it goes. I want to learn to grow sprouts, too. You can't go buying lettuce in the middle of the Pacific. Then there's yogurt. And we can grind our own flour and make pasta."

Tom continues his gaze over the bow toward the lights of the harbor.

"Are you listening?"

"You're right," he says, "We should start soon."

We already eat tofu occasionally in stir fry. Tom and I had tried to introduce this delicacy to Jeff and Lee while we still lived in Montana. One evening, when this hare-brained sailboat scheme was in its infancy, we invited them to dinner to share the news. As my son pushed pieces of tofu off to the side of his plate we told him of our plans to buy a sailboat and sail to the Caribbean.

"First the tofu, now this," he said earnestly. "You guys are losing it."

"Lots of people do it," I said. "You'd be surprised."

"Just promise me you won't go sailing in the Bermuda Triangle."

"How fast do you go when you sail on the ocean?" Lee asked.

"Oh, six, maybe seven knots," Tom said, as if they'd have a clue about a knot.

"That's seven or eight miles an hour," I said.

Jeff laughed so hard he cried, and we all joined him. "But you're in your fifties!" he said through his tears, "You'll never *get* there at that speed."

Since we have tofu under our belts, so to speak, I'll orient my current research toward cooking with other foodstuffs recommended for use offshore. I find a book, *Sailing the Farm*, which is fun to read and tells you how to turn your boat into a floating food factory. The book also provides instructions on how to make your own tofu. At the library I search out a book on cooking with legumes. I already have a crockpot. It's good to experiment with new recipes while you still have shore power. Making pasta will have to wait, but I buy mung beans at a health food mart so I can try my hand at growing sprouts.

First I nurse the sprouts to life in a wide-mouthed pint jar, using a special lid with holes large enough to rinse the beans without losing them. I carefully rinse the little bean heads four times a day, and wrap the jar containing the potential sprouts in a towel to keep them warm during gestation. If only the sprouts will grow as fast as the mold in the corners of our lockers. Sailing in the cold and rain over the weekend makes it tricky to keep the sprouts warm. But after six days all the beans are sprouted. The seventh day I place them uncovered out on the back porch so they can catch the sun breaks and turn green with chlorophyll, which I understand makes them even more healthful. On the night of the seventh day I sprinkle the sprouts on top of a green salad. They're downright cute with their little green tails and don't taste too bad, either, in a moldy sort of way. In a matter of minutes, we eat the sprouts I'd so carefully nurtured for an entire week. The strangest part, though, is that the very next day our bodies begin their own sibilant symphonies.

Around this same time the inside walls of the boat become moist. Beads of water form and begin to trickle down into the bilge. Simply because of a handful of sprouts, our lives change over night. Quite possibly, things will never be the same.

The next week I buy a 25-pound bag each of soy beans and calico beans (that's all kinds of beans, all colors, in one bag). I find a bean stew recipe that calls for brown sugar, and follow the instructions on preparing the beans for cooking: first simmer the beans for at least 30 minutes, then store them in a cool place overnight. The cockpit is convenient. The next morning I chop and sauté an onion and several garlic cloves and toss in a little browned lean ground beef. I add a can each of diced tomatoes and tomato sauce, two sliced carrots, lots of salt and pepper, and 1/4 cup of brown sugar. I put all these ingredients into the crockpot with the beans, turn it on low, and leave it for the day. That evening the beans still aren't done. I set them out on the back porch in the cockpit again to spend the night. All the next day I cook them on high. They're done that night for dinner, and they're delicious.

The sibilant sounds intensify on THE SHOE and the condensation problem grows serious. We now have to pump the bilge twice a day. Sometimes Tom will flip the bilge pump switch on without telling me. While I'm cooking in the galley he'll go about his mysterious tinkering business.

Suddenly he'll yell, "Turn it off! Turn it off, quick!"

And I yell back, "Turn what off? Turn what off?"

"The bilge pump! It'll burn up if it runs dry!"

Where are some good hand signals when you need them? From now on we agree that Tom will babysit the bilge pump. I can't even hear the thing run or the water pour out the hull because of the squawking seagulls and all the other sounds on the boat.

Additional noises soon announce themselves. As Tom works on something or other under a floor panel, machine gun retorts blast off from his port aft quarter.

" Honey, what did you say?"

"I really like my new power tools," he says. I love that guy's sense of humor. I think I'll keep him. When he messes around with something out in the cockpit and I am, as usual, in the galley easily within earshot, I hear more sound effects from the captain.

"What was that you said?" I ask.

"I love you," he replies.

The week is filled with discoveries. We learn that the packing nut on the engine is loose and has been causing most of the extra water in the bilge. We also get wind of a previously unnoticed law of physics—that smells and noises expand to fit the space available. This is an unfortunate turn of events for someone who, in a former life, was quite possibly a canary used in gold mines to detect carbon monoxide. It doesn't take long to realize that we need a much larger sailboat—preferably one the size of a barn. Thirty-seven feet just isn't big enough.

We hear there's an Alberg sailboat rendezvous every year north of here. The organizer of the event reports that at the last rendezvous participants exchanged information on various topics, such as how to extend the length of the V-berth and how to maintain the Alberg's unusually deep bilge. I'm also sure the question "What kind of head do you have?" came up. It always does when sailboat people get together. If we make it to the next rendezvous I want to recommend growing sprouts in the bilge under the engine, where they'll stay warm and where you can grow a generous supply at one time. And even though it's indelicate I want to pose a very practical question: "How do you guys handle the problem of *breaking wind* after eating beans and sprouts? First there's the condensation problem it causes, then there's that other person in such a small area."

In the meantime, I've been checking with other liveaboards on this topic. My local research has been lively. One woman tells me that when she and her husband were first married she held her discomfort but her husband refused to do this because he feared it would make him sick. They almost got a divorce over the issue. Why don't more people talk about a topic that has such potentially high stakes? Marriages could be saved. She finally decided she wasn't going to suffer the pain of holding it in while enduring *his* free-for-all flatulence. So now she just lets fly and it's no big deal. Their two little live-aboard doggies do it, too. That's the consensus of all the couples I've interviewed on the subject. You either become very tolerant and lower your air quality standards or you don't live on a sailboat with another person, and certainly not dogs.

We find that the best defense is to go sailing immediately after eating beans or sprouts. It's a sibilant symphony out there anyway and we've discovered that our cruising speed picks up about half a knot. Maybe with this added tail wind we'll get to the Caribbean after all.

12

I ONLY CUSS WHEN I'M SAILING

It's not easy not to cuss, when you've had as much practice as I have. Oh, some of my best friends cuss, but Tom believes cussing is caused by a weak mind—one not smart enough to use the *right* words. "And it isn't aesthetically pleasing," he adds. So I try, I really do, not to cuss around him. But when we're sailing and the boat heels way over in the howling wind I leave Tom at the helm grinning his face off and go below deck, away from the water. I sit on the downhill side of the cabin and brace my feet on the opposite settee. The gravity always forces me backward against the storage lockers. Sometimes the hatch cover drips on me as I cry. I feel as if I'm being punished. My fear is ugly and I mutter several strings of cuss words, my mantras from the stump ranch dialect I once spoke so fluently.

Some sayings have a religious theme, others have outhouse overtones or relate to agricultural activities and smells. Often my cussing addresses the ancestry of certain humans. Tom is Norwegian, clearly of the Viking stock that went about marauding on the high seas, while I am of peasant, inland, German farmer stock. I'm even shaped a bit like a potato. And my genes like land. So far I endure sailing to get there, but for Tom, we're already *there* when we're sailing.

I believe my fear of water began with a ferry ride on a warm spring North Idaho day in 1948. It's my earliest recollection.

"I hope the brakes hold on this son-of-a-bitch. They're not very good," my mother said, as we rolled to a stop on the ferry and climbed out of our old DeSoto.

The ferry, nothing more than an oversized raft, would take us from Thama across the Pend Oreille River. I can still hear the clank of the chain pulling the ferry, and feel the breeze on my face. My mother's big hand held mine as we stood near the car. With my little sister, Laurel, in her other arm, she chatted nervously with Aunt Irene. Every few minutes she'd glance over at the car, sigh, and say, "I hope we make it across."

The tires of our car rested a couple of feet from the front edge of the ferry and the deep, dark water we were crossing. I stood next to one of the tires and stared at it, willing it to stay in place. Why didn't my mother do something to make the brakes hold, to keep the car from rolling off into the river? It was a big job, but on my own, with all the willpower available to a three-year-old, I kept our car in place on the ferry. My relief was enormous when we finally reached the other side and the safety of land. I'm told I slept all the way home.

Every time we go sailing Tom reassures me. "We can*not* tip over in these conditions. This is a bluewater boat with a full keel. It is physically impossible for us to tip over."

"But I'm on board. Anything can happen."

Being a sensitive sort of guy, he continues his efforts to comfort me. "We'll keep sailing as often as possible, even in winter, and you'll see for yourself. You'll cheat death often enough that sailing will become routine. It'll be no big deal. You'll learn to like sailing. If you don't I'll take you to the Marine Exchange and trade you in for a model that does." I do know a joke when I hear one. Tom likes me too much to trade me in; I'm quite sure he likes me almost as much as the boat.

But I know the waves, steep and pushy, are hiding something. The water is a bog with quicksand that will pull me to the bottom under dark, mysterious currents.

My mother usually spoke her mind, with frank, colorful, and sometimes inventive language. Yet this robust woman who talked so big was afraid of many things, including the howling of wolves and coyotes and catching a draft on her neck. For her, bodies of water any size, even mudpuddles, held hidden terrors. We didn't learn to swim when we were children because Mom was convinced we'd drown.

Oh, she could be brave. Like that day we drove home from town in a thunderstorm and arrived to smoke pouring out of our old log house. I can still see her leap from the car, yelling to my older sister, "Marian, you come along and help." Into the thunder and lightning they ran. My little sisters and I could not believe our eyes. We waited in the car and watched them go in the front door of the smoking house. Would we ever see our mother or big sister again? We screamed and cried for them to come back. Finally Mom slammed the screen door aside and barged out the front door, coughing, pulling a large object behind her, muttering to herself. Marian followed close behind. We stopped screaming, wiped our eyes, and watched them drag a smoldering mattress across the yard through the pouring rain, and down the steep bank into the frog pond. This woman, who feared getting chilled because you could catch your death, climbed back up the bank, slogged through the rain and mud to the car and said, "Goddamn lightning struck Laurel's bed. Good thing we were in town."

It was a good thing, too, for we slept and played upstairs, often lying on our beds talking to our dolls and fighting with each other. Mom said it might be bad luck to leave Laurel's bed where it was so we moved the frame with its new second-hand mattress across the room. When it rained we put a bucket under the hole in the roof until Daddy could patch it. But the old mattress just lay there in the frog pond. My sisters and I often stood on the bank, peered over the edge at the offending item, and said to each other, "Goddamn lightning."

Within a year we moved to the valley below the log house, onto land Daddy called a stump ranch. A few years before, all the ponderosa pine trees had been cut and most of the slash burned, leaving behind a field of stumps. Daddy built us a new house on a slight rise overlooking the valley. My vocabulary of cuss words grew while I played with scraps of lumber and overheard the things Daddy said when he hit his thumb while pounding a nail, or sawed a two by four too long or too short.

And eventually we forgot about the mattress rotting in the frog pond over on the far side of the valley. It's probably still there, nearly fifty years later, a key component in some strange ecosystem that's been named a research natural area by the University of Idaho.

Maybe now, like the mattress, I'll end up as part of the ecosystem here in the waters of North Puget Sound, because when an object begins to tip, to slide, to fall, it rarely stops. I had managed to keep the old DeSoto from rolling off the ferry that time, but somewhere along the line I lost my powers. Love couldn't stop the car sliding on an icy mountain road that night over an embankment with my grandma inside, and nothing could stop what followed—the wreckage, the death, the incomprehensible loss.

Roaring sounds make me particularly nervous. When the wind wails through the rigging and gusts into the swollen sails, when the waves make the mast shudder, it sounds too much like the stovepipes of my childhood when they would catch fire and clean themselves. At these times—a couple times a year—I'd be watching a western on TV, working on a paint-by-number set, or leafing through the Sears catalog. I'd be as close to the stove as possible, my body scorching hot on the side nearest the stove and freezing cold on the other side. Suddenly the chimney would glow red like a caboose and the stove would roar as if a freight train were about to crash into the living room. Instead, my mother charged into the room and said, "Oh, hell, it's that stove again."

My father sat rocking nearby in the chair he occupied by the stove every winter when the woods were shut down. "Ah, it'll cool off pretty soon. Always does."

But with neither insulation nor a proper through-hull fitting for the rusted six-inch stovepipe, it's a miracle our house didn't burn down.

And when we're sailing and Tom says, "We're safe in this boat, can't you get that through your head?" I try to remember that my father was right. The stove always did cool off. We always survived the chimney fires. So maybe I'll advance to sailing unafraid with the boat heeled way over in gale-force winds in a lightning storm, and just maybe I won't cuss anymore.

13

ARRIVALS AND DEPARTURES

This morning's job is to balance the underwear account. Just as I begin tossing socks on the pilot berth, Tom arrives home from work. Something must be terribly wrong; it's only 10:30 a.m. and he works until 5:00 p.m.

"Melanie called me at work," he says, staring at the pile of socks on the settee. I watch his mouth as he continues, "Marian has a brain tumor and is scheduled for surgery." Everything blurs. Who cares if we have 30 pairs of socks on board and only two pairs of underwear each. Nothing matters, nothing at all, except that my big sister faces brain surgery.

I run to the pay phone to call Melanie, Marian's daughter in Wyoming with whom she's been staying. "She's right here. You can talk to her," Melanie says.

Marian sounds upbeat and I try to do the same. "They're doing tests. Surgery is Wednesday," she says, matter of factly. We talk back and forth about how we all thought she'd just been depressed, and isn't it good to know what's really wrong so it can be fixed. It's like talking on the phone with someone in Alaska, where there's a longer-than-normal delay between what you say and the other person's reply.

When it's time to hang up I say something like, "I love you very much. I'll talk to you in a few days." But I know I might never talk to her again. Why did I act as if she were dealing with a hangnail? I could at least have said, "Marian, I'm sorry I cut the hair off your doll that time. Yes, it was me. I did it and I'm real sorry."

I call our sister, Laurel, in Priest River and learn that all the sisters and many of their family members are driving down to Wyoming to see Marian. I'm quite certain she'll receive more love and attention now than she's ever received in her life. Why do we wait? It reminds me a little of leaving my job this summer. I'd felt somewhat invisible for months, yet when I announced my departure date everyone suddenly treated me like I was a most fascinating person—one who'd be sadly missed. Relationships I didn't even know I had intensified to a state of frenzied, undying love and affection. It was weird. It was wonderful.

In a half-hearted way, I continue with my errands and galley duties. Captains have to eat and a boat must be kept tidy enough so you can find a place to sit down. But I feel immobilized—slow, vacant, drifty—pretty much the same symptoms Marian had exhibited for months. It's like I have a sympathy tumor. I wait. And I think about my big sister. She was supposed to be around forever, at least as long as I was. Marian has a habit of twirling a clump of hair on top of her head while she talks. Is the tumor under that spot? Had 55 years of this habit somehow caused the tumor?

As I sit quietly thinking about Marian, I recall the spring weekend we spent together a couple of years ago at her place in North Idaho. It was before she became so tired and disinterested in life, before she began acting lost. We each got a kit at a fabric store so we could make quilt squares to enter in a quilt lottery—a random drawing. No matter how unsophisticated your design ended up, you had a chance to win a splendid quilt (which neither of us won). The next day we raked her yard and burned grass. That night Marian found a Washington State lottery ticket she'd forgotten about in her purse. When she checked it with the winning numbers she discovered she'd won $60,000. We hopped in her car and drove as fast as we could to the mini-mart in Newport, Washington, where she'd bought the ticket. As she drove I talked her into letting me help her spend the money—we'd take a trip to Switzerland together, that is after she got a new well dug and bought a sports car. But when we got to the mini-mart the young attendant said, "I'm sorry, but you didn't win anything. You read the numbers wrong." Our disappointment lasted only a few minutes. In thinking back about it, spending that money she

didn't even win turned out to be some of our happiest moments together.

My new friend, Lisa, stops by the boat. I try to act like nothing
is wrong. No need to burden other people with worries about my sister. We talk about many things, including the importance of being
healthy on a sailboat, and I casually ask what she knows about brain
tumors. Then I begin to cry and I tell her about my sister. She takes
my hands and prays aloud for Marian at some length. I feel immea-
surably better. Later I pray on my own. I pray to God; I request assistance from "the universe;" and I send several May Day calls to my
guardian angel, even though she's on probation for previous lack of
assistance. This scatter gun system of prayer just has to help. My requests are simple: *Please let Marian be her old self again. Please give
me back my sister.*

Our new friends, Carl and Christy (alias C²) are scheduled to
come to dinner. Although several weeks behind schedule, they're
still working hard on their boat so they can leave for California.
They've been eating nothing but peanut butter sandwiches for days
because they're too busy to stop and cook. Tom and I feel nurturing
toward them, and envious, too. After all, they'll be basking in the sun
this winter and we will not. Carl and Christy arrive at 8:00 p.m.,
after it's too dark for them to work on their boat. At dinner we learn
that they met in Durango, Colorado, at an arts and crafts fair.
Christy saw Carl playing in a bagpipe band and asked him to teach
her how to play. They've been married 12 years, and they still play
the bagpipes.

"Looks like we'll leave next week, maybe Friday. We're having a
cockpit coaming built," Carl says. He announces a new departure
date every time we see him, and each date sails past leaving C² and
their boat, URSA MAJOR, behind in their temporary slip up at the front
of the harbor.

The subject changes to heads. Even at dinner time this is a favorite topic of men who own sailboats. A boat toilet, properly called
a head, of course, can be so very mysterious. Sometimes when you
most need it to work you pump and pump and nothing happens.

"What brand of head do you have?" Tom asks.

"Well, our head's the greatest," Carl replies proudly. "They say you can flush an overcoat through it."

I catch Tom's eye. He smiles, for he's always on the lookout for some high-tech item to buy for the boat. We ask them lots of other questions, too, since we're in a state of preparation for sailing to the Caribbean in a few years, that is if I can overcome my fear of sailing in Bellingham Bay. The ocean seems so big and scary. I hope we all know what we're getting ourselves into. At least the evening with C^2 takes my mind off Marian.

On Wednesday, surgery day, I call the Wyoming Medical Center in Casper.

"They did more tests because the doctor wanted more information," Melanie tells me. "The tumor is about the size of a golf ball, and a main artery goes through it. Surgery is rescheduled for Monday. We're taking her home to Lander for the weekend." She also says the sisters and their families have all come and gone. At least the C word—cancer—hasn't been mentioned. I wonder how they'd know yet? More waiting. As usual, we'll go sailing over the weekend.

Tom's son Daniel arrives Friday night about 8:30, en route to San Francisco to do a chef's internship. We immediately set sail in the dark across Bellingham Bay for Inati Bay. Daniel has never sailed before and he likes it right away. He knows exactly what his father means when he issues some sailboat instruction. Must be the Norwegian genes.

We all talk a lot about food for the next 24 hours.

"You should try a raspberry shooter some time," Daniel says. "You hold up a fresh raspberry, squirt chocolate sauce into it, and shoot it into your mouth."

I want one.

"Maybe," he continues, "when I'm done with my internship I'll buy a sailboat, too, and be a cruising chef. I could cater to rich people who'd come aboard my boat for a sunset cruise and a gourmet meal." We talk about names for his business. He could call it *The Kitchen Table Sailboat*, but that's too prosaic; *The Sailing Gourmet* isn't too bad; or maybe *The Gimballed Galley*, although surely that's a cliche by now.

The wind blows briskly as we sail along on Saturday. The sail from Inati Bay over to Eagle Harbor on Cypress Island is mostly pleasant.

By the time we leave late in the day for Bellingham the barometer has dropped and I feel like an elephant is sitting on me. As we cross Bellingham Channel the winds roar down on us from the Gulf of Alaska, interrupted only by islands the size of pimples in relation to the size of the wind. With both sails full up in the howling wind the boat heels way over, and Tom stands at the helm grinning and chatting happily with Daniel. I retreat below deck and sit glumly on the downhill, starboard side of the cabin and brace my feet on the opposite settee. Gravity forces me back against the storage lockers. My fear is ugly and I mutter several of my favorite heavy-weather sailing mantras. The hatch cover drips on me as I cry. Why do I feel like I'm being punished?

As we barrel along across cyclone alley I realize I have to go to the bathroom. I make my way slowly to the head by holding onto the overhead grabrails. Once inside the tiny cubicle I brace my head against the wall opposite the toilet for balance. I pull down my pants, lean back and squat down approximately where the seat is supposed to be. My head remains braced on the wall so I won't slide off the pot. When I pump the handle to flush, I pump only air because the boat is heeled over so far to starboard. "Piece of crap toilet," I growl as I plaster my face and chest against the wall and slither back into my pants. By this time I feel queasy and take two alka-seltzers before climbing back up into the cockpit, where I glower in my corner under the dodger.

As soon as we're back in our slip, Daniel departs for San Francisco.

Later Tom and I talk, as we often do, about how I'm doing with sailing.

"Sailing is like life," he says. "It isn't always fun."

"But," I snarl through the tears and snot, "you *gotta* do life. You *choose* to go sailing because it's so wonderful and fun!"

"I really enjoyed the conditions we sailed in today," he says. "It helped me learn to be a better sailor." I glare at him and say nothing.

"And I don't know what you're so afraid of," he continues. "It's far more dangerous to drive across town to the grocery store than it is to sail on the ocean."

"If I hear that one more time I'm going to get seasick all over you," I state calmly, emphasizing each word.

"Do you want to leave here? Is that what you want?" Tom asks.

"That isn't a very helpful thing to say. You know I have no place to go." I blow my nose. This discussion, and the honeymoon, it seems, are both over.

I'll bet Marian isn't thinking "you gotta do life." She's probably desperately hoping she'll get to do life some more. My biggest hope in the world is that she be allowed that opportunity. The weird thing is I'm sort of getting used to the *idea* of Marian having a brain tumor. But it also makes me feel as if all our efforts are absurd, like we're just dumb, fat chickens scratching in the dirt of life. Suddenly "chop!" off goes your head. Next thing you know you're in the stew pot.

Monday is another low barometer day. As the storm passes inland it seems to take most of the air with it and I'm left yawning, tired, vulnerable. When it's 2:00 p.m. and time to call the Wyoming Medical Center about Marian's surgery, I'm overcome with emotion and feel in need of life support. I dial their number and breathe deeply so I can talk. An elderly volunteer in ICU tells me, "She's just being brought down from the recovery room. Why don't you call back in an hour?" I am so frustrated because I can't talk with anyone about the results that I run all the way back to the boat through the rain and wind. At least she's alive. At 3:00 p.m. I call again, practicing deep breathing to avoid sobbing at the nurse who says, "Marian is doing well and her vital signs are good." I want to hug her over the phone. Then I talk to Melanie. The tumor was benign and soft enough for easy removal. I am relieved beyond telling, but then on the way back to the boat I fall apart all over again because it was so mean and unnecessary that she got the tumor in the first place.

The mad pace of errands resumes. Since I'm so efficient with my chores and errands my list becomes longer, my assignments more advanced. The newest task is to find 3/8" Plexiglas for the fixed port-holes (the large ones you can't open). The old glass is scratched and dull, and they leak. We must install the new portholes before the weather turns colder. To find the right quality and thickness Plexi-glass requires numerous phone calls and visits to glass shops and hardware stores. My search takes me to a glass shop in the small town of Lynden, a Dutch village, very Christian Reformed and quaint. It requires one trip to take the old panels and another, a few days later, to pick up the new panels. Lisa goes with me on the second trip. As we drive there we agree how wonderful it is to see only pastoral farm land and mountains—no water or boats. The highway passes over a pond at one point, but we both focus straight ahead and pretend not to see the water.

While I pick up the new Plexiglass panels, Lisa goes shopping. When we meet back at my truck she reaches into a sack and pulls out a fake, shiny blue iguana about 8" long, with black beads for eyes.

"It was half price," she says, "and you need a pet on your boat." Lisa is definitely a sweetheart.

When we return to the harbor, I see that an astonishing thing has happened. There's a gaping hole in the marina, as if half the boats have vanished. Carl and Christy have finally left in URSA MAJOR. I can't believe they're gone. They've been preparing to leave since I arrived the end of August. Stopping by their boat to see how things were going was part of my routine. At least we have a forwarding address for them and a promise that all letters will be answered.

"This time it's for sure," Carl had said the last time he announced a departure date.

"We'll stop by the evening before," I said, not believing him.

"We'll probably be going crazy by then."

"Oh, we can help with that."

Tom had stopped by their boat, but I had not. Now I walk the long dock home to THE SHOE where I hold my blue iguana, whom I name *Sydney*. While I'm sad that Carl and Christy have left the harbor, one departure I *can* celebrate is that of Marian's tumor. I have my big sister back.

14

MAKING ADJUSTMENTS

John Denver spent my twenty-first birthday evening with me, although he didn't know it. That night he was performing with the Mitchell Trio at the Cellar Door in Washington, D.C., where friends had taken me to celebrate. The show was fun, uplifting, joyous. Now, sadly, John Denver has died in a flying accident. Deejays have been playing his song, *Rocky Mountain High*, and the tune runs through my head as Tom and I walk along the dock. Oh, to be on some mountain top in Montana, or anywhere. After nearly two months on board THE SHOE, I'm barely holding things together. Due to recent events I've about reached the end of my halyard with this liveaboard lifestyle.

A handsome couple walks toward us on the dock, he of distinguished gray hair, she of petite size and demure bearing. Two model liveaboards, elegantly dressed. Mature Ken and Barbie dolls.

"So, how are you adjusting?" the wife asks me.

Immediately, I start in jabbering like someone pulled my string. "Oh, fine, but I'm in the doldrums today. I didn't have time to write a thing, although I'd been on a roll until this week. Wrote three stories last week, then nothing. Our new diesel heater spit soot all over our boat inside and out and I've been cleaning ever since. I may never write again. Otherwise I'm okay. I'm fine, really."

Tom and the couple stare at me wondering, I'm sure, if I will ever stop talking. Abruptly, I stop. I say to the man, whose mouth is still hanging open slightly, "I see someone took your parking space." Now everyone's attention is on him.

About the soot. One night recently Tom and I arrive home to

our boat to see foul, black diesel smoke pouring out of the chimney. We push back the companionway hatch cover as smoke flows past us. Flames are shooting out from under Dick, our new diesel heater. Tom switches off Dick's pacemaker (the pump that feeds fuel to him) and, after we open all the hatches and portholes, we collapse on the settee to assess the damage. My eyes burn and I feel hopeless. A film of diesel soot covers every surface. We're lucky the boat didn't catch fire. Or are we?

Certainly Tom had carefully installed the heater. Just in case, I ask, "You did follow all the instructions, didn't you?" This inquiry isn't well received and apparently doesn't deserve a response. Tom knows how to do many mysterious things. I should never ask such a foolish question.

When everything cools down a little, including us, Tom climbs above deck to inspect the chimney and cap. He discovers that both are completely clogged with soot. We proceed to clean out Dick's internal organs as much as possible, then Tom adjusts the pacemaker with a screwdriver and reboots Dick. This produces more hideous diesel fumes, so he turns him off. When we picked up the diesel heater at the marine store I had happy thoughts of being a warm person. I had hoped this heater would be capable of "running us out of the house," just like a good wood stove.

But now I'm cold, and I can't possibly sleep on the boat in this mess. Since we hate to spend money on a motel room, however, we just shake out all the flannel bedding and rearrange it in the V-berth. I take two aspirins and go to bed thinking about what I'll be doing for the next several days—cleaning all surfaces top to bottom, and washing all bedding, clothes, curtains, and cushion covers. As I finally drift off to sleep, I am comforted by John Denver's liquid voice crooning away in my head about leaving on a jet plane.

The next evening, after scrubbing soot off the walls and laundering every washable item, I am not my usual cheerful self. When I'm not feeling too thrilled with life Tom can be especially attentive. Every few seconds he says something like, "I'm sorry you're having a hard time." When I say nothing he says, "Poor baby. I'm sorry you didn't have a very good day." On and on, as I quietly go about cooking dinner in my little hobbit kitchen. Then he says, "Are you crabby?"

"What makes you think I'm crabby, for chrissake?"

Silence.

Later I tell him in my kindest, most groveling way, "Thomas, darling, it would be so much more helpful to me if you'd simply acknowledge my less-than-wonderful mood and allow for it. Otherwise it makes me feel sorry for myself."

The weekend is coming. In spite of the mess still to clean up and numerous long-neglected chores around the boat, Tom wants to go sailing right after work Friday, as usual. This means motoring or sailing across Bellingham Bay after dark through crab pot buoys, their lines just waiting to get tangled up in our rudder. The boat could also plow into a partially submerged log, resulting in a sink or swim odyssey in 50° water. And if we do survive the crossing, we'll anchor at Lummi Island with the help of our searchlight—which has a short in it and works only when it's in the mood. To make matters worse, it's cold out there this time of year.

Sure, I agreed to come to Bellingham for a couple years to prepare for our escape to the Caribbean, but when I signed up for this unlikely lifestyle I didn't think I'd be spending two years in the first and second stages of hypothermia. Sailing in the Pacific Northwest can be chilly even in summer and here I am, freezing my hinder off Friday night through Sunday every fall weekend. I need time out, preferably in a sauna.

"We need to stay here and take care of some things on the boat," I say, stomping my size ten Converse tennis shoes. "And besides, I want to learn how to cook a new bean stew recipe and sew some curtains."

Tom acts like he's just been kicked in the stomach; however, he's basically a good person and finally says with a deep sigh, "Okay, we won't go, then."

On Saturday morning beans simmer on the stove while I retrieve my portable sewing machine from our storage unit near the harbor and set it up on our table in the saloon. I begin to sew new curtains for the boat. The curtain fabric is cream colored and all I have to do is hem each side of the 12 little panels, sew on a fabric tape with built-in snaps and sew in some tucks. I've heard that when the curtains and the walls are the same color your boat will seem larger. It's worth a try.

Sewing isn't one of my better skills. When Tom and I were preparing for our trip to St. John, I sewed us each a pair of string pants, pants you pull on and gather about your waist with a thick string sewn into the waistband. We wore this comfortable island attire nearly every day on our trip. While they appeared stylish on tall, lean Tom, on me they looked like a full sack of round items. When a friend saw photos of our trip she said, "Whatever were you wearing?" I like to think the problem wasn't in my sewing, that it was the choice of fabric coupled with the garment's style.

As the morning progresses and Tom goes about his preparations for tinkering, he keeps banging his head. Whenever he's on the boat he really ought to wear his bicycle helmet. A goose egg grows on his forehead to match the one on the back of his head behind his starboard ear, and his face is streaked with soot from cleaning Dick for the third time. He also keeps banging his port elbow, the one that always hurts a little anyway. He never bangs the other elbow. With Tom in a self-mutilation mode I'm doubly glad we aren't sailing this weekend. But then he'd probably be just fine if he were sailing instead of imprisoned here in the harbor doing chores.

Tom had purchased new hacksaw blades so he could saw through a bolt holding down an impotently placed cleat on our dock, but now he can't find the hacksaw handle. He gives that up and begins to search for a roll of mechanic's wire with which to secure Dick's new stovepipe to the deck. When he reviewed Dick's installation and operating instruction booklet, he discovered that we need four feet of stovepipe and he'd only installed two and a half feet. The wire would keep the wind from blowing away the new addition to the chimney.

Tom takes all the tools out of the coffin-sized locker on the starboard side of the cockpit. No wire. He then sits on the port locker lid amidst the tools, and stares out to the east. Every few minutes I look up from my sewing. He doesn't move. I worry about his eyes. It's important to blink once in a while, otherwise they'll dry out. Fifteen minutes later he backs down the steps into the boat to resume his search for the wire. He sifts through his project box behind the navigation station. Not there. He stands and stares out the fixed porthole for five or six minutes. Then he looks in the tool boxes under the settee. Not there either. He stares another three or four minutes at a red toolbox. At least the length of time is decreasing and I can stop worrying about his eyes drying out. Then he crawls on the floor in front of me, lifts up the floor panel, and the wire isn't there, either. He stays on all fours and stares at the floor for two or three minutes. Slowly he gathers himself up into a mostly upright position and goes into the head. I hear him pump the toilet handle once, then silence (I can tell he's staring), then he repeats this activity—pump...stare...pump...stare—about a dozen times. He walks slowly back over to the companionway, his pants still unzipped, and stares out over the jetty at the top of Lummi Island.

"What's wrong?" I finally ask. No answer. "Well, let's go to the hardware store and buy what you need."

"Okay. But I need some junk food, too."

At least he's talking.

We walk along the dock to the car and drive with great purpose to the hardware store. I wait in the car while Tom goes in to purchase the eyebolts and wire. After he returns with a sack of stuff we drive to a nearby hamburger joint for a bag of burgers and fries, then to a park near the harbor to eat and watch the action in Bellingham Bay.

"Sailboats...racing," Tom says, gazing longingly at the cluster of white sails in the distance as he chews a French fry.

Bravely I say, "It sure was funny how you kept staring when you couldn't find the wire."

He stops chewing, swallows, and says slowly, sadly, "I forgot to buy the wire."

On the way back to the boat we find a different store, walk in together holding hands, and buy some wire.

Back at the boat Tom secures the chimney to the deck using the eyebolts and wire. He then finds the hacksaw and manages to butcher the cleat off the dock, followed by an hour of smoothing the mutilated cleat with a file. He also washes the soot off the deck of the boat, then installs a smoke alarm and a carbon monoxide detector below deck as recommended by the Coast Guard. I sew more curtains while my experimental bean stew recipe simmers away on the stove. You have to cook beans for a very long time.

On Sunday morning Tom cooks breakfast. We don't have a toaster due to the lack of counter space, so he's learning to broil toast on a cookie sheet in the propane cookstove. As he reaches under the stove to pull out the cookie sheet from its storage area, he shoves his hand into some cooking slobber that has run down the side of the stove from the simmering pot of beans. After the initial disgust wears off, he calmly cleans up this new mess. He then places two slices of bread on the cookie sheet and slides it onto the first rack under the broiler. The top of Lummi Island reclaims his attention.

"I smell something burning!" I yell, as the new smoke alarm shrieks. Tom races over toward the piercing noise, disables the alarm, then dashes back to the oven, opens the door, and tosses the black, smoldering toast out into the cockpit among some sooty rags and sponges. He places the stove's rack down a notch. Making toast at this lower elevation in the oven takes longer but produces superior results, something like Melba toast. After slathering the toast with margarine and honey, Tom resumes his thousand-yard-stare out toward the bay. Honey and margarine drip down his arm, past his bruised elbow and onto the companionway steps.

Sunday evening the wind howls, it rains, and we have noisy indigestion from the bean stew. It's a cozy, intimate time, except that the carbon monoxide detector keeps blinking and squealing. Dick behaves quietly, however, and keeps us warm and snug inside the boat, even as a few chunks of old soot spew out the chimney onto the recently washed deck. I read aloud as Tom mends our 140% genoa sail, the one that's been in a bag on the pilot berth for several weeks. What a lovely way to spend a Sunday evening. I think I could learn to like this sailboat lifestyle.

15

DOCK DOGGIES, CRUISING KITTIES, PARROTS AND THEIR HUMANS

I suppose I should be thankful that I have Sydney, since I no longer have my beloved Fatty cat. Sydney, the fake shiny blue iguana with black, faceted beads for eyes, eyes that see everything. Sydney is definitely a male. It has something to do with his attitude. He's kind of cocky and self assured, even though he's a bag of beans wearing a blue *lamé* overcoat.

Sydney is on probation. One evening, after another cold crossing of the bay, Tom assigned me the task of lighting Dick. The little pocket flashlight I carry for security and a feeling of independence was growing dim. I would need it, however, at a critical moment when starting the stove. First I flipped on Dick's pacemaker, over by the electrical panel, then turned Dick's bellybutton knob all the way to the right. After a few minutes I opened his chest plate so I could shine my flashlight down into his gullet to see if it was black and wet. If so, I'd know he was primed with sufficient diesel fuel so I could light a match and produce a flame. But, in my less-than-wonderful condition, I shined my weak little flashlight into my own eyes instead of down inside Dick, then wondered why I couldn't see anything. I looked away with crossed eyes, and there was Sydney, sitting on top of his favorite book, *Cruising for Cowards*.

"Way to go!" he sneered. I couldn't believe it, and just when I needed a friend the most. So, now he sits on top of the radar unit guarding the companionway, where he cannot watch me light the stove. He stares at the door while Tom stares out the fixed portholes or the open companionway. Sometimes it feels like a wax museum here on THE SHOE.

When Sydney misbehaves, all I have to do is stroll the docks and meet the pets that belong to other boaters. We have a surprising diversity of pet fauna down here at the harbor.

Last summer THE SHOE was in a temporary slip, over on F-west dock. A very old wood powerboat bobbed in the slip next to ours, and a woman stayed there with assorted friends and a Great Dane named Equus. Sometimes Equus didn't get enough walks to suit his needs, and as soon as he and his human stepped off their boat onto the spur dock between us, Equus would take a leak on the carpet there that looked like green grass. At least he usually (but not always) waited to do his other business elsewhere. The first time the proud new owner of a permanent slip on the *other* side of us docked his elegant sailboat, he stepped off the boat right into a huge pile of dog droppings.

"My God, do they allow horses on this dock?" he grumbled. His little kitten sat like an ornament on the deck of his boat, watching everything.

Equus was the tallest dog I'd ever seen, and obviously very intelligent. He liked me. Recognizing a fellow co-dependent, he would lean against me whenever he got close enough. I felt acknowledged, understood and loved. And his way of leaning was so much like surrender that I could almost hear him singing *Only You*. But, over the next few days, I could see clearly that he leaned indiscriminately against anyone who would scratch behind his ears. Once I met him and his human walking on the main dock. She and I were walking along making idle conversation while Equus tried to walk along and lean against me at the same time. Suddenly Equus stopped, arched his tall back even higher into the sky, and lifted his back legs off the dock. His human yelled gleefully, "Here it comes!" as she moved deftly into position and held a small brown plastic bag under his tail.

Mark and Lisa, who also live aboard, have a doggie named Pepe, a Pomeranian-rat terrier cross with a Doberman attitude. He doesn't just think he's a big dog, he knows it. Lisa reported that the first time Pepe met Equus he stood directly underneath his head, glared straight up at him, and growled like a bear. Equus stood his ground as he looked straight down at Pepe, his ears wing on wing.

Pepe is so small that those prissy Flemish rope arrangements present sufficient vertical relief for him to lift his leg. Pepe hangs out with another dog named Rika, who is much larger than Pepe but whose legs are the same length. They share a common leash and sometimes get all tangled up.

One beautiful fall day Pepe and Rika rode with Lisa and me up to Mount Baker. Pepe even hiked like a big dog, but when he got tired he took advantage of his little dog stature and allowed me to pick him up and carry him, at which time he showed his gratitude by licking my nose and trying to clean my teeth.

On another occasion, Pepe and Rika and their humans, and Tom and his human (that's me) buddy-boated to Saddlebag Island. We dinghied to shore, where Pepe and Rika chased each other around the dry bushes and golden fall grasses like circus dogs. They ran so fast—the little dog that thinks it's a big dog and the big dog with the very short legs—that all we could see was a blur. It was like a mouse chasing a rhino in a mirage on the African plains.

Recently I met a new dock doggie—a very tall, offwhite dog with short hair named Squid. Squid and his human, a helicopter pilot, just got a permanent slip on G-west.

"Squid is a healing dog," his owner said, as Squid nudged my crotch. "She goes to hospitals and convalescent centers to visit sick people."

"Oh, my goodness. Well, that's just wonderful," I said, trying to hold Squid's head at arm's length. But Squid is a big, strong dog. His ancestors were quite possibly sled dogs.

"Sure is a friendly dog. What kind is it?"

"Pure yellow lab. She's just a tall one."

Squid is an elegant addition to the harbor, one I'm always happy to see.

One morning about 5:00, Tom was drinking coffee and doing his thousand-yard stare out one of the fixed portholes, when a black cat walked past on the deck of our boat just inches away from his face. As he tried to re-focus his eyes on the cat, Tom's eyeball muscles got quite a workout, suffering something like *fall arrest*. He reported later that all day long, objects close up looked a little blurry.

Tigger, the kitten who belongs to the man with the sailboat next to us over on F-west last summer, was trained to a leash. Every night he took his human for a walk all the way up to Gate 3 and back. But sometimes when his owner is away at work Tigger disembarks and wanders loose. On a cold, rainy day at the end of September, Tigger fell overboard. Lisa took him to her boat for the rest of the day, where he terrorized Pepe and Rika.

Jack is an older gentleman who lives on a large sailboat moored at the end of the boathouse near our dock. An African Gray parrot named Sinbad rides on a stick Jack has affixed to his shoulder with a hose clamp. The last time Tom was out on our deck and Jack walked past without Sinbad he said to Jack, "How're you doing?"

"Oh, I'm doing all right," Jack said, slowly and thoughtfully.

"How's Sinbad?" Tom asked.

Silence and deep thought on Jack's part. "I was trying to think if I asked him."

"Does he talk?"

"Not yet, but I did teach him to whistle *Row, Row, Row Your Boat*."

This kind of parrot *can* learn to talk. Mark said his dad has an African Gray, too, and one time his dad was in a serious discussion with a family member at the dining room table when the parrot jumped up on the table, walked over to his dad, and said, "You wanna play?"

One Saturday morning I met another parrot, a huge green-winged macaw, sitting on the shoulder of a big, burly, bearded guy walking toward me on the dock.

"What's his name?"

"Bullwinkle," he said, "but when he's down here on the boat with me his name is Chicken of the Sea."

"Does he ever fall off?"

"Oh, no. He even rides the motorcycle with me."

Another time I saw Chicken of the Sea and his human, walking to his little red sports car we call The Parrot's Porsche.

"Is it cold for your parrot?"

"No, he's good down to twenty degrees."

"He's so beautiful, just gorgeous," I gush.

"Oh, and he knows it, too. I don't even tell him any more; don't want him to suffer delusions, you know."

"Does he talk much?"

"Naw. He's the John Wayne of the parrot world."

One morning our friend, Jeff, who lives on a boat near ours, showed up at THE SHOE all out of breath and looking a little haggard.

"Last night the weirdest thing happened," he said. "I heard a noise and thought someone was stealing my dinghy, so I jumped up, banging my head, of course, and peeked out the porthole. I couldn't see anyone so I opened the hatch cover and quietly crawled along the deck to the bow in my underwear and peeked over the edge. A big otter was trying vigorously to climb into my dinghy!"

Just then, for no apparent reason, our boat began to rock wildly. Jeff's eyes got real big. "Oh, no!" he said. "He followed me."

In addition to Pepe and Rika, Squid the healing dog and the parrots Chicken of the Sea and Sinbad, we have Mousetrap, a shy kitten; Luke Dockwalker, a cute Australian shepherd-golden retriever cross, rescued from a Humane Society shelter in Juneau, Alaska, by his cruising humans; and Nick, a Portuguese water dog. With all these charming pets strolling the docks, not to mention the seagulls, herons, Canada geese and occasional wild animals, I don't need a real pet. I guess I'll just keep Sydney, my sometimes surly sailing iguana.

16

THE CATCH OF THE DAY

I'm sitting on the settee, trying to drink coffee without spilling it while the boat rocks wildly in another gale. We should install seatbelts. The room fan hums, distributing heat from the diesel heater, which is behaving admirably today. Dick's pacemaker clicks and groans, bumpers rub the dock, and lying out back in the cockpit is a whole, partially frozen tuna.

The tuna has been out in the cockpit for 24 hours. Now that the fish is mostly thawed I'll put it in a second plastic bag and flop it into our ice box. Lisa purchased the whole flash-frozen tuna, all 12" x 24" of it, from a fishmonger over at the commercial docks. We'll buy the next one. The idea is that we'll clean and fillet the tuna and give half of the meat to Mark and Lisa.

After work, Tom carries the tuna out to the corner of the dock. When he cuts into the fish it's all mushy and he can find nothing firm to grab hold of, nothing to fillet. We end up with about a quart of what appears to be a fish by-product. There are no tuna steaks. It's a sorry offering, and Mark is surprised when we hand him the little bag of fish meat. We bake our share. It sets up fairly well and tastes good with liberal squirts of lemon. Someday, when I have both the time and the equipment, I'll catch my own tuna.

When I was a kid, fishing was an important pastime and source of food. Creeks ran through my childhood along with a couple of rivers—the Priest and the Pend Oreille. I often fished up Riley Creek. I'd rise early, walk alone through the woods, then along the neighbor's fence line and down a steep bank to the creek, where numerous trees had fallen and created small, deep pools. I usually got my fishing line tangled up in the alder trees, but when I did get my hook and angle worm into the creek, the trout I caught were pathetically underdeveloped. I didn't care; I loved to fish. On my twelfth birthday my dad took me fishing to show me how to stalk big fish without getting my line tangled up in the trees. He taught me to crouch low in the stinging nettles and sneak up to the bank without the fish seeing me. When I dropped my line into a deep hole I caught the biggest trout ever, about eight inches long. I didn't get my line tangled once. Daddy and I caught a few more so we could say we "caught a mess of fish," and Mom cooked them for dinner that night. It was the best birthday present Daddy could have given me.

My family's favorite fishing hole was a slough near the confluence of the Priest and Pend Oreille rivers. We sometimes caught bullheads by the light of a bonfire but mostly we fished during the day. With my simple fishing pole made from a lodgepole pine sapling, I'd cast out a line. The line held a red and white bobber, a lead sinker, and a fishhook onto which we pushed squirming, fat angleworms dug from our backyard or a bank at the slough. We caught perch, sunfish, and sometimes huge bottom feeders we called tench. I don't know what they really were; maybe carp. We didn't eat them, but because they were so big I longed to catch one. I spent many pleasant hours staring at the bobber, listening to the red-winged blackbirds sing, and every now and then pulling in a perch or sunfish.

One day when we were fishing at the slough I was thinking how I might go crazy if I didn't catch a fish pretty soon. A boy named Tommy from my class at school was fishing nearby. I didn't like him. Once, when we had to dance together in gym class, he said, "Why do you bounce around so much? Are you trying to fly?" Suddenly my bobber took a dive and stayed down. I pulled hard. Whatever was on my hook pulled back harder, and I slipped and fell in the mud.

I scrambled to my feet just as Tommy ran over to help me land the fish. He grabbed hold of my fishing pole, his hands right above where I gripped the pole with all my might. Working together, we lifted the pole in the air as we backed up. Even though I felt acute embarrassment at being so close to Tommy, we made progress as we tripped over each other's feet. Then we saw it—an enormous tench about 18" long. A real lunker. When we got the fish up to the bank, Tommy ran to grab it. Just when he reached down with both hands, the monster fish broke the line and disappeared. I wanted to cry but I knew he'd tell the other kids at school, so I said, "Oh, I'll just catch me another one." I never did catch a tench. But I forgave Tommy for asking me, that time we danced together in gym class, if I was trying to fly.

One time Mom and Daddy took us fishing at Blue Lake, up in the woods northeast of Priest River. At Blue Lake we usually fished from the shore for trout, even though we mostly caught lily pads. This time my dad spotted an old rowboat someone had dragged up into the trees beside the lake. Daddy pulled the boat out into the water, maneuvered it alongside the shore and said to Mom, "Hop in, Vi." They took their fishing poles and Daddy rowed quietly through the lily pads around a point of land, out of sight. My sisters and I stood on the bank feeling abandoned and left out. It was quiet and scary in this isolated place. To make matters worse we heard wild animal noises coming from the direction in which our parents had disappeared. Certain we'd never see them again, we skipped rocks and picked on each other, arguing about how we'd find our way home. Just when we began to whimper and sob, here they came, smiling and talking nice to each other. They hadn't even caught a fish. Now that I think of it, this was the single most romantic memory I have of my parents.

As we finish carrying our cargo from the Bronco up the stairs to our storage locker near the commercial fishing docks, a huge fishing boat motors into the harbor and ties up to a dock at the edge of the parking area. Seeing our little four-wheel drive vehicle, the captain of the fishing boat comes over and offers Tom twenty dollars if he'll pull their fishing net off the drum so they can repair it. After some discussion Tom agrees to do this in exchange for two big salmon. Dragging a fishing net out across the paved street into a parking area doesn't sound like much, but the net proves to be hundreds of feet long and ponderously heavy. Once Tom starts to pull the net he has to put the Bronco in 4WD low and lock in all the hubs. Now that our transmission makes funny noises, we've decided not to catch any more fish with the Bronco.

It so happens that Brent, a friend Tom works with, has made plans to move to Brazil, where his internet sweetie lives. Brent comes to dinner one night and brings three slightly used saltwater fishing rods and reels. We strike a deal with the money given to me by the other landscape architects when I left the Forest Service. I now own almost everything I need to catch big fish. I'll make my own lures, some as big as tree ornaments with fake eyeballs. Big fish will come chasing after me, begging to be caught. Over dinner Brent tells us about his fishing experiences in Alaska, where he caught halibut.

"They call them barn doors up there because they're so huge and flat," he tells us. "When halibut are born their eyes are in a normal position, one on each side of their head. As they grow large they lay over on their sides and both eyes migrate to the top of their head. That way they can spot lunch when it swims above them, and nail it. When you catch one it's a lot of work to haul the thing up off the bottom. They're heavy. Then, when you do finally get it up near the top of the water, it'll take a dive back down. If you do finally manage to drag the fish back up to the boat, you have to shoot it in the head before bringing it aboard, or when it flops around it can tear up the boat or break your legs."

"How big do they get?" I ask.

"The Washington record halibut catch weighed about 350 pounds."

"If Rae Ellen catches one that big," Tom says, "we'll just tow it along behind us like a second dinghy."

17

PREDICTIONS

Tom insists that I learn what he calls docking skills (and I call take-offs and landings). Friday afternoon I back the boat out of the slip as instructed, in reverse instead of forward. One more accident-free event. Tom motors toward the harbor entrance and I watch the safety of the slip grow smaller then disappear as we round the rock jetty to enter Bellingham Bay.

We left on another positive note, that of actually having completed a boat-related task. We successfully made a *pendant* out of a seven-foot piece of 3/16" stainless steel cable (#719) and a nicro fastener with an eye thimble (a crimp-on fastener with a smooth surface to protect the cable from wear). During this effort, I deftly handed Tom every tool he requested and even crimped a fitting with a borrowed three-foot-long, double-handled device. What a surprise when we completed this half-hour job so quickly—in only an hour and a half.

"This particular pendant makes up the difference between the smaller jib sheet that we have on for winter and the top of the mast," Tom explained.

"Oh, do you mean that in the span where we no longer have any sail we now have a pendant instead?"

"Yes."

As predicted the weather is unusually warm and sunny, for a day in November. Tom unfurls the jib sheet and raises the mainsail. We sail across Bellingham Bay in friendly five-knot winds and arrive at Inati Bay just at dusk. As usual, Tom is at the bow to drop the anchor and I'm at the helm. Inati Bay has a braided waterfall that splashes down a cliff and disappears into the beach, and with only one other boat present we can anchor near the waterfall. Tom is wearing black gloves and his Army surplus, olive-colored jacket. His hand signals are difficult to make out against the dark island vegetation and rocks. That's the excuse I give later, but to be honest I've forgotten some of our hand signals in the two weeks since we last sailed. When he points straight up it takes me quite a while before I recall what to do. It means I should shift into forward gear, but instead I put the engine in reverse. Then I get confused.

Tom doesn't appreciate having to say anything above a whisper while we're anchoring. It's tacky and unseamanlike, especially when people on another boat might hear you.

"Will you please *talk* to me? I don't know what you mean!" I finally yell. I always feel so *at risk* if some small thing goes wrong or I don't understand what to do. Tom stubbornly continues to use hand signals.

"Will you just *tell* me?" I yell louder, muffling my cuss words. When he finally tells me what to do, he does so calmly, inaudibly.

"*What!!??* " I scream.

Finally we get anchored. When Tom turns off the engine we hear only the waterfall, splashing peacefully nearby in the quiet dusk. I feel safe, even cradled.

"Good job, sweetheart," Tom says, and actually means it.

When he does this it makes me feel like a seal in training that almost got it right, and he, the trainer, is taking a positive approach—that maybe if he gives me a compliment or a dead fish for my efforts, I'll keep trying and eventually succeed. I believe this is what the word *patronizing* means. Over the years, I've had some experience with the word. A boyfriend I had once, for fifteen minutes back in 1965, said I acted patronizing. "Well, thanks," I said, "What a nice thing for you to say." Then I went home, found the word in a dictionary and discussed it with my roommate. A young woman from Twodot, Montana, she had thought the word meant "saintly." Together we decided I didn't really like that guy after all, and I'd be better off patronizing someone else.

Now, when Tom says, "Good job, sweetheart," I want to bark

like a seal and slap my chest with my flippers. But, really, I must ask him not to thank me when I don't do very well. It annoys me and reminds me that he operates somehow in a different time zone while I'm still back on the stump ranch. Tom is usually excruciatingly patient and gives me the benefit of the doubt, all of which is admirable. He should really be with someone else—someone not afraid of water and noises and spiders—maybe a sweet, demure entomologist who likes wind. They could sail all over heck in search of pelagic bugs, and in heavy weather they could fight over who gets to go up on deck and change the sails.

The night is elegantly quiet, except that I dream a foghorn is blowing. This turns out to be something in my nose causing a honking sound as I breathe deeply. What a relief, for if we awoke to fog Tom would want to weigh anchor immediately and practice sailing in it.

Tom is making toast this morning to the tune of the smoke alarm. So many mysteries on a boat. We're also listening to the marine weather forecast on the VHF radio. Among other things, the male voice on the black box reports *a six-foot swell with a six-second period in the Strait of Juan de Fuca*. Once upon a time I prayed for a six-second period, but this particular report reminds me of what I have to look forward to out on the ocean—six seconds between six-foot swells, and worse.

My favorite VHF report is always what the weather is doing off *Point No Point*, a real feature somewhere out here in the marine environment. I love the name of the place, and feel a solid recognition of it—having spent entire decades there, and never near water. But the current decade may just win the purple ribbon for *place*. When I first agreed to this nautical lifestyle it was only so I could live on a sailboat during the winter at St. John. At first, we planned to buy a boat down there. I pictured a roomy sailboat already anchored at Coral Bay, the hull safely encrusted in barnacles. That didn't work out. When you've been so brave or foolish as to try to make a dream come true, why is there always such a big difference between the great idea and what really happens? Now we have to sail to St. John on the ocean, and Tom talks almost daily of other exotic coves and ports where he intends to anchor—places he reads about in sailing magazines.

"If others can go there, so can we," he says.

"Yeah," I reply, "but they aren't married to me."

Inati Bay is a peaceful, sheltered spot to stay all weekend, but Tom wants to leave and flirt with disaster for two more days out in the San Juan Islands. We review our hand and arm signals and enjoy a smooth departure into Hale Passage. Our destination: Matia Island near Sucia.

Hale Passage is a bit narrow for tacking back and forth and we're under power because the slight winds keep changing direction. With strong winds predicted from the northwest later, we'll probably set a double reef in the mainsail, unfurl the small jib, and use up a boxful of tacks sailing back and forth across the southern end of Georgia Strait.

Ahead we see a white Foss tugboat pulling an empty barge dozens of times larger than the tug. Foss tugs are like sheep dogs, and barges and tankers are like sheep—apt to go off sideways with the slightest breeze. Yet the tugs herd them with deftness and skill. A ring of automobile tires hangs from the rails of the tugs to serve as bumpers. Now the tug reverses its engine to let the barge catch up with it. Just as they touch, a guy jumps off the tug onto the barge, removes the towing cable and ties the barge onto the tug. The tug then escorts the barge to the loading dock at a rock quarry on the north side of Lummi Island.

"One time," Tom says, "I watched two Foss tugs nudge an enormous cargo ship around 180 degrees right next to a dock. I expected to hear Beethoven."

It's a good idea to stay out of the way of Foss tugs. They're working vessels and require lots of operating room. In the Coast Guard's Boating and Seamanship class that Tom and I are taking, we learned to always treat a working tug as the *stand on* vessel (the one other vessels stay clear of). We already know that it's wise to take their wakes head on. Otherwise they can swamp your boat. Tom says our boat could handle these waves just fine, that we really wouldn't need to steer into them, but he does it anyway.

After the channel is clear and we are further out in Hale Passage we see a different kind of tugboat, a little Nordic tug, behind us on the right. We recognize it as the boat recently purchased by the couple who sits next to us in the Coast Guard class. These tugs are for recreational boating, and this one is cream and green and cute, like a tugboat in a children's picture book. They've just changed her name to GLADYS ALLEN in honor of his grandmother who lived to be over 100, and who was sprightly and high-spirited until the end.

"GLADYS ALLEN, this is THE SHOE," Tom says on the VHF radio.

They don't know who we are, apparently, but after Tom repeats the radio call they answer and we switch to channel 68. Tom tells them we're table mates at the Coast Guard class and that we're studying for our upcoming exam. They say they are, too, ha! ha!

"Oh, no. They're gaining on us," Tom says. He'll do almost anything to avoid being passed by another boat. Back on the radio, he says, "Fall off to our port stern so we can take your picture." It works. They drop away and assume different little tugboat poses, back and forth behind us. It's like we're pulling *the little tugboat that could*— this vessel half as long as THE SHOE that's worth twice as much.

We're now sailing along in the southern Strait of Georgia, where the winds are from the west and fairly steady. My guess at the wind speed would be 15 to 20 knots, but then Tom says I'm usually about 10 knots over on my estimates. Anyway, at our speed of 5.5 knots we're not heeled over much, although the boat is bucking the two- to four-foot waves.

We approach the southeast side of Matia Island on the lee side, with a deep orange sunset off our bow. Maybe because it's so beautiful and peaceful, I offer to take down the mainsail alone. I crawl along the deck with one hand on the grabrail until I can hug first the mast, then the boom. After loosening the halyard, I wrestle fistfuls of the stiff Dacron sail down until it spills off both sides of the boat and nearly touches the water. You always need three hands on a sailboat. It's a tricky deal to hang onto the boom and, at the same time, take charge of a sail the size of a football field. But I lift weights and Koraks are sturdy and strong, so I just keep grabbing armfuls of sail and whomping it onto the boom until I can tie it together in a few places. This is called either *faking* or *flaking* the sail. All I know is that I fake it, and this time I truly deserve a dead fish for my efforts. If only I had two free flippers, I'd pummel my chest in applause.

"Good job, sweetheart," the captain says as I stroll proudly back to the cockpit.

"Thank you, it was no big deal." I think I like this guy after all.

When we motor around to the west side of Matia we see that little Eagle Cove is too rough to anchor in due to the westerly winds. We motor across a channel to Sucia Island, where we slip along through the smooth, glassy surface of Fossil Bay and head toward a mooring buoy. On the first try I successfully snag the buoy's ring. This is easy to do when the person at the helm practically stops alongside the buoy. Tom is getting pretty good at this sailboat stuff.

Soon the stars twinkle and a waxing moon illuminates the wind-sculpted trees on the horizon. We'll be protected from all winds except southeasterlies, which aren't predicted. This is good. I'm not interested in spending another wild night like the one we survived in neighboring Echo Bay. Southeasterly winds weren't predicted that time either, so I'll keep my fingers crossed.

For dinner we eat Mediterranean stew, steamed muffins and chunks of cheddar cheese followed by one of Tom's specialties, Tom's Yippee Yogurt Apple Muck—apples steamed with raisins, mushed together, and mixed with honey vanilla yogurt.

"Sailing today wasn't too bad, you know," I announce with my mouth full of muck. Tom smiles but before he can reach for a dead fish to reward me I add, "It was actually a little boring. I missed the old adrenaline rush I get when I think I'm going to die."

My smug comfort lasts only until Tom turns on the VHF weather channel to listen to the latest weather prediction. *Hurricane force winds are expected off the coast of Vancouver Island and could affect the weather in the Strait of Georgia and other areas of North Puget Sound.*

Tom, wearing that *let's go chase squalls* look, says, "Now we'll have some real sailing on the way back tomorrow." We learned in the Coast Guard class that sustained winds over 64 knots qualify as a hurricane. I didn't even know we could have hurricanes here. For some reason Tom always hears more on the VHF radio than I do. He explains the forecast. "A very deep low pressure system is on its way down from the Gulf of Alaska. It's a counter-clockwise wind system. At the same time, a high pressure system is moving out from the land into the vacuum created." What vacuum? How does he know all of this? I must study weather. I must study everything. The exam for our Coast Guard class is this Wednesday night.

The weather is warm this morning here in Fossil Bay, but we can't afford the time to inflate the rubber dinghy and go ashore to hike. We agreed to study *Aids to Navigation (ATONS)* and learn about buoys, lights and markers for the Coast Guard exam. Since I'm comatose after 8:00 p.m., I slept during some of the classes, and we haven't kept up on our reading. Now we must study and I feel incarcerated. I gaze longingly out the prison portholes, recalling the wonderful hike we took on the island last March—the hike that made me think having a sailboat would be a worthwhile thing to do, even though my first sailing experience was so bad.

"We'll go ashore a lot over Thanksgiving," Tom reminds me.

We leave Fossil Bay around noon because of the predicted hurricane force winds. I'm worried sick over this, but after we sail out into the Strait of Georgia the wind dies and we have to start the engine.

"This is a stupid turn of events," Tom says. But I'm relieved and sit smugly under the corner of the dodger. I reach for my new placemat chart of the San Juan Islands, purchased so I can more easily keep track of where we are and learn the islands by their shapes. The map is more convenient for this purpose than the large nautical charts. Even though the scale is small, the little chart in my hand indicates depths in fathoms. Orcas Island is now off to starboard, and there are Barnes and Clark Islands off our port bow with Mount Baker immediately above them, sharp as a quartz crystal. How unusual to see absolutely clear blue skies in this piece of landscape, this time of year.

"How deep does your map show it is here off Orcas?" Tom asks.

"I'm telling the instructors in the Coast Guard class that you navigate off a placemat." He can't always tell when I'm kidding. One couple is taking the class because, on their first outing in a chartered powerboat, they used only a Washington State highway map to navigate around in coastal waters. They got as far as Anacortes before running aground in the mud at low tide. I could like these people. By now we've all learned in class to use real nautical charts, to map our courses and read the tide and current tables. Armed with all this new information, none of us should run aground again.

The wind returns; I'm guessing 15-20 knots. We're sailing along just fine on the south side of Lummi Island, when Tom notes a serious threat, one that requires an urgent need to increase our speed. Behind us, a sailboat curls through the whitecaps like a snowplow. It's clearly gaining on us. Tom takes out all the reefs in the mainsail. I hate to see this happen, since he had promised to leave them in until next summer so I wouldn't have to act hysterical anymore this fall.

We're now cruising at 6.5 knots on a south-southeast course, and I'm at the helm. Soon we must aim east-northeast toward Bellingham Bay. The wind is strong, so instead of jibing to change course Tom instructs me to turn clockwise and do a nearly complete circle. This seems peculiar, but I do what I'm told. Just when I start to think this is kind of fun, the boat tips way over in a gust of wind. Instinctively, I steer away from the offending breeze. This is the wrong thing to do, of course, but we survive and resume a new course skipping along at 6.75 knots, a respectable clip for THE SHOE.

"This is so peaceful," Tom says. "There's something so right about deriving motion from just the wind."

Sinclair Island is now a low profile off to starboard. Vendovi is higher, more abrupt in shape and straight ahead. Our immediate goal is to pass between Carter Point on Lummi Island and the Viti Rocks, then hang a left and head for Bellingham.

"According to my placemat, we can squeeze between the island and Viti Rocks," I say.

"I've been through it many times. Your prediction is accurate."

But now, of all times, Tom needs to use the head. The man has no bladder, just a loop in the tube between one end and the other.

"Hurry up!" I yell as he leaves me stranded at the helm, the boat heeled over with a full mainsail and jib billowed out to one side. It's strangely warm for a November day, probably thanks to El Niño, and I'm sweating and cussing as THE SHOE and I leap and snort toward Viti Rocks. No delusions here—the boat is clearly in control. I just hang onto the wheel and hope for the best. It was in this area that a 50-foot fishing boat capsized one night recently in heavy weather with five unfortunate men aboard. Apparently they found themselves in a "quarter following sea" situation, where big waves can catch one quarter, or corner, of the stern and upend the boat, leaving no time to make a distress call on the radio. This is what I'm thinking about when THE SHOE suddenly makes a serious run for the north. We're zeroed in on Lummi Island and it feels like I have Moby Dick on the line, or at least a halibut as big as a barn door. For some reason a strange image enters my head—that of a loaded logging truck, barreling downhill out of control. I correct the course back toward Viti Rocks, but this lasts only a nanosecond before the boat makes a powerful run for the south, and we're not even fishing. Where am I? The twilight zone? The Bermuda Triangle? Tom finally strolls casually toward the companionway, looks up at me and says, "Check to make sure the gearshift is in neutral. I could hear the propeller turning when I was in the head." After I make the adjustment, the boat is much easier to steer.

But the sailboat behind us is gaining ground. We're considered the *stand on* vessel, however, because we're still in front. Maybe if we go around in circles again they'll get confused and back off. But this wouldn't be good seamanship, so we stay on our course. Tom tries everything he can to make us go a little faster. He adjusts the sails and all the lines and halyards, until I'm worn out just watching him. In spite of his heroic efforts the pursuing sailboat shoots past us going about 10 knots, as if we're at anchor. Tom sits down, calmly taking the helm in one hand.

"Like Wes told me, if they pass you, you were never racing them in the first place," he says with great dignity.

We wave at the big sailboat and its six humans.

"Well, no wonder!" Tom says. "It's a 52-foot racing boat with Kevlar sails. And their jib isn't even properly trimmed. Look at that!

The jib car is too far back on the track making the angle on the jib sheet too small. See how the jib is luffing?"

We proceed north across Bellingham Bay, behind the big sailboat. Just as the sun sets we pass between the day marks (ATONS), the red one on our right (red right returning), and enter Squalicum Harbor. Tom easily noses THE SHOE back into its narrow closet space. With the bow line in one hand I leap gracefully onto the dock and coax the boat forward, but not too far this time.

"Good job, sweetheart."

"Thank you, Captain."

18

TURKEY BLUES

"Do you have any turkeys less than seven inches high?" I ask at the meat counter of our favorite grocery store. "I brought my tape measure."

"Follow me," the clerk says. "You did say seven inches."

Finding a Thanksgiving turkey small enough for our boat's propane stove turns out to be easy. But could I cook the turkey without burning it?

My first attempts at using the oven were less than successful. When I'd finally worked up enough nerve to make muffins, I fiddled with the temperature gauge for nearly an hour, until I thought it would stay right around 350 degrees, then I popped some bran muffins into the oven. After a quarter-mile dash up the dock to the laundry room to throw some clothes in the dryer, I hurried back. Even as I turned onto our dock I could smell burnt muffins. But where was our boat? I got all the way to the end of the dock, and no boat—at least not THE SHOE. At the time all sailboats still looked alike to me, but I couldn't even find the coil of green water hose that served as a landmark. Then I realized I was on the wrong dock. Thanks to the gentle southeast winds, a low, dark cloud of burnt muffin smells advertised my status as a boatfrau still dry behind the ears. I ran to our dock, turned right after the water hose, and climbed aboard. So much for *those* muffins.

Since I have an incinerator for an oven I'll have to stand watch over the temperature gauge while the turkey cooks.

Fog is predicted for Thanksgiving morning. We'll leave the harbor right after it clears, that is if Tom can wait that long. Instead of fog, however, we awake to a bellowing 25- to 35-knot wind.

"We might be able to sail all the way to Stuart Island today, in this wind," Tom says, clearly pleased with the weather.

But first a shower. As we stroll hand in hand to the bathhouse Tom jokes about leaving the slip in these high winds—how we smash into several boats, careen off docks, wreck things. We love to joke around like that.

We think we're real funny, until it's time to leave. Tom is at the helm while I'm on the dock with the lines in my left hand, walking the boat backwards in the slip.

"Better get on right now!" Tom yells.

The second I take the giant step aboard, Tom guns the engine in the hope that we'll scoot clear of the other boats. At exactly that moment, however, a ferocious gust drives the bow of our boat against the neighbor's dinghy, suspended from the back of their powerboat. Our plow anchor hooks the dinghy like a fish.

"Hurry! Take the helm," Tom yells as he dashes to the bow to extricate the two boats. But it would take the jaws of life or a Foss tug. With the bow held fast, the wind blows our stern around against the next boat downwind, the one I call THE SWORDFISH BOAT because of its long bowsprit poking out into the channel—the very bowsprit that instantly locks horns with one of our stanchion posts. The wind screams louder.

"Accelerate forward!" Tom yells.

When I do this, THE SHOE attempts to climb onto THE SWORD-FISH BOAT, as our anchor rips at the corner of the hooked dinghy.

"Turn the helm the other way!" Tom yells.

When I do this all the boats let go at once and I stare, paralyzed and in shock.

"Reverse. Put it in reverse!"

I shove the gearshift lever back and THE SHOE skulks away from the scene. After I push the lever into forward gear, we slink along the inside of the jetty toward the west entrance of the harbor. At least I'd remembered which way reverse was this time, and our own dinghy, in tow behind us, is still in one piece.

"I just bought that guy a new dinghy," Tom says. "And our stan-chion post and bow roller are bent, too."

While I'm still at the helm he pulls off the bumpers and bow lines, and slams them into their lockers. I turn the wheel and we motor out the harbor entrance, into Bellingham Bay. Even Tom's eyes bulge out when he sees the size of the waves. A large, heavy object swells low in my chest. We have survived a departure from hell only to come out here and drown.

"Shit! The waves are as big as the house I grew up in," I groan.

"They aren't *that* big," Tom says, matter of factly.

As instructed I steer into the swells while Tom unfurls about 75% of the jib. My view ahead through the vinyl dodger window is first all boat, then all waves, then boat, then waves.

"That's all the sail we'll need today," he says, then takes the helm and steers us on a broad reach in the valleys (of the shadow of death) between the waves. Each wave bullies us, shoves us first in one direction then the other, while Tom works the wheel constantly to keep us on course.

I sit on the low side of the cockpit hyperventilating and staring dumbly at the walls of water marching toward us. At the top of each roller I can see for miles, like I'm *The Fiddler on the Roof*. We're surrounded by an entire housing development of waves. I move to the other side of the cockpit under the dodger where I can no longer see the waves coming toward us, only the receding waves, the ones we've already survived.

When the top of a wave sprays into the cockpit Tom ducks like a boy dodging a snowball.

"Sure is salty," he says, licking his face as water sloshes over his boots across the cockpit floor to the drains. The boat rattles, creaks, rumbles and bucks through the wind and waves like a wild bronc at a rodeo. It doesn't matter to me that the waves aren't really as big as houses, that they're only the size of chicken coops.

"That's it! I'm only going as far as Inati Bay," I announce, panting.

No reply.

After about five minutes, Tom says, "I'm worried about how wet the V-berth is getting."

If I don't go down to check for water, I know I'll have to take the helm so Tom can do it. Almost anything would be better than that. Somebody has to go below. We've had leakage in the past just from the rain.

As the boat plunges along at six knots I slowly disengage both my foot and the leash on my safety harness/lifejacket from the binnacle, the post in front of the helm supporting the boat's compass. When I open the companionway hatch cover, I'm not prepared for what I see: debris scattered all over, water running down the gutter through the saloon, and Sydney lying face-down in it all. I lower myself into the cabin, hindered by the bulk of my rain gear and the need to hold onto something every second. I toss Sydney into the sink. He seems defeated, indignant, diminished. I can relate. Making my way to the forepeak, I hang onto the overhead grabrail. When I lose my footing I swing out sideways like a monkey in a tree. After my feet drop back to the floor I continue my snail's pace forward, rescuing important papers and unpaid bills, shoving them into dry lockers above the settee.

When I reach the V-berth I see water spilling onto our bed and the floor through an unsecured porthole. Hanging on with one hand, it takes me several minutes to fasten the porthole with my free hand. I'm in a washing machine. Even more alarming than my growing seasickness is the pounding of waves, crashing into the hull all around me. I make my way back to the companionway while hanging onto the monkey bars, knees slightly bent, ready for anything.

Back on deck I resume my position under the dodger, reattach my leash, and place my left foot on the binnacle. In addition to my fear and loathing I now have the flu-like symptoms of seasickness. How can any normal person think it's acceptable to spend even five minutes in these conditions?

"Well, look at that!" Tom shouts, ducking spray from the top of a monster wave. "Three windsurfers over there, toward Fairhaven. We're headed right for 'em."

But I don't care if Alan Alda is dropping by in a helicopter, unless he's planning to rescue me. "Well, don't run over 'em," I holler back in my worst fishwife voice. I continue to stare in the opposite direction, my rapid, shallow breathing punctuated now and then by a seasick burp or one of my choicest sailing mantras.

"You won't believe this. They're leaping off the tops of the waves, then crashing into the drink. I've never seen anything like it," he says, excitedly.

I can only shake my head. Surely none of this is happening.

Then we have to change course, tack a different direction, and I must take the helm.

"Tell me *when*... say *now* when it's time to turn, okay?" I scream. "Don't pull any of that fancy sailboat talk on me."

"Okay."

"Okay what?"

"Turn now!!! "

So I do. And after he finishes with the jib sheets he asks, "Do you want to keep the helm for some experience?"

"You must be kidding!" I say in my mean and ugly voice, then resume my position under the dodger glaring at the dark, steep waves, my mouth hanging open.

I'm limp as a sack of chicken feed except for my left foot on assignment with the binnacle. I'm also pulling tightly on my leash, just for something secure to hold onto. My glasses are wet with salt spray and I have no idea where we're headed. If we're only going to Inati Bay maybe Tom is trying to extend his sailing time. After all, Lummi Island is only seven miles from the harbor—just next door as islands go—and he's never considered it a destination, just a brief overnight stop like a Motel 6 on our way to some real island in the San Juans. But I like Inati Bay. The bay faces north and it's protected from steady southeasterly blasts, like this one.

Even though I sit slack-bodied, my mind is very busy. Every few minutes I review exactly how to activate my lifejacket— *now, just reach up under your right boob and pull the handle.* I remind myself that I can't swim very well, and that the water is ice cold.

"Are you all right?" Tom asks.

I do not answer. Why would he ask me a question like that?

It's time to tack again—that noisy, chaotic out-of-control turning through the wind to change direction, while we plow, buck, snort and heel way over. Slowly pulling myself up using the binnacle as a handle, I move around into position behind the wheel while Tom grabs the jib sheets.

"Turn *now!*" he yells.

Just as I turn the wheel both of my feet slip out from under me, putting my bottom in intimate contact with the post supporting the helm. I can't see where we're going from my new position on the floor of the cockpit but I have a job to do—I'm saving our lives. So I maintain my death grip on the helm at 10 o'clock and 2 o'clock, and say every cuss word in my repertoire. The boat goes around in a complete circle, jibing, dipping wildly from side to side, forward and back, water flying everywhere, until Tom takes the helm from me and I pull myself up.

"Are you all right?" he shouts again.

"Stop asking me that stupid question! *Of course* I'm not all right!"

After crawling back over to my cowering place, I resume my rapid breathing, staring and burping. This is never going to be all right for me. I'm not going on the ocean. It sounded okay at first, and so many people do it, but if sailing is like this even occasionally my nerves just won't take it. I hate myself and my fear. I know I'll miss out on a big adventure, new scenery, interesting people. I guess I'll have to watch it all on TV or see it in the movies.

We're finally at anchor at Inati Bay on Lummi Island. My bowels are loose, my brain is in neutral and I'm physically and emotionally shot. I'm lying on the settee with two hot water bottles and a blanket in the cold darkness of a Thanksgiving afternoon, on a boat with very little heat. At first I complain about water dripping onto my face. Tom keeps wiping—first the vent hole in the ceiling, then the hatch cover, then the porthole—everything is dripping. Water dribbles from the wall-mounted bookshelf, too, and the bottoms of all the books are wet.

I think over the past week. After Dick, the diesel heater, acted up again we sent him packing. This time he'd gone too far—bringing six fire trucks to Gate 3, a fire-fighting tugboat alongside THE SHOE and a dozen helpful firefighters crawling all over our boat. A commercial fishing vessel had reported seeing black smoke pouring out of the back of our boat. The harbor office called the fire department and then Tom, who drove all the way across town to the marina thinking THE SHOE was toast. But while Dick pretty well fried himself and there had been flames, nothing caught fire. It was a miracle. The resulting diesel film and stench in the cabin had meant days of cleaning for me, again. The heater should not have malfunctioned. Tom had just cleaned soot out of the heater three days before, a task you're not supposed to have to do very often and which he'd done numerous times. Tom wants another diesel heater. He thinks the one we had was faulty, but rather than risk another fire I prefer to be cold and damp.

This has to be the worst Thanksgiving Day in my 52 years. If we had a cell phone I'd call a bed and breakfast on the island. I'd dinghy ashore and have them come to meet me at the end of the road above Smuggler's Cove. It's supposed to be only about a half mile up an old road from here.

Tom sits in the dark at the other end of the settee on the small side of the L, immobile, staring into the dark. Water no longer drips onto my face and I doze while the turkey stews in its juices in the oven.

Every fifteen minutes or so I ask Tom, "What's the oven temperature?"

"290 degrees."

"Will you turn it up slightly?"

Next time I ask him the answer is "400 degrees."

"Would you turn it down a little?"

Every time, like a robot, he reaches over and turns the knob slightly. We are like this for the entire time the turkey cooks, from 1:30 to 5:00 p.m.

When I finally drag myself upright to finish cooking dinner I discover that I can hardly walk. It's like I aged thirty or forty years on the trip across the bay. Maybe my hair turned completely white as well, like some Ripley's Believe It or Not character. I hang onto grabrails and edges of things, and make my way slowly to the galley. Every joint aches. When I remove the turkey from the oven, open the bag and pull on a leg bone, it comes free easily and the meat falls away into the pan. It's cooked perfectly—overdone, just the way we like it. I steam yams, make both a green salad and a fruit salad, and open a can of cranberries. Thanksgiving dinner is ready. Slowly, I move back and forth the few feet between the galley and our little table, which drops down from the wall and rests securely on the floor. Tom sits, frozen, at the end of the L. We neither talk nor make eye contact, and eat our dinner in silence after not giving thanks.

Later, as I stand at the counter in the galley removing the rest of the turkey from the carcass, I think about Tom's mother, Alta, who is having Thanksgiving dinner in Bigfork, Montana, with Tom's ex-wife, *what's-her-name*, and several of Tom's children. What if Tom and I had gone there to be with them instead of sailing? It would have been so much more pleasant. While I overate, I would have listened quietly and politely to their conversation, and I wouldn't have looked at *her*, even though I'm sure she's a very nice person.

Tom is fiddling with the little alcohol heating stove that West Marine generously loaned to us for the weekend. It's not much, but it's our only source of heat.

"I've decided I am not going on the ocean," I say.

"Well, I believe this is the highest setting on the stove," he replies.

I throw the pot of turkey bones, skin and gristle over the side of the cockpit, to feed the crabs, to feed next summer's catch of the day. That's if I'm still around here then.

Tom is doing the dishes now. He stops, stares at the companionway for several seconds, then says, "What's the point of having a sailboat if *you* won't sail on the ocean?"

"Well, I can fly to meet you and go through the Panama Canal, then we'd be in the Caribbean," I offer. "Remember our agreement last spring before we bought the boat—that I may not be ocean-going material, that I might have to do it that way."

He says nothing. His disappointment seems bottomless. He is 54, after all. He's tried many other interests on for size but only recently discovered that it is sailing he wants to do, and all over everywhere, too, just like his Viking ancestors. Now he finds himself married to a sailing-impaired person—in the way and a hazard to the safety of the boat. For Tom it seems that anything less than the whole dream is so limp and pale it's not even worth doing.

"You do have options, you know," I say. "You could divorce me and find a more suitable mate."

"I can't believe you can be so casual about us—like we aren't even important."

"Well, maybe you could *com-pro-mise* and adjust to my *dis-abil-ity*. Let it be all right for me to fly to meet you so we can do some island-hopping together. Keep in mind, this whole thing was an experiment, a lifestyle on probation."

We pull out the settee and rearrange the cushions to make up our bed in the saloon. The down comforter and flannel are wettest around one edge and Tom volunteers to take that side. He turns out the alcohol stove. I'm cold at first but begin to thaw as we lie close for a little while. Tom is always warm. He likes to say he has extra warmth in the form of BTUs (Big Tommy Units). Soon it's balmy and moist under the cumulus covers, as if we're already in the Caribbean. Becalmed, we drift to sleep to gentle goodnight kisses and the almost imperceptible amniotic rocking of the boat, safely anchored beneath the winter moon.

In the morning we awake to a clear blue sky and very little wind. My body still hurts all over and I walk stiffly. When Tom rubs my back with warm massage oil, the source of my aches and pains turns out to be bruised ribs and hip joints.

"Well, you did take quite a pratfall yesterday at the helm," he says.

"What do you mean pratfall? I fell on my butt!"

"Yes, and hard, too. And you hit the side of the lazarette. That's why I asked if you were all right."

"Oh! At the time I didn't notice. I had a job to do! I'm sorry I screamed at you."

Tom rubs my shoulders. "You did very well yesterday, really you did."

I do not believe my ears. It seems like maybe we were on separate boats, maybe even on other planets having totally different experiences.

"It was the worst Thanksgiving Day of my entire life. I did not do well at all! Why do you say that?"

"Because you're brave and you keep trying."

It's 10:30 a.m. and Tom is cooking bacon and eggs. He's in a much better mood. There's nothing quite like time spent warm and close saying "Oh my goodness!" and "Holy Buckets!" to soften disappointments and restore communication. Tom now calls this place I'm Naughty Bay—a very fine destination.

As he cooks breakfast he talks about all that I'd be missing if I don't sail on the ocean. He believes my decision is a temporary one based only on yesterday. I don't say that it isn't just yesterday. He thinks if I keep trying I'll come about. Denial can be so comforting. He makes toast in the oven and, as usual, produces one good one for every two pieces of bread. When he opens the hatch cover and tosses the burnt toast out the companionway we both listen, quiet and still, to hear the splash. It's the morning after Thanksgiving for the sea life, too. We eat breakfast while water drips from the hatch cover onto our plates. I joke with him about how he uses toast as an excuse to eat butter and jam, but he says I use food as an excuse to eat salt. He's got me there. He knows about the chunk of cows' saltlick I kept under my pillow when I was a child, until my mother found it.

He looks longingly out at Bellingham Bay then up toward Hale Passage, which would take us to Sucia Island. Denied as he might feel, he knows enough not to suggest we go sailing. After yesterday I need some still, quiet time. It's one thing if you're immigrating across the ocean in steerage through storms on the Atlantic, like my Grandma Frieda did at 16, but to make a lifestyle of it? I don't think so. It's safe and peaceful here. We can read, write, eat, go ashore, hike and talk.

Tom carefully removes his nearly-new sextant from its wooden box. This is a device you can use to take sights on the sun, moon, stars, and planets. After taking two or more sights to measure angles (in degrees, minutes, and seconds), you can use an almanac of some sort to find the exact position of the various heavenly bodies at any given moment. It's a trigonometry problem, and mariners throughout history have used this method to pinpoint their location in order to make landfall on the right continent. For some reason related to the higher math and science of navigation, you don't actually sight something, you "bring it down to the horizon." Tom is now trying to bring down the sun. Let's pray he doesn't succeed.

Lummi Island is nine miles long and about a mile wide—a quiet island with only a few services at the north end in addition to several homes, cottages, and the bed and breakfasts. We row our new, used dinghy from the boat over to the waterfall that disappears into the beach, then we row to shore. Stepping onto land is, quite simply, glorious and wonderful. The sky is crystal clear, intensely blue, and we hear an occasional bird singing as we hike uphill along an old road past ferns and moss, Douglas firs and alder trees. Back home in Idaho my father would take my sisters and me for a walk in the woods while Mom cooked Thanksgiving dinner. She was a good cook, and on that particular day of the year she wanted us out of her hair. Daddy always took his rifle on our walks in the woods, in case we jumped a deer. But we talked and laughed and held onto his hands and jacket, and never once saw a deer on those walks. By that time of year in North Idaho the ground was always covered with snow, but today on Lummi Island the ground is covered with a layer of wet leaves. It feels good to move my sore body but, after an hour of slowly huffing and puffing uphill, I'm tired. When we stop Tom takes our picture, just like he used to do on the mountain tops of Montana. He arranges the camera on a stump, sets the timer, pushes the button and runs as fast as he can, leaping and grinning, to pose next to me. Sometimes he makes it in time.

Last year on this very day we hiked the Reef Bay Trail on St. John in the Virgin Islands past dripping mosses and giant ferns, Tayer palms, and 100-foot kapok trees with termite nests in them as big as brown bears. How desperately I want to hike that trail again, but with so much ocean to cross between here and there, I may never get back to St. John.

Tom and I eat leftovers for dinner. After doing the dishes he takes the sextant above deck to bring down a star. I'm now alone with the wall clock ticking loudly nearby. When was the last time I heard a clock ticking? Almost never, for I've been rushing around, working or fixing something, cleaning, selling things, not staying still long enough to feel soothed and sheltered by a clock's faithful, steady beat. Right now Tom and I are at a standstill in so many ways, unable to weigh anchor and rush off into the weather to careen off docks or islands. Instead, we're safely secured to the bottom, to ground, in a few fathoms of water. Time has stopped to wait for me here in this invisible and peaceful stillness. What are the new opportunities, now that former goals seem so unattainable? Maybe I should set Tom free to sail off into the sunset while I rent a little apartment. But we've had such fun together. We've talked and shared so much, both good and bad. And what about our dreams?

Tom climbs down the companionway steps, the smile of success all over him. "I practically brought down the entire Milky Way," he brags.

"You sure like your new toy."

"Sweetheart, this is an important navigational tool. You know that."

"Yes, I do. Maybe I'll learn how to use it myself some day."

Before bedtime I read aloud to Tom from *Sailing Alone Around the World* by Joshua Slocum. On page 193 I read this: *But where, after all, would be the poetry of the sea were there no wild waves?* Funny how the mind works, for just as Tom begins to salute old J.S. I stop reading and say, "You think you're disappointed? What about me? One reason I married you is that you could dance. We haven't danced since we got married—not once in four years."

The ceiling and walls are wet with condensation, and water drips now and then onto our heads as we make up the bed. Without the little stove turned on it's wonderfully cool outside the damp comforter and flannel covers, yet tropical and snug underneath. I sleep like a sedimentary rock. In the morning the boat is even wetter and drippier inside.

After such a clear, calm and pleasant reprieve yesterday, the cloudy, windy weather is back this morning. We will cross the bay to Bellingham this afternoon so we can mop up our lives before Monday—wash the salt water out of everything at the Laundromat, clean the floor, wipe the rest of the diesel film out of the lockers.

First we'll eat. We open a jar of Caribbean jelly, carried close for the past year specifically to have this Thanksgiving but forgotten until now. Busha Browne's Twice Boiled Guava Jelly is a smooth, light-colored product of Jamaica that tastes like grape jelly, only more mild. Tom successfully makes toast without burning one piece. It's a sad morning for the sea life, and when he opens the hatch cover to look out there's a huge seagull sitting in our dinghy, no doubt waiting for a piece of burnt toast to come sailing out to him. Maybe the bird thought this was a garbage barge or that he finally struck it rich and found The Source of All Burnt Toast off Lummi Island.

Off and on we listen to the radio. "It's a waltz," I say. "Hear it? One-two-three, one-two-three." Tom surprises me by pulling me up off the settee. We dance the waltz in a circle in the few square feet of the saloon, even moving in time to the beat.

It's time to head back to the harbor. Tom prepares the boat to sail while I store all books, bedding, papers and clothes in plastic bags. I'm tired and spacey. Earlier, while I was securing stuff in the V-berth, I almost fainted—an unfamiliar feeling for a sturdy person such as myself. Tom decides it must be the fumes from the alcohol stove, so he turns it off. Maybe it's just that I'm worried about the trip home. If we make it across the bay alive there are all those boats in the harbor to crash into. No one will be there to help us dock. I long for another clock-ticking-loudly sort of day, but we have all that cleaning ahead of us and must also deal with the wreckage from our unfortunate departure.

Winds in Bellingham Bay are 25 to 35 knots again, just like Thursday. Several times during the roughest part of the trip home Tom says, "Oh, I feel so happy and safe out here. This boat will take care of us. I just realized that! It's so wonderful!" He's almost euphoric. Now I know for sure he's an alien creature. No wonder he gets such a bang out of bringing down stars. Or maybe he's just a member of that human sub-species, the silver-haired salt, who suddenly must take up sailing.

Then a strange thing happens. We're running along directly with the wind and waves while a seagull flies along a few feet overhead. Maybe it's the one we saw standing in our dinghy this morning waiting for a handout. Anyway, everything is incredibly quiet and peaceful, and I have the oddest most pleasant sensation that we, too, are flying in the air. I'm almost embarrassed to admit that this is a magical experience, one I could definitely grow to enjoy.

But as we approach the harbor I can hear the wind screeching, clanging, belching through the hundreds of masts. All too quickly it's time to dock. Because of the strong wind, Tom decides we'll tie up at the end of G-west dock instead of trying to enter our slip. While the boat moves toward the dock he gives me instructions so I'll know what to do. I nod to Tom at the very same time as I'm whispering, "Dearest guardian angel, if you're out there..." As if summoned, an enormous harbor seal pops his head up out of the water only a few feet from the boat. Holding onto a shroud with one hand, gripping the bow line with the other, I watch the seal. He cocks his head sideways and looks intently at me. Our eyes meet for several seconds. The seal's eyes are dark and shiny, enormous and perfectly round, and I see that he is wise and confident. Then he disappears. At that moment I know, with complete certainty, that everything will be all right—that as Tom noses THE SHOE into the wind I will leap gracefully onto the dock with the bow line and secure us safely to a cleat. Then, when he tosses me the stern line, I will catch it too, and quickly snug the line to a cleat so that the back of the boat won't blow out into the channel. And that is exactly what happens.

19

A CLOCK TICKING LOUDLY

Recently, life has felt like an expensive working vacation—one where you pay a lot of money plus your own airfare to visit a different country. You join a team that rebuilds a trail or a retaining wall, and this turns out to be the part you read in your vacation brochure about learning the new culture.

Sunday evening Jeff invites us to dinner at a pizza place. He wants to hear about our recent sailing adventure. He'll bring a new acquaintance, a young South African physician named Niki Stilwell. Jeff tells us she's been visiting a friend who recently purchased a sailboat and that she'll be flying home to South Africa in a few weeks. After spending much of Thanksgiving weekend together cleaning, mopping, and doing laundry, Tom and I could benefit from contact with humans other than ourselves. Besides, it'll be wonderful to eat something besides turkey leftovers.

At dinner with Jeff and Niki, Tom tells *his* version of our Thanksgiving outing.

"We did manage to scrape up the neighbor's dinghy a little when we left, but we had a great sail. On the way over to Inati Bay the waves were as big as any I'd ever seen. The boat handled beautifully, though. In fact, yesterday on the sail back to the harbor I began to realize that the boat will take care of us. All in all, it was an excellent learning experience."

Then I tell what *really* happened, starting with our dramatic departure—the ripping, the tearing, how we locked horns with the swordfish boat.

"Oh, that's just a part of sailing," Niki says, shrugging.

"And," I continue, "when we were crossing the bay in that horrible storm, after I crawled below deck to close the porthole and after I fell down in the cockpit when we were tacking, I decided that I am absolutely not going out on the ocean."

"Oh no!" Niki says. "Don't judge ocean sailing by what it's like sailing around *here*. I grew up on a sailboat. We sailed around the world. You'll adore ocean sailing—mostly you run with the wind in the trades where it's warm. It's just magnificent."

I stare at her, dumbfounded and speechless. Clearly she's one of *them*, but she sounds so...convincing. Tom looks as pleased as the night he brought down all those stars with the sextant.

"Let's go sailing together when I come back from South Africa," she says.

Everyone but me cheers and clinks their water glasses.

Tom soon begins to work long hours, about 60 hours a week. It's dark when he leaves for work and dark when he comes home, and on his only days off, Sundays, he has things to fix. The issue of going sailing again doesn't even come up. I'm in heaven.

My daily routine is quiet and reflective. I rise at 5:45 a.m., write in my journal, read, sort through recipes, cook, and think about the things Niki said.

When I heard the wall clock ticking the day after Thanksgiving, it became clear to me that I needed to unfasten my seatbelt. It isn't just the wreckage left behind when we departed our slip Thanksgiving morning, or the tough trip across Bellingham Bay in the gale. It's all the changes we made to accommodate this new life; the loss of that old, familiar life. The drift of psychological flotsam is still demanding to be processed, sorted, put in its place.

Both my parents passed away within the last few years and I've become acutely aware of time. I'm 53. Let's face it, my life is at least half over and I'm feeling selfish about how I use what time I have left. To make matters worse, in the past week or two I've noticed my hair is lighter. Tom nicely tells me he thinks I'm becoming more naturally blond. Truth is, I'm getting grayer by the minute and it's probably the result of my recent sailing experiences. When conifers invade an aspen stand, ecologists refer to it as "colonization," and that, it seems, is what's happening to my brown hair.

The awareness that I'm now the one on the front lines—with no parents to shield me from my own mortality—did help give me the courage to quit my job so I could do the kind of work I really want to do, and live where I really want to live—in the warm, lush Caribbean. Now here we are in Bellingham, and the price for sailing to the tropics might be too high.

I lost a couple of friends because of my decision to move aboard a sailboat. They listened in disbelief when I shared the news and couldn't seem to relate to me afterwards. I might as well have told them I was going off to Australia to wrestle crocodiles. Like Tom says, maybe they weren't such good friends after all. A sad thought.

Loss and change do bring new opportunities, of course. During this time of reflection I become friends with Niki. She's one of the most fascinating individuals I've ever met. We talk about many things related to sailing and life. One day I ask her, "What do you think about the risks of ocean sailing, about dying out there?"

"Well, you probably won't die while sailing. Almost no one does," she replies. "But even so, dying isn't the worst thing that can happen to you. It might be the *last* thing, but it's not the worst. When you grow up in South Africa you come to realize that."

This is one of the most amazing things I've ever heard. I lose sleep over it, and finally conclude that you have to be in love with the sea to entertain the thought of dying in it. I'd rather be eaten by a grizzly; however, when I stop to think about it, that doesn't sound so great, either. Would falling off a mountain top be better? So much to ponder. Mostly I'm simply not ready to die yet, now that I'm finally working at my chosen career—a non-paying but enjoyable job as an internationally unknown writer. I want to see my articles and books in print. I want to know how things turn out with this sailing life and how our novel-in-progress, *Hollis and the Wild Woman*, ends up. After all, I've grown so close to the main characters. But if I were to disappear at sea, my sisters would absolutely never forgive me. I can just hear Patsy at the memorial service: "I *told* her to stay close to shore!" And Marian would reply, "Well, I told her to get off that stupid boat and find an apartment. She never would listen!"

Another time I say to Niki, "I've noticed a strange thing lately. I'm not feeling sad like I usually do this time of year." Since she's a physician I thought she might find this somewhat interesting, especially given my feelings about my recent near-death sailing experiences. By all rights, I should be downright depressed.

"I believe people need adrenaline in their lives. Think about how wild animals live, for instance. Maybe sailing is like shock therapy for you," she says, thoughtfully.

Never before have I thought I needed white-knuckle fun to be happy.

More sleep loss. She *does* offer an enhanced global perspective, somewhat broader than my rural, North Idaho view of things. It's odd how she got tossed into the mix of life here, like an exotic spice that causes you to sit up and take notice at the dinner table.

Before Niki leaves for her vacation in South Africa she tells me, "Remember, mostly you sail the trades and float with the wind and the waves—it's just lovely. And you'll meet the most interesting people out there sailing around."

Tom and I don't really celebrate Christmas. In the past we've decorated outdoor trees with suet ornaments for the birds, but we have no trees down here on the docks and, except for burnt toast, we don't feel like feeding the seagulls. We do exchange Christmas letters with friends. The Xeroxed letters we send and receive are a lot like personal annual reports. Our friends, C², report from San Diego. After they left here in September they experienced serious electronic difficulties and major storms off the Washington coast, but managed to sail as far as Portland. In their determination to get closer to Mexico they swallowed their pride and had their boat, URSA MAJOR, trucked to San Diego while they took Amtrak. Christy says in her letter, "We're planning to sail to Mexico as soon as we can."

"You take time to smell the roses," writes my sister, Marian, bossier than ever now that she's recuperating from her brain tumor surgery. Hers was a mighty scare—much bigger than a frightful little sailing trip. I understand her message, although I do believe everyone's roses are different. Maybe I should identify mine so I won't forget to smell them.

I reach some conclusions about my fear of sailing. While it's true I'm dealing with fears picked up in childhood, more important is the simple fact that I don't know what the hell's going to happen next when we're sailing, or even what I can do to help make things go smoothly. This is difficult for me. I've always needed to mentally prepare myself for new things. But having something a little different for breakfast is one thing, learning to sail is something else. Everything about sailing is alien, mysterious and scary; yet when I try to learn, try to help around the boat, I find I have absolutely no facility for it. What I learn one weekend is gone the next, like I've never heard of it before. Then there's the fact that I don't even trust Tom's driving, and now he's The Captain. I'm just along for the ride in howling winds and huge, steep waves in a very weird vehicle that's only happy when it's tipping over. And there I sit, clinging to the binnacle post, not even qualified to be a backseat sailor.

When Tom and I are on land or safely secured in the slip, we're equals once again. I am whole, good-humored, poised, self-assured, positive and courageous. When we're sailing I feel completely the opposite: afraid, tearful, anxious, intimidated, panicky, and angry to find myself in a situation where I feel so *less than*.

Dead reckoning is a method sailors use to map their intended course of travel on a nautical chart. Where you have been determines where you now are on the map. By using a protractor and a scale like a ruler you can determine what compass bearing to follow. In sailing, as in life, there is a pull on the compass away from true north. If you don't pay attention to this magnetic deviation when plotting your course, you may never arrive at your destination. You might even crash into hard objects. I will learn to plot our course on the nautical charts. I'll also read the how-to-sail books that stare down at me from the little bookshelf on the wall. I want to take charge of my life again and learn as much as possible about sailboats and sailing. Maybe if I learn more about sailing I'll be more comfortable out there in Bellingham Bay—maybe even on the ocean.

It's true that I may discover I'm not cut out for a life of adventure and risk on the high seas. I might end up hollering "Uncle!" There's only one way to find out.

During this period of contemplation I try to bond with THE SHOE. They say it happens, but I believe it occurs more easily between man and boat. My theory is this: while a boat is difficult to handle, it's still easier to handle than a woman. That's why men develop such a strong bond and always call the boat *she*. It's also one reason why the husband sometimes continues to live on the boat after the wife has had enough sailing around the world, careening off islands and mountainous waves, thank you very much, and announces that she will now live in a real place on land. Sure, maybe my theory's all wet, but one thing I do know is that THE SHOE and I haven't yet become one. Maybe it's because I'm still trying to figure out how something that weighs 16,800 pounds can even float.

Tom, on the other hand, has begun to bond with THE SHOE. He's terribly loyal and defensive about her sleek, traditional lines as well as her ability to cut through waves instead of bob about like some sailboats do. He seems offended when I lust after much larger, beamier boats. Yes, I believe our boat did better on Thanksgiving Day than many boats would have. I'm the one who didn't do so well.

All in all my nervous system enjoys a pretty good rest. I begin to sleep so soundly that some mornings it's as if I'm waking from a coma, and I groan like a dreaming dog by a warm wood stove. I'm even feeling up to a little sailing again, but only if the weather is halfway decent. For Christmas we're talking about sailing the route we had planned for Thanksgiving: from Bellingham to Inati Bay, Inati to Stuart Island, Stuart to Friday Harbor on San Juan Island, then back to Bellingham. With four whole days, maybe we'll be at a peaceful anchorage long enough to hear the clock ticking loudly. This would be a fine way to spend our first Christmas on the boat.

20

THE CHRISTMAS ROUTE
OF *THE SHOE*

"Maybe we should have asked the insurance company to send us a whole handful of those accident forms," I say to Tom on his fourth attempt to back THE SHOE into our slip.

No reply. He is busy jamming gears and cranking the wheel. Finally two men walking by on the dock offer to help. I toss each one a dock line and together they pull us home.

"I would have had it. It was just a matter of time," Tom says later. "Backing the boat in was good practice, and look at how the boat is positioned. When we leave for our Christmas sail, all we'll have to do is drive forward out of the slip."

On the day before Christmas we have no wind. What a relief. I stand on the dock, bow line in hand, confident that our departure will be pleasantly unremarkable. Tom accelerates. I'm ready to climb aboard, but why isn't the boat moving? The main dock shudders slightly. Surprised, Tom turns to look behind him. "Well, no wonder. It's that goofy little stern line, still tied to the dock."

At this same moment I spot SHOESTRING, our new dinghy, resting upside down on the dock near a piling. Without him, we'd have been prisoners on the boat for four days. We do need someone to watch over us.

Fifteen minutes later we're motoring across Bellingham Bay on flat water. Just before dark we pull into Inati Bay, only minutes ahead of another sailboat, and head for the cherished anchorage near the waterfall.

"Boy, that was a real milk run," Tom says.

We drink some hot wine, a once-a-year treat on Christmas Eve, and Tom makes his annual batch of fudge.

A few weeks ago, after Thanksgiving, we replaced our faulty diesel heater. The new heater's name is also Dick. When we're at the slip Tom keeps the boat as warm as an old folks' home. At night he closes his eyes and tells me about the palm trees dancing in his head while I doze nearby, book in lap, mouth open. In the tropics I'd be catching flies.

But here, at anchor on Christmas morning away from shore power, we can't use the room fan to distribute Dick's heat.

"I can see my breath," I say, taking a swig of coffee.

"That's impossible. You're dreaming you're back in the tundra."

"If it isn't true why are you wearing your down jacket?"

Without replying Tom pushes aside the curtains on the fixed porthole so he can spy on the other boat. He announces that it's foggy out, that the other boat is covered with frost and so is THE SHOE. Why am I not surprised? At least my feet are in the tropics because I'm wearing a *toe warmer* in each shoe. This small luxury makes a huge difference in how I feel about winter sailing.

The boat swings gently around. Now we can see the waterfall. It's been raining the past week or two and the waterfall is a vertical arrangement of braided streamlets, forming strands of water like tinsel. Two separate waterfalls cross about a third of the way down the cliff. This is all the Christmas tree we need.

The people on the other sailboat put out several crab pots, apparently hoping to catch their Christmas dinner. We had put out a crab pot one evening, then didn't sleep well that night because we worried about actually catching some and having to kill them. We talked about the little ghost crab we'd watched that afternoon on St. John. Checking our borrowed crab pot the next morning, we were relieved to find it empty.

For breakfast this morning Tom cooks whole-wheat orange-pecan pancakes. Then, since I've decided to become more involved in the mechanics of sailing, I unfold our nautical chart for the San Juan Islands. When I first heard the term *dead reckoning* at our

Coast Guard class I thought, "How appropriate." It really means something like deduced reckoning, but the term became altered, much like "halyard" came from the term "haul the yard." Anyway, to chart our intended course we first need to know where we are. No problem. We're at Inati Bay, our home away from home. I draw a pencil line on the chart from the mouth of Inati Bay up through Hale Passage to the south end of Georgia Strait. Then I calculate the compass bearing using a clear plastic protractor, noting the magnetic deviation (20 degrees east of true north for our travel area). We'll steer this course using the large compass that sits atop the binnacle post in front of the helm.

Next I match a scale on the edge of the protractor with the scale indicated on the map to estimate the distance of this leg of our trip. Where this leg ends and the next one begins is a waypoint for us, or a point along our course. I draw several connected legs to take us to Sucia Island, staying clear of other islands, rocks and shallows that are shown on the chart. Tom then checks my coursework, figures out the longitude and latitude for each waypoint, and enters this information into the Loran, our electronic navigation aid. This unit uses low-frequency radio signals to tell us our geographic location in longitude and latitude. The Loran is also useful for telling us such things as how long it will take to get from where we are to the next waypoint, if we continue at the same speed. Since it's foggy out, Tom also fires up our radar unit. We have all the information and electronic equipment needed to reach Sucia Island, fog or no fog. I'll record our course changes and keep track of our time, military fashion, in the boat's new logbook.

I'm wearing most of my Korak clothing: Sorel boots with felt liners and extra felt footbeds, two pairs of wool socks, fresh toe warmers; knitted ankle warmers, insulated long underwear, jeans, and green rain pants; turtleneck, flannel shirt, wool sweater, black polar fleece jacket, and an oversized army surplus rain poncho, gathered at the bottom. I'm now a large green sack of potatoes wearing a combination safety harness/lifejacket and a furry hat with ear flaps. I'm ready for a day of cold, rainy, white-knuckle fun.

No wind. We motor out into the fog, our visibility about 1/8 mile. The companionway is open. From his position in the cockpit at the helm Tom can see the radar unit that sits on top of the navigation station. On the green screen we can see our exact location in relation to land and other objects like boats, even buoys. If we steer carefully on our course and watch the screen for edges of land and other boat blips, we shouldn't run into anything.

We motor into mile-wide Hale Passage at six knots. This seems a little fast in these foggy conditions, but then we do have the radar unit. At exactly 1100 I crawl below deck, slow as a snail in my bulky attire, to enter the next waypoint in the Loran. When I go back up to the cockpit I take some photos. The fog is denser now, but I can still see the bow of the boat.

Oh no! The radar screen just went blank and we're approaching Gooseberry Point, where the ferry crosses from the mainland to Lummi Island. Tom slows the boat to its lowest speed of three knots while I reboot the radar unit. When the image returns to the screen he tells me to set it to show coverage at two miles, with each distance ring at 1/2 mile.

"Don't you want a larger scale on the screen, with Hale being so narrow?" I ask. No reply. He's standing at the helm, his eyes fixed straight ahead. When I look back at the screen I yell, "Why does it look like we're heading for land?"

"Well, you could say that in a more helpful manner, especially when I'm up here having vertigo!"

After things settle down a little, Tom tells me what happened to him.

"I looked up at the top of the mast to see if it was still visible. It was. When I did that, though, I felt like the boat was turning so I immediately started to correct it. But when I looked at the compass I saw that I was correcting it in the wrong direction. The boat might not have changed direction in the first place."

"Oh," I say, "That's when I yelled that it looked like we were headed for land. And we were, weren't we?"

"I began to wonder if the compass was even working," he continues, "since the radar had blanked out for a while. Felt like I was in a bottle of milk. I finally realized I'd have to stay calm and sail by the instruments, like I did when I was flying. I'd have to look at the compass, the radar, then the Loran—over and over in that sequence—to stay on course."

1155. Steering 295 degrees magnetic into the fog toward waypoint 7. We'll begin our second leg at 242 degrees to waypoint 9, located between Matia and Sucia. We have light winds from the east-southeast, but not enough to sail. We're now out of Hale Passage in the south end of Georgia Strait. The shape of the sun is visible overhead through the fog, suggesting that the sky might clear soon. Our destination is Fox Cove on Sucia Island. I've seen pictures of its fantastical mushroom-shaped sandstone features. Even in dense fog we can maneuver into Fox Cove using our instruments, that is if we've drawn our course accurately and the radar unit doesn't blank out again.

1245. The fog clears. Since it's still early, we decide to skirt Sucia Island and continue on to Stuart Island.

"Snap a line on the chart, matey," says the captain. This reminds me of all the chalky, orange lines we snapped on all those boards back in Montana when we worked on the brothel. So I reach for the tools of the nautical chartwork trade, run a couple of lines using the protractor, and scale off the distance, then take the helm while Tom checks my work for accuracy. This time he adjusts my course lines, since I've kept us so far from islands that I added about an hour to our travel time and nearly spilled us over into Canada. He enters the new waypoints into the Loran. Someday I'll learn to figure out that latitude/longitude business so I can enter the waypoints myself. When Tom resumes his position at the helm, I take more photos—*Puffin Island With Fog Bank*, then capture snowy Mount Baker, looming above Sucia in the afternoon light. It occurs to me that this is my first Christmas without snow. After daydreaming about cross-country skiing for a few seconds, I decide that life's not too bad without snow.

When we motor past, no one is anchored or moored at either Echo Bay or Fossil Cove on Sucia Island. What a strange, exotic Christmas Day. With no one else out boating we agree that for today, at least, we own all the San Juan Islands.

1340. Saturna and Pender in Canada's Gulf Islands are off our starboard bow. We're motoring along 1/4 mile from Canadian waters. Waldron Island in the San Juans is off our port bow. I finally know port from starboard. It's easy—port is left (as you look toward the bow) and has the same number of letters. We're drinking tea and eating fudge. How lovely it will be when we can turn off the droning, vibrating diesel engine.

At 1435, several seals poke their heads above the water into the cloudy bright mist. We're on a course of 217 degrees to waypoint 16 at Prevost Harbor, our destination on the north side of Stuart Island. We see a tanker headed toward us, and it must be enormous because it doesn't yet show on our radar screen, set at a range of four miles.

We arrive at Prevost Harbor at 1530. What a surprise to see three large powerboats and two other sailboats already here. I'm at the bow doing my hood ornament imitation, holding a boat hook ready to snag a mooring buoy, when I make eye contact with a bright light coming straight toward us from the southeast. A float plane? There isn't room in the harbor for one to land. While we coast past the mooring buoy, which I don't hook because I'm staring down the airplane headlight, the bright light lands at eye level beyond the harbor. Apparently the island has an airstrip. I hook the mooring buoy on the next pass, and Tom kills the engine. Ah, silent night.

Removing our safety harnesses, we quickly prepare to go ashore while we still have daylight. The prospect of stepping onto land makes me giddy, and I joke and laugh as we board the dinghy. Tom climbs over the side of the boat and into the dinghy first, then gives me careful instructions. "Just step down into the middle of the dinghy, squat and grab the gunwales for balance while sitting all the way down." I turn around, get on my knees, begin to step down then retract my leg, several times. I feel so ponderous in all these clothes.

"Don't be so nervous," he says. I will risk a lot to make it to land, so I finally step down into the dinghy and hang on tight as Tom rows with his back to the dock where we'll tie up. Now its my turn to give *him* instructions.

"Row to port, now to starboard, no, the other starboard."

We dodge the mooring buoys and boats and arrive at the dock.

Now the tricky part—disembarking. I finally manage to flop my upper body onto the dock and drag first one flipper up and then the other, like a fat seal. A big cabin cruiser sits nearby at the dock. I see a curtain move. This must be entertaining for them.

Next time, I swear I'll wear a lifejacket. We learned in the Coast Guard class that lots of drownings occur in dinghies because they're such tippy beasts, and people like us don't always wear lifejackets.

We lumber uphill from the dock on a mossy trail beneath giant cedar trees, firs, and madronas with reddish trunks shaped like elephant legs. This part of the island is a state park, and areas have been leveled for tent camping. We follow a trail to the northwest onto the ridge between Prevost Harbor on the north and Reid Harbor on the south. Reid has dozens of mooring buoys as well as small floats where you can dock your boat and have a picnic. The horn of a buoy blows every few seconds near the entrance to the harbor. We're glad we chose Prevost, with only a few mooring buoys and no horns.

In the moist, foggy late afternoon light of Christmas Day we stroll into the woods along the path. The slight dripping sound of the rain is peaceful and calming. At the wood steps that descend to the head of Reid Harbor, we stop. Tom stands and gazes out through the branches at the clouds for a long time. I head back up the trail. A mossy boulder at a junction invites me to sit and wait in the mist and decaying leaves, in the glorious and eerie hush. A gentle restfulness surrounds me as I reclaim lost time, and I feel rooted, as if I've always existed in this tranquil place. Maybe Tom, too, is finding refuge in the soft, vaporous silence and droop of cedar boughs. I feel limp and thankful. Tom's dark form appears on the trail. He reaches out his hand and pulls me up to him.

Back on the boat I warm our precooked German Christmas dinner: sauerbraten, hot German potato salad, braised red cabbage, green salad, and home-made bread. Vinegar flavors most of the food groups in our meal. My German ancestors would be proud. And since I cooked enough for a small German outpost, it's good that our food has big flavors. We'll be eating it for several days.

The morning after Christmas, the sky above South Pender in the Gulf Islands glows red like coals—a sailor's delight. Classical music plays on the car stereo Tom installed in the navigation station. As the boat swings slowly on the mooring buoy, the scenes out the portholes shift by the second—a ballet of wind-sculpted trees and puffs of fog.

After a lovely late breakfast prepared by Chef Thomas, we don our warm clothes and rain gear to explore the island all afternoon. The guidebooks tell us about a one-room schoolhouse in a clearing and a cemetery a bit farther on. Even farther, at the northwest tip of the island, is Turn Point Light Station—a five-mile round trip.

After successfully boarding the dinghy, we row to the dock and climb out without incident. It's raining steadily, but I'm not cold. Tom is wearing his light hiking boots.

We find the ridgetop trail, which ends at a narrow country road near the little old white schoolhouse. Children once came to school here on Stuart from nearby Speiden and Johns Islands, rowing as much as three or four miles across an open channel in all kinds of weather, then walking overland a half mile or so to the school. At the cemetery a dozen assorted headstones show that former residents were of Scandinavian and German ancestry, and a large white cross marks the grave of a Civil War veteran. I hope none of the graves are of children who didn't make it across the channel to school.

We continue on the road and follow the signs to Turn Point, slogging along the dirt road through the rain. My socks are mostly down around my toes, but it feels so good to be out in the fresh air among trees that I can ignore the discomfort inside my boots. A few horses and Hereford cows approach a fence near the road, either curious or hoping for a handout. Farther along we see evidence of recent logging; abandoned old farm implements, including a potato picker; an old pull-grader for "floating" the road; and three deer.

As we approach Turn Point the road goes uphill, then down. The wind-blown trees arch and reach in all directions, true to no one prevailing wind. We pass bluffs of conglomerate rock formations—outcrops of pebbles held together tightly in a mix that appears to be concrete. Neon green tiers of moss and miniature ferns cascade down the hillsides and rock faces. We stop, as if beckoned, to peer into the mysterious shadows of the stunted greenery, two Gullivers with limited-time visas who have stumbled across the remnant of an earlier geologic era. Reluctantly we pull ourselves away from this peaceful intrigue to walk on into the mist. We talk of returning in late spring to take photos and sketch, knowing it won't be the same, won't be so magical, as it is today. Maybe on a sunny day we'll discover different enchantments.

At the light station we find several elegant clapboard structures, including a house like the one in *Anne of Green Gables*, only cream-colored. The views are vast and overwhelming—Haro Strait, the Gulf Islands and Vancouver Island beyond, in low clouds. How lovely it would be to live here. Walking around on the luminous grass and moss, we approach the edge of the cliff and look down at the kelp beds. A bald eagle flies up in front of us, shuddering in its fear and haste to leave. If only we had seen it, we would have kept our distance. Several small birds like chickadees flit about near the ground. The rain continues.

The setting is so spectacular it's difficult to leave, but I'm cold. Like a statue in the mist near the cliff, Tom stands in a grove of large conifers, his eyes fixed on the waves washing against the rocks below him. He can do this for hours. I yell several times. He doesn't hear me. I yell louder still, in my big, fishwife voice, "Tom. I'm getting cold, let's go back." He glances up and seems to hear me, but he doesn't move. When I start walking up the road he finally joins me.

"The sea was caressing the rocks," he says, dreamily. "I wanted you to see it."

His poet's eyes and heart see so much more than mine.

Back at the dock we find that our dinghy has six inches of water in it, and we have nothing with which to bail. Tom climbs into the dinghy first, and in dancing around to avoid stepping in the icy water with his already wet, cold boots, he nearly tips the dinghy over—not once, but twice. After all his chiding me about my extreme caution, I now hesitate to get into the dinghy with *him*. Maybe his judgment has been impaired by the cold or from watching the sea caress the rocks. But it's getting dark; I'm wet, chilled and hungry; and once again I forgot to wear a lifejacket.

We survive the dinghy ride, even though Tom nearly kisses the water again while climbing out of the dinghy onto the boat. It's getting dark and, except for the near-death dinghy ride, it was a great outing. We drape our wet gear all around the saloon. Now everything on the boat is moist. After our second Christmas dinner, which tastes even better than it did last night, we work together charting the course for tomorrow's travel to Friday Harbor on San Juan Island— a distance of 13.2 nautical miles. Tom enters the waypoints into the Loran. We'll leave at first light.

Zero wind again this Saturday morning, but at least we have no fog. We depart the mooring buoy at 0755. After an hour we motor past the channel where the children once rowed to school.

Tom unfurls the jib. Still not enough wind to sail, so he furls it. We're now approaching Flattop Island to port, part of the San Juan Islands wilderness, where birds nest and people aren't allowed. Farther south in San Juan Channel we see Shaw Island, where nuns operate both the ferry landing and the store.

At Friday Harbor we motor toward the visitors' docks, dressed like we've been dodging icebergs up north. Slowly, cautiously, Tom approaches a slip. I'm standing at the shrouds, a death grip on the bow line, ready to leap onto the dock and tie our horse to the nearest hitching post. I realize one is supposed to *step* off the boat onto a dock, but THE SHOE doesn't always get close enough to the dock for me to be graceful. Now our boat aims for a badly placed electrical panel.

"Can you jump off from the bow?" Tom asks. I do not believe this is happening. But I head toward the front of the boat, tripping over the bow line I'm dragging along, and climb up and over the metal rail around the bow, the bow pulpit.

I poise there in my sloth apparel, utter a prayer and a mantra, then leap, barely clearing the dock between the electrical panel and an enormous, tar-covered piling. I search for a cleat. No cleat. I push the nose of the boat away from the electrical panel. If I were small and petite I could be crushed between our logging truck of a boat and the panel. If you'll recall, I'm pushing 16,800 pounds. As I lean against the hull with all my strength, the stern of THE SHOE drifts over into the dock of the adjacent slip. Fortunately, that slip is unoccupied. Our boat is now, more or less, parallel parked along the main dock; however, due to a design flaw the two slips aren't quite wide enough for a 37-foot boat to do this.

Taking a deep breath, I cuss again and take a chance. I toss the bow line around the tar-covered piling, run to the other side, grab the wet line, coax the boat toward me and finally tie the bow line to a cleat on the dock. Then Tom ties an extra line onto the stern line to make it longer. When he throws it to me I catch it, miraculously, and pull the boat's stern back to our dock. People in nearby visitor slips watch as they drink wine (yes, it's still morning), and I believe they take bets. Now the bow line is too loose, so that when I pull the stern over to the dock the bow makes another stab at the electrical panel. I continue to cleat off the stern line.

Finally, we're secured in the slip. I go below and begin to peel off layers of wet clothing, shaking my head, cussing shamelessly.

Tom pokes his head down the companionway, and coolly, calmly says, "The current is kind of strong here. What did you think of our docking?"

"There isn't enough insurance in the whole *world* to cover us in this boat. What a stupid way to spend time and what a good way to get maimed or killed."

"We're still learning," he says. "We didn't even wreck anything this time. Why can't you be more of a sport?"

But I want to be on land, and I want a shower. We gather clean clothes and shower supplies and head to the harbor office, walking along the dock holding hands, as usual. We hold hands out of habit, even when we aren't speaking to each other.

"Hi, how are you doing?" Tom says to the onlookers, who move aside and watch us walk up the dock. Tom always does this—struts away from a scene like it didn't even happen. Or he'll act like it's just part of the learning process, and a dandy little experience it was, too. Why do I get so angry? How long will my nerves hold out? How many more of these dockings do I have in me?

On our way to the harbor office we walk past a short, stubby sailboat named SPEED QUEEN. It even looks like an old wringer washer. I try hard to stay true to my bad mood but finally sputter and laugh

out loud. I simply cannot stay in a funk very long with all this foolishness and absurdity around. Seeing the SPEED QUEEN somehow
gives me hope. Maybe we *will* learn to dock the boat.

"You know, your bad mood is nothing more than a little bird fart
in a hurricane," Tom says, reassuringly.

After our showers we return to the boat for a third meal of leftovers. As we eat, I can see the whale museum from the boat—a tan
two-story building with a brown roof and a black and white orca
whale painted on the second story gable end. After we kill all the leftovers, we walk up to the museum. Last July, between Sucia and
Matia Islands, Tom was lucky enough to see a pod of orcas surfacing,
and he tells the curator at the desk about his sighting. We also tell her
about the strange meows we heard on a moonlight sail in early
September. We take turns trying to imitate the sounds.

"Oh, that's the signature sound of the K pod!" she says, obviously happy for us. We *had* heard whales that beautiful night. She
shares some of her own experiences with orcas here and grey whales
in the Sea of Cortez. We all get teary-eyed. By now my bad mood is
gone, and we head out the door to find good coffee and a bookstore.
After visiting with several friendly shop owners, we walk hand in
hand through the charming streets, past trees brightly lit for Christmas, and onto the docks that lead us back toward THE SHOE.

"Next time we come here I hope our arrival will be a little more
elegant," I say.

"Next time we'll just anchor out in the harbor and row to shore
in the dinghy."

On the last morning of our trip before leaving Friday Harbor,
Tom does the course work and enters the waypoints for the six-hour
run back to Bellingham. Earlier Tom had said, "I got up twice in the
night to adjust things on deck—or did I? I know I moved the dinghy
once because it kept bumping into the boat. Gee, what did I do out
there the second time? I hope I'm not losing my faculties."

I've been sleeping so well lately that I didn't even hear him in the
night. And, after our recent arrival and departure episodes I, too,
hope he isn't losing his faculties—especially as we head out into the

perfect storm to go home. The harbor here is well protected from southeast winds, but I can hear the howling over the tops of the masts.

While Tom fixes bacon and eggs for breakfast we listen to the marine weather forecast, which states: *Small craft advisory for Hood Canal and Puget Sound. Winds 10-25 knots, waves to four feet. Rain likely.*

"Sure, we're a small craft," Tom says, anticipating my concern. "But our boat is seaworthy. They're just letting us know it's not going to be a bluebird sort of day, that we probably won't need to use our light-air sails."

After a delightfully unspectacular departure, we sail with both the jib and reefed mainsail up in variable winds, light rain, and low clouds. Wisps of fog decorate all the islands we pass. Three eagles fly overhead toward Cypress. A few other sailboats are out cavorting in the brisk wind.

Today I feel more comfortable with sailing. By charting our course and measuring the distance we'll sail, I can now see that the conditions won't change suddenly. Sure, we might go into or out of a wind shadow, but I can anticipate those times and prepare for them. Gale force winds and monster waves will probably still scare me, and I do have to work on my attitude about our arrivals and departures. But sailing might be a decent way to spend time after all.

Soon we have to tack. I take the helm while Tom manages the sheets, those lines you pull to switch the jib from one side of the boat to the other.

"Okay, put the helm over," he says.

But which way should I turn the wheel? I'm supposed to *know* this. "Well, aren't you going to tell me which way to turn?" I ask.

"You know. You always turn toward the direction the wind is coming from, then through it to the other side."

So I turn, but I turn too slowly and we nearly stall out. When the boat recovers it tries desperately to go in a circle.

"You have to turn the wheel *smartly* so that doesn't happen," he says. He really *is* amazingly patient.

Sometimes trying to handle THE SHOE feels like trying to walk a very large, untrained animal.

By early afternoon we're running easy with the wind across Bellingham Bay, although THE SHOE is rolling from side to side. To make this more comfortable we drink tea and eat fudge. When we arrive at the harbor Tom decides the conditions are tame enough for us to enter our own slip, and that he'll back the boat in. It's going well, for a change. Then I see it.

"SHOESTRING's trailing behind us. He'll get crushed!"

Tom immediately lets go of the wheel and jerks the dinghy away from between the neighbor's boat and ours. SHOESTRING is now close behind us, and as we back up he's perfectly positioned for another good crushing. I'm ready at the shrouds with the stern line, cussing and praying that we won't wreck our dinghy and that this time Tom will trick the boat into place next to the dock so I can jump off, tie the line to a cleat and stop the beast. Amazingly, everything turns out okay. We dock without smashing up our dinghy, we miss the neighbor's boat, and we don't crash into the main dock. But once again I'm a nervous wreck.

"What did you think about our docking?" Tom asks, obviously proud.

"I can't believe we forgot all about SHOESTRING."

"He was fine. I kept him out of harm's way."

"Huh. We just got lucky again."

"Look at it this way, our bow is pointed out for a another quick and easy getaway. What a great way to start the New Year."

21

THIN ICE

January advances on us with a cold snap that intensifies every feeling, especially feelings not worth having. Time slows to a glacial crawl. When it's darkest and coldest in these wet northern climates, a nanosecond can take an hour to pass. This week in mid-January is a week like no other, during our first winter on the sailboat. With the wind screaming through the harbor, when we need each other's warmth the most, our marriage chooses to pitchpole and head for bottom.

Now that I can't even reach out to the only person I know very well here—my husband—the West Coast feels like the edge of elsewhere. Oh, to be some other place—a small apartment inland, perhaps, with big windows and a parrot, because a parrot is good company and won't hurt you.

The wind chill factor is minus 15 degrees at the harbor. Tom is away over the weekend at Fort Lewis for National Guard training. I'm glad he's gone. Only an electric heater is running; I can't turn the new diesel heater on to help keep the place warm because it backdrafts in high winds. If Tom doesn't drive me crazy, Dick will. I go to bed early on Saturday night wearing a turtleneck, long underwear, a polar fleece neck gator, and two pairs of wool socks. I hug a hot water bottle and listen to the screaming wind, to bumpers moaning and screeching against the dock, and lines rattling above deck as I read a book about explorers in the Arctic whose boats froze in the ice and buckled into kindling. I wonder if Squalicum Harbor is suffering a freak El Niño weather phenomenon and THE SHOE is being frozen in and crushed. But then, it really doesn't matter.

The cold snap continues.

Tom returns, and for the coldest week of winter we continue our efforts to heat up the atmosphere with hot words, yelling, tears, and cussing. Our marriage can only go in one direction; it can't sink any lower. Tom is wearing his shiny black combat boots, and I have reached for my can of pepper spray. I want to call in *The Horse Whisperer* to teach me how to approach our wild animals with kindness, generosity, and love—to help heal our wounds, soothe us, and whisper loving words in our ears.

To make matters worse our diesel heater backdrafts, again and again.

"It isn't the heater's fault," Tom says. "When the wind blows over the boat it can cause a suction effect on all the vents and openings that is greater than the stovepipe's ability to draw. The already-burned fuel is forced to backdraft, driving the diesel fumes down into the cabin. This puts out the flame in the firebox, and when the flame re-ignites it causes a mini explosion and more fumes."

Every time, at the moment of the explosion, the smoke alarm leaps into the chaos with a piercing, ear-splitting squeal. I believe that this new heater is related to the first one, the heater that nearly caught the boat on fire twice before it was replaced. It's that cross-generational phenomenon of dysfunction we learned about in counseling. We're somehow awarded all the unresolved despair and sadness of our forebears. We carry this debris around with us, and every now and then we haul it out and dump it on those nearby.

Our grievances are so oppressive that it seems we'll lose everything good. No words are left unspoken. Previous messages echo with new clarity and meaning and cause the ice on the dock next to the boat to melt. Things are touch and go during this week of emotional housekeeping, of dissolving old resentments from our marriage and from distant times—hard objects in each of us that had become lodged and frozen in place.

The word *scarification* comes to mind, for only when a seed is scarified in some way (cut, moistened or cracked by heat) can it germinate and grow away from its encasement—its sealed, resistant state—to flourish. The scarification then becomes something forgotten. Its shell falls away and a new, healthy plant emerges and, if nurtured, it will thrive.

By the time the cold snap ends in patchy morning fog and drizzle followed by afternoon sunbreaks, our marriage is not only afloat but doing better than ever, as if the arctic week from hell never even happened. Now that the weather is warmer, time is melting away and flowing a little too quickly—as we begin, once again, to talk about our future.

22

INTO DAMP AIR

In spite of the weather fronts approaching from the Gulf of Alaska and Japan, we're enjoying damp but unusually mild and balmy weather, thanks to El Niño. As early spring arrives, crocuses bloom, buds swell, shrubs and trees blossom, and for several days the sun breaks turn into entire days of blue skies and warm temperatures. I take my long underwear and wool sweaters up to the storage unit and bring back my spring and summer wardrobe. The weather feels subtropical compared to our last winter in Montana.

The weather is never boring, and some mornings I discover that the patch of blue sky I see out the porthole is only the reflection off the neighbor's blue tarp. Other times an especially deep low pressure system slides onto shore and the wind screams through the south harbor entrance. Then the boat rocks and rolls in our slip, and if I'm cooking I have to gimbal the stove to maintain a level surface for the pots and pans. This is good training for the ocean passages in my future.

One late afternoon a howling wind bursts into the harbor, driving sheets of rain and waves against the boat. Tom arrives, slams open the hatch cover and yells over the wind, "We'll have to hurry! We don't have much time."

"My God, what happened? Did Mount Baker blow?" You never know. It *is* a volcano.

"No. A cold front moved down from the Gulf of Alaska and bumped into the warm air in the Sound. That's why we're having this big gale."

Tom tightens the winter lines on the stern and bow and snugs them to cleats on the dock. The wind howls all night. The halyard chorus sings, water sloshes, bumpers groan, and THE SHOE tugs against the dock lines while we try to sleep.

One day I receive an important-looking envelope from my former employer, the Helena National Forest. A buyout of several thousand dollars is being offered to employees to encourage early retirement and reduce the workforce. The catch is that I would give up my opportunity to regain federal employment. The offer shakes me up and causes me to rethink my life. Maybe I *should* jump ship, go somewhere else and live on land. Or should I stay and use the money to pay for some needed work on the boat? In my ambivalent state I really can't decide. So I sleep on it.

The next morning I make my decision. I'll stay and use my inheritance from Uncle Sam to upgrade the boat. Besides, the buyout wouldn't amount to enough money to get me very far if I did cut and run.

While I bustle about the galley preparing dinner, Tom hovers over a borrowed laptop computer entering THE SHOE's boat repair and maintenance list.

"This is just overwhelming," he says, shaking his head. "Three pages, double spaced, 51 items, and the list isn't even finished."

"Don't forget, we've got to find a way to protect the boat from your head," I say. "Did you include that?"

"I'll just wear some little bumpers all the time," he says, sighing.

Tom soon begins to poke around our boat in earnest. He uncovers entire mini-subdivisions of hoses, wires, switches, tanks, pumps, valves and hoses lurking behind panels, under seat cushions, and down in the bilge. Unmasked, THE SHOE is a spaceship. And each item knows the rules. If it's patient, it too will get an opportunity to malfunction. No wonder our maintenance list is so long. Luckily, Tom enjoys being Mr. Fixit. Sometimes he even seems happy to find a new boat mystery, a complication, although he claims this is absolutely untrue.

One day Tom decides to investigate the main water tank, located under our bed in the V-berth. Because the edges of the V-berth cushions are always damp and often downright wet underneath, he wonders if a hose might be leaking. We do hear sloshing noises under us when the water tank is partially empty and the wind rocks the boat. Sometimes we even wake up wet behind the ears, as if we've been camping in the mountains on a dewy night.

But the tank doesn't appear to be leaking. The moisture in the V-berth is simply more condensation. When Tom takes the top off the aluminum tank, however, he finds that the interior is badly corroded and contains curious mucilaginous bits and pieces—some sinkers, some floaters. In addition, the ribbed white plastic hose that fills the tank is all moldy. The boat is 26 years old, after all, and I guess tanks and hoses don't last forever. But the designer must have meant for the tank to be a permanent fixture because it's too big to remove from the boat in one piece. Tom screws the lid back down, replaces the hose, and leaves to buy a filter for the water faucet in the galley so I'll shut up about the goobers I saw in the water tank.

Nothing on a boat is as simple as it first appears. It's so very much like life.

On Valentine's Day I stop cooking dinner to help Tom lift one of the smaller water tanks out of the bilge in the saloon. Together we muscle it up through the companionway. Because of the corrosion, the tank is only a step away from being a colander. Tom and a friend will build a new stainless steel tank to replace it. They'll practice on this tank before attempting to build a replacement for the larger tank under the V-berth, the one we might have to saw in half to remove from the boat.

Over Valentine's Day dinner Tom gazes at me tenderly, smiles, and says, "You know, I've been thinking. We've just got to get a 45-pound CQR anchor. That's all there is to it."

He used to be the romantic one.

We always eat dinner to the tune of the little pump under the floor panel that pushes diesel through a hose over to Dick. When the pump, Dick's pacemaker, pushes fuel into the hose it sounds like a chainsaw way off in the distance. One day while Tom is retrieving some tools from under the floor panel next to the pump it makes its goofy groan as if it's scolding him. He whacks it with a wrench. The pump immediately falls silent.

"I guess I showed him who's boss," Tom says, holding the wrench and grinning up at me like one of his Neanderthal ancestors.

"Well, it won't work with me," I reply. In my defense the little pump groans back to life.

Repairs on THE SHOE continue every weekend. And we thought moving to a sailboat would simplify our lives. Boy, did we get fooled.

One Saturday Tom begins to install a new electrical system.

"I wonder where all these *other* wires go?" he says, looking behind a panel.

"Can you get electrocuted?" I ask.

"Well, it's only 12 volts."

When I ask Tom what he's installing he tells me (and I quote), "It's a high-output alternator that will more adequately charge our new deep-cycle, six-volt batteries. The interface board, that's its brain, will monitor battery condition and tell the alternator control (the regulator) what to do. I'll put the specs into the monitor and it will keep the batteries charged properly."

"Oh, I see."

"The batteries will last longer that way. The charger-inverter I'm putting in next is two machines in one. I'll wire it into the 110 shore power so that when we aren't running the alternator, the battery monitor will talk to the charger instead. The inverter part is for when we're away from shore power. I'll wire it back into our 110 system so we can run our coffee pot, power tools, and computer. The system inverts 12 volts to 110 volts AC."

"Oh, uh huh."

"And after this work is done we'll be more comfortable when we're at anchor. We'll be able to run a fan to distribute heat around in the boat. Your feet won't be so cold."

"Well, then, let's get to it."

For entire weekends, while Tom works at installing our new electrical system, the companionway steps lean against the settee. The sink and counter top are stacked on top of the icebox. We use special unassisted climbing techniques to enter the boat or to exit into the damp air. But I can't leave for long. As the chief petty officer I have to respond to various requests like "Can you find a 10-amp fuse in the little red plastic toolbox under the settee next to the batteries?" or "Will you come out on the dock and stand on the adjusting arm while I saw the end off so it will fit?" or "Will you bring me a Band-Aid and the triple antibiotic?"

On a good day the boat interior could pass for a teenager's bedroom. During the time of the electrical re-fit, however, the boat resembles one of the harbor Dumpsters.

Each day during the week Tom drives to his machining job and I walk to my little writing studio. I love my on-shore office in a big old blue building next to the railroad tracks. The floor is level and the room doesn't move. The building was once a chicken factory. Even better than that, a sign out front said *chicks available*. The floors of the larger studios, where chicks were hatched and raised, slope to the center and have drain holes where they washed out the chicken shit. My studio, 8' x 10', was probably one of the executive suites. Chicken business could have been conducted from a space the size of my studio.

Early in February we take our mainsail and jib to Port Townsend, a couple of hours and a ferry ride to the southwest of Bellingham on the Olympic Peninsula. Tom attends a weekend sail repair class with Carol Hasse at Port Townsend Sails, where he learns to do stitches and patches and to sew hanks on sails. While he does this I soak in a huge clawfoot bathtub at a bed and breakfast. I also spend hours at a used bookstore perusing book titles with my head heeled over 30 degrees to starboard, after which I can't straighten my head until I walk around town for an hour.

Over the weekend I go to the sail loft several times. At the class, Tom and I meet a Canadian wildlife biologist who specializes in pelagic birds. She and her partner plan to buy a steel boat in which to do bird research in the North Pacific. If the ocean freezes them in, a steel boat will withstand the pressures of the ice. Seems like a daring thing to do. Another couple lives on a boat at Coeur d'Alene, Idaho. One evening they came home to find their boat sitting at the bottom of the harbor in 15 feet of water. A plug in their hull had popped out during a freeze-thaw event. Both the owners and the boat have recovered and this summer they're trucking the boat over to Anacortes, Washington, about 60 miles southwest of Bellingham, to prepare it for ocean cruising.

We leave our mainsail at Port Townsend Sails so Carol's team of sailmakers can install a third reef. When we're sailing in heavy weather, we'll be able to use this third reefing system to reduce the size of the mainsail even further. Tom also hopes this will reduce my hysteria in gale-force winds.

Three nights a week Tom picks me up at my studio and we drive to a health club. On the way we usually stop at West Marine for more hose clamps or electrical tape, then at a supermarket for a snack and a cup of Starbucks coffee to share. We sit in the car in the parking lot to talk and munch on a bagel or some nuts, while watching the action around us. One evening we see a man trying to chew the price tag off a bouquet of flowers wrapped in clear plastic. Another spring evening we watch an elderly man ride his cart full of groceries across the parking lot to his car, clearly having a good time. Then a young man arrives at the entrance to the store riding a skateboard and pushing a baby stroller.

Another evening a couple we know from the harbor walks past our car. We wave to them and they disappear into the store. Half an hour later they walk back past us with their groceries. We wave again.

"Won't your car start?" they ask.

"We're hiding from our boat," I say.

We work out at the health club so we'll be able to crank on the winch handles, flake the mainsail, and raise the anchor without wrenching some body part or pinching a nerve. And I must stay agile and deft enough to leap onto distant docks when we tie up the boat. But often, after we make all our other stops and finally arrive at the health club, we park out front and just sit there and talk some more. People walk past, go in, work out, return to their cars—and we're still sitting there. Sometimes we have a disagreement.

"You have a good disposition," Tom says. "I appreciate that."

"That's ridiculous. I'm a cranky, troubled person. You're trying to pick a fight, aren't you?"

"No, I mean it."

"Me, too. Let's go get some junk food."

We don't know why we sit in the car like that. Maybe because it's a warm, safe place, one that sits still when parked and doesn't have mold in the corners. Usually we talk about Tom's work, my writing, people we've met, our families, books, and what needs to be fixed next on the boat. And we're comfortable facing forward. That way we don't absolutely have to make eye contact. This is good, especially when you're telling the other person that if they do a certain thing one more time you're going to go stark-raving mad.

When I was a child on the stump ranch I didn't talk much, and I liked to be alone. On summer days I often disappeared down to the field beyond the house and sat in a rusted old car, and pretended I was big. Just to make my fantasy more real I ripped two chunks of foam rubber out of the seat cushion to put in the front of my shirt. In an instant, I became a bosomy woman of the world. My breasts would never be larger than they were those summer afternoons spent driving a classic car through the field of stumps and wild strawberries out into the future, a future I never dreamed would include a sailboat.

It still seems unbelievable that I live on a sailboat. It took so much planning and dizzying effort to pull this move off, and here we both are. We've been married four and a half years and we've lived together a total of six months—on a sailboat. It's a good way to size up your mate.

When we want to communicate with other liveaboards and they aren't home, we affix a plastic baggie with a message in it to the lifeline of their boat using a giant clothespin. In this way we invite people over to talk about condensation and the weather and to share harbor news.

We often invite Jeff to dinner. A bachelor of about 40, Jeff is always curious about what we eat, where we sleep, and so forth. He says he likes to sleep between two blankets on a narrow berth, like he's a sandwich.

"It just feels right," he says. "I don't know what I'll do if I ever get married."

"That's easy," Tom offers. "You just do whatever the first mate wants you to do."

"I'll tell you what," Jeff says, "If I can talk someone into marrying me, she can even be the captain."

Another friend tells us that in the middle of the night one weekend a powerboat caught fire and scorched the two boats on either side. When the harbor office called the owner in the night, his wife answered and said her husband was out of town. When the firemen got to the boat, however, there were two people—the husband and a woman—standing naked on the dock. Now the rest of us, whose lives are less interesting, refer to this as The Incident on the Hanky-Panky Boat. It gives us all something to talk about during an intense low pressure system, one not followed by sun breaks.

More disturbing news is that WILD THING, one of the biggest sailboats in the harbor, sank off the coast about 90 miles southwest of Cape Flattery. The owner was sailing solo on his way to an around-the-world race in his custom-built racing machine. He escaped into his liferaft when his million-dollar boat began to sink. After 12 hypothermic hours in the raft, he was picked up by a Panamanian freighter. This sinking doesn't exactly ease my mind about sailing on the ocean. It's true that 30-foot waves and 50-mph winds shouldn't have sunk a boat of that testosterone level, but we read that the boat's ballast had shifted in the storm. Now it's gone—the tallest mast in the harbor, the boat everyone walked to the end of the dock to see, the boat with the toilet seat welded onto the stern rail.

Otherwise it's fairly quiet this time of year down here on the docks. Canada geese fly past every morning at 7:20 gabbling to each other. What are they saying? Where are they going? A few lone seagulls hung out all winter at the harbor. Now that it's spring, their noisy relatives are returning, squawking, bragging about their winter vacations, and sizing up potential mates. A bald eagle sometimes flies over the marina causing the seagulls to go crazy, and we occasionally see a brown pelican sitting on the jetty as we walk back and forth between our car and the boat.

Once in a while we liveaboards enjoy a little hanky-panky of our own. One night, as Tom and I stroll homeward on the docks through the damp night air, the water is flat calm and everything in the harbor is completely still except for the mast of one sailboat, rocking from side to side, its bumpers rubbing the dock. Soon after we climb aboard THE SHOE, two boats are pitching and rolling in their slips.

23

SAILBOAT SCHOOL

All I wanted from the start was to live on a sailboat in the Caribbean, one safely encrusted with barnacles, one you could take on a trip once in a while to a neighboring island. But it turned out that we began our sailboat lives here in Bellingham. Now, it's true that the waters of Bellingham Bay and the San Juan Islands are a good training ground for offshore cruising. The area's unpredictable weather provides numerous opportunities for sailing in dead calms as well as fog and heavy weather. And every now and then, the conditions are perfect.

I still have a long way to go before I'm a skillful sailor. For instance, the last time Tom and I were sailing in a gale and I was at the helm, Tom finally gave up saying "turn to starboard" and said, sighing, "just turn right." In my fear and confusion I said, "which right?"

With most of my limited attention span and energy spent surviving our sailing experiences, I haven't actually grasped many of our sailboat's technical facets. Oh, I've learned a few things. I single-handedly observed that a rudder is that doodad at the back of the keel that aids in steering the boat until either a dock line or a crab pot buoy gets tangled in it. I also know that you don't say *pull up the anchor*, you say *weigh the anchor*. Then you *bend on* a sail before you turn the helm smartly through the wind so the boat doesn't lose momentum, stall out and *get in irons*.

In the Coast Guard's safe boating class we took last fall we learned to tie the king of knots, the bowline. I also discovered that rope is only called rope at the store where you buy it. Once you get the rope anywhere near your boat it becomes the name of its purpose: halyards raise something (usually sails); sheets control some-thing (usually sails); and lines attach things (like your boat to the dock).

And I finally learned that when THE SHOE tips, or heels, it will not go all the way over. In my 53 years, when I've begun to tip or fall I never once stopped in midair and recovered to an upright posi-tion—not on a tipping chair, not while slipping on ice, and not dur-ing a tumble over the head of a pony. I know this for sure, after sailing in too many gales with too much sail bent on. Another real-ization is that once you hoist or unfurl a sail, you must use the sheets to shape it so the leading edge of the sail, the luff edge, won't flutter. Other sailors watch your luff edges to see if you know what you're doing.

Before I gained all this knowledge, limited as it is, I had thought the boat was in control; now I'm sure of it.

Tom recently found time to take stock of all the sails that came with the boat. This sail inventory, located in bags under our spare tires in the storage unit, turned out to be a storm trysail and a storm jib—two handkerchief-sized sails about right for sailing in really snotty weather. Now that it's May and the weather is generally milder, we're ready for some heavy-weather sailing.

It's time for me to put aside my fears and add to my sailing repertoire. I need a new attitude. I'm going to learn to sail the boat myself. If things don't go well, I'll just sail the biggest piece back.

On a sunny, clear day in early May, Mark and Lisa sail with us to Inati Bay. Before we leave I take charge and turn on our marine radio to listen to the weather report, only to find I still can't understand what the voice is saying on this squawk box. When it says *variable winds* I still hear *terrible winds*.

We anchor at Inati Bay and eat a picnic lunch in our cockpit. It's nice to have a back porch when the weather's perfect. After lunch we weigh anchor and head back toward Bellingham. I'm at the helm.

"Now, turn into the wind while we put up the main," Tom says as he and Mark head up on deck.

"Which way should I turn, port or starboard?" I ask, pleased that I can conjure up these terms after not sailing for several months.

They both stare at me in disbelief to see if I'm joking. I'm not. The wind, of course, only comes from one direction at a time, yet I can't always tell which direction that is and I forgot to look up at the Windex, our wind direction indicator. I can't remember these things from one weekend to the next, let alone one season to the next.

While Tom and Mark are above deck, I'm at the helm standing with one foot on each side lazarette, doing my Ben Hur imitation so I can see over the dodger. Lisa tells me that instead of a wheel they steer their boat with a tiller (a long handle that extends into the cockpit). Whoever is steering stands in the cockpit and guides the boat by holding the end of the tiller between their cheeks. To turn the boat, they sway their hips slightly to one side or the other.

"It works real well," she says, "and we haven't once had to have it surgically removed."

As we enter the harbor I'm still at the helm. For the first time, I think I'll take the boat into the slip. But as we motor closer I can't even *find* our slip. When I finally locate it I can see clearly that the slip is much narrower than our boat, so I chicken out and abandon the helm. Tom is ready for this and deftly takes the boat in while Mark stands on deck with the dock lines and I stand at the stern, gripping the backstay, embarrassed yet again.

On the Friday before Memorial Day, while a storm brews and seagulls mate on top of the boathouse near our slip, we prepare the boat to sail to Stuart Island, where we spent last Christmas. I'm determined to participate more actively in this sailing thing. As I follow Tom around the deck while he readies THE SHOE for our trip, I fill three full pages with notes and sketches. First you remove and store the blue canvas covers that protect important boat features (windlass, mainsail, binnacle, instruments, winches). To unhook shore power you have to deal with breakers and pigtails, locking collars and plugs. All steps must be conducted in a careful sequence and each item stowed in a specific way, in a specific place. Then you remove and coil (just so) the bow and stern spring lines (extra dock lines). The halyards and other lines must be moved from their stowed positions and readied so sails can be hoisted. Additional steps involve pulling pins; detaching and reattaching snap shackles; loosening and/or tightening winches; pulling on topping lifts; installing lifelines; and flipping switches on battery knobs and panels so you can operate the engine and read the depth and speed instruments. Finally, you insert the gearshift handle and start the engine. Three pages of instructions. I've never before paid much attention to these above-deck preparations. Tom always did it.

My job has always been to ready the inside of the boat for sailing—a big job that involves storing and hanging items, or otherwise causing all the loose stuff in the cabin to vanish. When first faced with this task, I recall how daunting it seemed. But I got good at it, and fast, too. Items too numerous to mention now disappear, magically and quickly, sometimes never to be seen again. With my new knowledge of all the above-deck preparations required before leaving the slip, I understand clearly now why most boats never leave the harbor, and why some liveaboards haven't sailed in years.

We enjoy a successful departure from our slip even though it's raining, thundering and lightning. Tom is unconcerned about this abnormal weather phenomenon since the black clouds are off to the north, and we are heading west. Tom is at the wheel while I'm at the bow trying to extricate the bowline which has become bunched in the chock. While I loosen one end of the line and pull it all the way through the chock, Tom decides to motor around among the fishing trawlers in the commercial docks so he can practice maneuvering in tight spots. Finally we clear the jetty and head toward Stuart Island. After several hours of alternately sailing and motoring, we arrive at Stuart Island and anchor at Prevost Harbor.

"Wouldn't it be lovely here on a sunny spring day?" we had agreed last Christmas as we hiked from Prevost Harbor to Turn Point through fog and pouring rain. The day after Christmas on Stuart Island had been drippy and otherworldly, mysterious and magical.

Today, the Saturday of Memorial Day weekend, it's cloudy-bright and warm. We dinghy to shore and hike through acres of giant sword ferns under old growth Douglas firs to a single-track country road. The conglomerate rock bluffs on both sides of the road are now covered with moss and low ferns that are parched and shriveled due to abnormally dry weather in the recent months.

At the lighthouse station on Turn Point we sit near the edge of the cliff on the headland that juts into Haro Strait. After we eat our sandwiches, Tom lies down on the grass to rest, while I stroll around in search of something to sketch. Just over the top edge of the cliff I see clusters of exquisite plants hugging the rocks. Reddish leaves form a rosette at the base of the plants and at the top of each short stem are cream-colored flowers, also in the shape of a rosette. How odd to see a plant with nearly identical leaves and flowers. I walk over to Tom to bring him back to the cliff edge, and he follows me to see the unusual plant.

"Orcas!" Tom yells, pointing out into Haro Strait. "Over there."

A parade of orca whales swims past from northwest to southeast, around Turn Point. Two whales breach. Their entire bodies zoom straight up out of the water, splash over onto their sides, and disappear. The orcas mostly swim under the water, surfacing occasionally to breathe, then dipping below the water again. A few adults have one or two baby orcas swimming near their sides. For several minutes we watch the water intently, unable to tell where or when a whale will surface. One surfaces, moving fast, quite a distance away now. Ecstatic about our sightings, we settle down to sketch. But soon we hear the low, echoing tuba sounds of whales breathing. Another dozen or so orcas swim past below us around the point. We watch, spellbound.

When it's time to leave Prevost Harbor I decide to weigh anchor for the first time. Tom coaches me before and during the exercise. First I remove the chain keeper pin on the front of the bow roller, then stand at the bow and point in the direction the anchor rode goes down to the anchor. As Tom motors forward slowly I pull the wet anchor rope (rode) up onto the deck. When the bow is directly over the anchor I give Tom a palm down signal and he puts the engine in neutral. Then I cleat off the rode and feed all the loose rope down through an opening under the windlass into the chain locker, and put the windlass handle into its notch. I uncleat the rode, wrap it twice around a winch-like affair on the side of the windlass, and operate the windlass handle back and forth to winch up the remaining rode. When the chain appears I know there's only twenty feet of rode to go.

After I push all the remaining rope down into the chain locker, I catch the chain in the teeth of the windlass and, sweating profusely, continue to operate the handle forward and back to bring up the chain.

As the boat inches forward, the anchor dislodges. I continue to pump the handle to bring both the chain and the anchor up onto the bow while Tom motors THE SHOE out of Prevost Harbor toward Bellingham. After doing this I understand why it's called "weighing anchor." Bringing all the rode and the heavy anchor up onto the bow is a lot of work—and we were only anchored in five fathoms (about thirty feet). If I'm going to be raising the anchor, we'll have to install an electric windlass.

Sailboat school continues. This time, as I back out of our slip a little heavy on the throttle, Tom stands on the dock holding the dock lines. The boat roars backwards at an angle, threatening both the neighbor's boat and the dock. Fortunately, Tom is able to scramble aboard as the bow zips past. So far so good. Next I'll try to dock the boat at the fuel dock. I motor along outside all of G dock, waving at people as we make our way. Before we approach the fuel dock Tom tutors me on how it's going to work. I'll motor past the dock, swing the boat in a huge circle, and sidle up to the dock on our starboard side. This requires that we miss SHAWMANEE, the elegant 57-foot fer-rocement charter sailboat at the end of F-west dock, then aim our boat for the pilings near the fuel dock. Just before we ram into the pilings, I must turn away and aim for the fuel dock. Tom continues to talk me through all this while we motor along at our lowest speed of three knots. I can do this.

Oh, great! Here come three tiny sailboats enjoying a sailing les-son. Not only are the students facing the other direction, they never once glance toward us. All three of them sail along blithely and dumbly, closer and closer, on a collision course with THE SHOE.

"Reverse it. Reverse it!" Tom yells.

"Okay! Okay!"

I squat down to wrestle with the gearshift, unable to see where the boat is going while doing so. The sailboat people remain totally oblivious to our presence until they tack, at which time they flash happy expressions of confidence as they dip past us only a few feet away. They all have perfect teeth and not a care in the world. They must know that since they are under sail and we are under power they are, each one of them, a *stand on* vessel, the vessel with the right-of-way. Finally the little sailboats pass and I continue on, taking aim toward the pilings. I turn gradually and soon we bump gently, more or less, against the dock.

"Good job," Tom says. I say nothing. I flash no perfect smile.

Yet I am glad for one thing: we're the only boat at the fuel dock. By the time we purchase our $30 in diesel fuel, however, six boats have arrived. But wait—here comes a seventh, an institution-sized powerboat. We must leave immediately so the other boats can buy fuel. I pull away from the dock and quickly line up on a collision course with the enormous powerboat. Isn't that the idea? You're doing fine as long as you're on a collision course with *something*? So, once again, I drop down and shove the gearshift lever into reverse, then stand with my foot on the lever so it won't slip out of gear. We miss the huge powerboat, mostly because it wasn't coming in to get fuel after all.

This Friday afternoon we're on our way to Patos Island and Sucia Islands State Park. We've never explored Patos. Carrying my three pages of notes and sketches around between my teeth, I conduct the above-deck preparations for departure. An hour later Tom checks my work, makes a few minor adjustments, then starts the engine and backs out of our slip. For the next six hours we alternately motor and sail, as the wind dictates.

At Alden Point on Patos Island we line up the bow to enter Active Cove, a narrow sliver of water with abrupt cliffs on both sides and a gravel beach at the far end. Six eagles and two turkey vultures sit, like bumps with beaks, on a log that extends from the point down to the shore. Their eyes are riveted on THE SHOE as it sneaks past them into the cove, but the birds don't take flight.

After securing the boat to one of the three mooring buoys, we row to shore and follow a path through tall grasses past drifts of fragrant wild rose bushes. The wing beats of eagles sound overhead as we enter the woods and continue under giant Douglas firs, cedar trees, and on through acres of salal in blossom, buzzing with bees. We step over banana slugs and crawl over mossy logs, touching sword ferns that lean into the trail, until we come to openness and sky on the north edge of the island. The Gulf Islands lie north across a channel. Eagles sit in snags near shore; others circle out over the water, fishing. A cream and brown speckled seal lolls nearby on a rock.

When we return to the boat Tom reties our mooring buoy line. Some nights we've had trouble sleeping while moored because of clunking, banging noises, so he's trying something new. Removing our anchor, he sets it aside on deck, then rigs our mooring buoy line through the bow roller. We enjoy a quiet night in Active Cove.

In the morning I motor THE SHOE away from the mooring buoy. It's my first time. I watch the current and wind direction, and use the engine as needed to move away from, not over, the metal buoy. We exit Active Cove past the eagles roosting on the log. En route to Sucia I raise the mainsail. No big deal. When I attempt to unfurl the jib, however, I pull and pull on the furling line, wrapping one of the jib sheets around and around the furling unit like a maypole. Whoops! This particular rope is only used to *furl* the jib. I am trying to *un*furl the thing. I grab the loose jib sheet and begin to pull on it. But, no, first I'm supposed to wrap this twice around the nearest winch before pulling it, or a gust of wind can catch the jib and pull the sheet fast through my hands, causing a severe rope burn. So much to learn.

As we motor toward a mooring buoy in Fox Cove on Sucia Island we see a great blue heron standing on the water in the middle of the cove. His reflection on the still water all around him creates an optical illusion so that he appears twice the size of a normal heron. When he lifts off the water a small log surfaces at the spot where he'd been standing. His weight had completely submerged the log.

We dinghy to shore. Every time we climb into or out of the dinghy Tom reminds me, "That's *salt*water, you know! Don't get it *on* anything."

"You act like saltwater's a disease," I reply.

We hike past a Canada goose couple with five goslings swimming near shore. An eagle hovers nearby; I hope he won't capture a baby goose for dinner. Several people are sitting at picnic tables near their tents. It's a busy weekend in the islands, especially at Sucia. We hike on to Shallow Bay through evening light filtered by giant maple trees, drooping cedars boughs, elegant hemlocks, grandfatherly Douglas firs. Giant sword ferns and moss-covered cedar stumps edge the level pathway, glistening with old wet leaves as big as dinner plates. The path leads to a pebbly beach at the head of Shallow Bay. Our next few steps bring us next to the grandest drift of wild roses either of us has ever seen in one place. I love every one of our out-of-boat experiences.

On the dinghy ride back to the boat, the tide is right for us to row around the giant mushroom rock now standing about ten feet high in Fox Cove. After studying all sides of this strange, water-sculpted rock formation we sit quietly in the dinghy and watch the far shore. The tide breathes out, exposing a heron's upper legs. Waiting, poised to strike, the heron seems to have all day to wait. His prey leaps up behind him and swims lazily, unknowingly, toward the shadow under the stick figure where it looks safe. But the stick figure concentrates and, as if under tension, shoots downward like an arrow and seizes the small, innocent fish in its pliers beak. The large bird makes a short, hopping flight, lands on the beach, and shakes its head repeatedly to still the wiggling fish, then swallows it whole. The heron returns to the edge of the water and resumes its stick pose.

We've been curious about Ewing Cove at the northeast end of Sucia. From Fox Cove we motor over to Ewing. What we find there is a hideout surrounded by a sculpture garden of sandstone statues and outcrops with faces crafted by wind and water. Ewing Cove appears to be a gallery, a stage, and an exhibit hall, all at once. The small cove feels private, with only three mooring buoys and no one else here, although a campsite nestles out of sight at the head of the cove. We secure ourselves to a mooring buoy and settle into the cockpit to eat lunch. A platoon of seven Canada geese peek over a grassy crest, sashay slowly to the top of the hill in full silhouette, and honk low sounds as if plotting a siege. They huddle. The honking intensifies. Suddenly two geese break away and fly aggressively toward us. A scouting party? An attack? Surely the pair will sideswipe our stern. Instead they veer in a tangent, throw out their webbed feet and splash down behind us. As they swim around our boat, the two geese begin a gentle honking that sounds questioning. It's food they're after, and we share a piece of bread.

We hate to leave. "In the morning I think I'll just pick up the VHF and call in well," Tom says.

"I feel sorry for landlocked people," I say, and immediately look around to see if someone else in the boat could have said it. To make such a statement, when my heart is so firmly hooked up to land, truly startles me. But Sucia Island is that extraordinary.

They say you don't miss what you've never had. Well, it's too late. I've seen too many orca whales, great blue herons, Canada geese, harbor seals and bald eagles—quiet spectacles I would have missed had I not been on a boat. I can still see the magnificent frigate birds winging overhead on St. John, and the colorful fish swimming below me as I snorkeled over coral reefs. But I can no longer hear the night music of the frogs at the edge of the ocean. It's time to return to the Caribbean.

24

B. O. A. T.

When Tom and I have a disagreement he sometimes drives off, tires squealing, to a place where everybody knows his name—the West Marine store. Other times we'll be out doing errands and the Bronco refuses to go past this particular store without turning in. Today we almost make it past West Marine, when Tom suddenly applies the brakes and says, "I need some 5200." He pronounces it *fifty-two hundred*.

"What in the world is 5200?"

"It's a great adhesive sealant that bonds things permanently. When it cures it's like welding. You could glue an elephant to the dock just by putting some 5200 on his foot."

So we stop. I wait in the car and read while Tom is inside the store buying this magical new sealant. Other women are reading or just waiting in nearby cars in the parking lot, but their husbands eventually come out of the store carrying brown paper sacks full of marine items. They drive off. Still no Tom. My biggest fear, during these hours in the car, is that I'll finish the book I'm reading before he returns.

Waiting in the car reminds me of all the times my sisters and I sat in the car outside the taverns when I was a kid. We didn't mind too much, really. We filled our time counting the cars and logging trucks that went past Lou's Place or The Green Owl. Sometimes laughter, even our mother's laughter, would come floating out of the tavern along with the cigarette smoke and the smell of stale beer. After a while Mom or Daddy would bring us each a candy bar.

Now Tom brings me a sack with three charts, two tubes of 5200, an oil filter, engine oil, some pipe nipples and hose clamps, a receipt for $95.38—and no candy bar.

"What are the charts for?" I ask.

"Dan, in the store, thinks we should sail to the west coast of Vancouver Island for our vacation. He says Barkley Sound and the Broken Group Islands are real nice. If you decide you don't want to go there I can return the charts."

"Never heard of the Broken Group. Might be just fine if we can go hiking."

The next day at the library I find information on cruising the coast of Vancouver Island up to Barkley Sound, and read this: *Hundreds of ships have met their doom along the storm-torn shores of the Pacific Rim. The most ominous shores are between Port Renfrew and Cape Beale, an area generally known as the Graveyard of the Pacific.*

I wish I hadn't seen that in *The Pacific Rim Explorer* by Bruce Obee, or seen those other books that show shipwreck locations in Barkley Sound, on the edge of the Graveyard. I'd heard that dangerous places like this, called graveyards, were scattered across the Pacific Ocean. Now I find out one of them is between us and our vacation destination. It's true we need some ocean experience—with our goal of sailing to the Caribbean—but in one of the graveyards of the Pacific? When we sail we're either in a dead calm or a gale. Maybe we shouldn't go to this particular place. I read on and learn that, at 12,079 square miles in area, Vancouver Island is slightly larger than the state of Maryland. Each year between mid-May and early September cruisers circumnavigate the island counter-clockwise, taking at least a month to explore the island's secluded inlets. We only have nine days. Barkley Sound is as far as we can go. Seems a little risky, though, to kiss our first ocean waves in an area famous for its high number of shipwrecks.

Further research discloses that the best time to cruise the west coast of Vancouver Island is in June or early July because of a greater potential for fog later in summer. I read that the alternate spelling for the eighth month of the year is *Fogust*.

That evening Tom's face lights up when I tell him what I learned at the library.

"Sounds like a great place to test our boat and ourselves," he says.

"Can't we just sail to Sucia Island and spend a week hiking, sketching, and napping?"

"If we're ever going to sail on the ocean we've got to get some experience out there. Tell you what. You can be in charge of the sail plan. When you think we have too much sail up we'll reduce it."

"Well, I guess we might as well go and get it over with. At least we'll be sailing to the salmon-fishing hot-spot of British Columbia. I can try out my fishing gear and catch us some protein."

With only about a month to prepare for the trip, Tom springs into action. He arranges to replace our tired old rigging. This sounds innocent enough but requires the services of a person called a rigger, the purchase of new rigging and fittings, and extensive preparations before having the mast removed so the new rigging can be installed. Tom also decides we'll remove our roller-furling unit so we can switch to the more traditional method of bending on a jib, using hanks. We'll also install some additional hardware on the boom so we can finally use our third reef in the mainsail. In a summer gale situation, this third reef will allow us to reduce the sail substantially, eliminating the need to remove the mainsail in order to put up the small storm trysail.

Our sailboat has wire rope rigging that consists of a forestay at the bow, a backstay at the stern, and three shrouds on each side of the boat. This rigging, which holds up the mast, will be replaced with heavier wire. We'll substitute Sta-loks for the crimped-on fittings that now attach the rigging to the boat. I'm told boats are re-rigged about every ten years. Sta-loks cost more, but after they're installed it will be easier for Tom to make emergency repairs or re-rig the boat himself the next time it needs to be done.

"Friday at 1:00 p.m. we'll motor over to the boatyard to have the mast removed," Tom says. "That gives us a week to get ready."

"We could just go sailing in a big storm and get dismasted for free. Save $250."

"Doing it at the boatyard's less expensive in the end," Tom says, even though he knows I'm kidding. "And once the mast is down we can work on it."

"Work on it? What do you mean, exactly?"

"Well, after I remove the old rigging we'll clean and wax the mast. We also need to 5200 the masthead and the tri-color light, clean and rewire the steaming light, remove and clean the radar reflector, and add another electrical wire inside the mast."

"I think I'd like to go to Montana for a visit now."

"Well, I could really use your help with all this," Tom replies.

"You know I've talked about going to Montana in June for a long time. Of course, I could wait until August. But let me think about it."

"Sure," Tom says. "I guess I could manage here by myself if you decide to go."

Early in the week, before our planned dismasting, Carol Hasse from Port Townsend Sails visits us to review our sail wardrobe. Carol makes offshore sails for people everywhere in the world. She's highly organized and efficient, besides being personable and friendly. After she and Tom take some measurements above deck, they come below to discuss the sail plan. One of the world's most esteemed sailmakers sits in our saloon while I make muffins and ponder whether to go to Montana in a couple of days or wait until later in summer. Carol begins to fill out some kind of form on us and our boat. She needs some boat documentation information right off the bat, and Tom begins to search for the papers in his sock drawer.

"So, Rae Ellen, when are you thinking of leaving?" Carol asks.

"Oh, maybe Thursday," I reply, wondering how she knows about my trip.

"Offshore?" she asks, looking astonished.

"Oh, *that*. No, I meant Montana."

After the paperwork is completed and I feed Carol a hot muffin, she leaves with our main jib sail, a lapper they call it, to re-cut for use with hanks on our new rigging.

In the middle of the night as I grope my way past the electrical wires on a routine trek to the head, I make my decision. I can't leave Tom to do all this preparation and work on the boat alone. I'll postpone my trip back to the Old West. It's so nice to be needed.

I'm fooling around with the nightmare of electrical wires that are hanging down from the wall in the head, trying to read faded writing on brittle masking tape. My head is tilted at an absurd angle so I can see through my bifocals.

"I don't understand what I'm supposed to be doing," I yell. "My neck hurts and I can't untangle the blue wires from the red and the black ones."

Tom takes over the electrical project, asking me for the various tools he needs as he makes progress. I hand him the red-handled screwdriver, as requested.

Later Tom requests a specific hose clamp—an especially large one—and I find it. This makes me feel proud. I recently read a news article that claims an active learning mind helps to delay loss of memory. I hope learning about all this technical and scientific sailboat stuff counts for something.

Prior to departing our slip to motor over to the boatyard for our dismasting event, I secure all the loosened halyards to the mast so that the mast appears to be wearing spaghetti. We enter the channel at the mouth of Whatcom Creek. The dock for the boatyard is located about 15 feet behind (and upstream from) the stern of PELICAN, an enormous black barge outfitted with tanks and pumping equipment for use on oil spills.

The rigger meets us at the dock. He and Tom quickly loosen the backstay, and four of the six shrouds. The crane operator is ready and swings a cable with a rope on the end of it directly above the boat. Tom and the rigger then tie the rope into a noose around the base of the mast and snug it up just under the spreader bars. They quickly remove the bottom ends of the forestay, the roller-furling unit and the two remaining shrouds. All this loose rigging is handed over to the rigger's assistant, who steps onto the dock while holding it out of the way. The mast is tight, but the men jostle it back and forth and finally the crane is able to lift it up and out of THE SHOE. While the crane holds the top of the mast in the air the men walk the bottom end of it along the dock and up a steep ramp. I follow them. With the men guiding the mast, the crane operator maneuvers it onto a long padded cradle with wheels.

Within a few minutes, we are told to move our boat because another boat is scheduled at the dock. We race down the ramp and Tom hops onto the boat to start the engine while I stand on the dock with the lines. As Tom accelerates backward and we move away from the dock, I scramble onto the boat. But the tide is moving out of the channel into Bellingham Bay on a brisk current and we are propelled against the stern of the barge PELICAN.

"Take the helm!" Tom yells. "Give it full throttle while I try to fend us off."

With all his might, Tom tries to push us away from the barge, but it feels like we're being sucked under. I pull the throttle all the way back, determined to cheat the hulking beast. With agonizing slowness we wrench THE SHOE away from the barge without a scratch and motor out into Bellingham Bay.

"I hate those close calls," I say. "They make me absolutely furious."

"It was really no big deal," Tom says. "It's normal to have to fend off something once in a while."

"Never in a million years will I get used to fending off anything, let alone a metal barge the size of a shopping mall."

We motor THE SHOE mastless and sleek as a cigarette boat, back to the harbor and into our own slip.

During the next week we spend our evenings at the boatyard working on the mast in the cold and wind. We're surrounded by various hulls of wood, steel and fiberglass in all stages of repair. Some of them look like they've always been here, up on blocks. Bearded, elf-like men live in two or three of the oldest, most derelict boats.

Tom removes the old rigging from the mast. The mast is as long as a telephone pole and every inch is filthy, even has mold growing on it. Funny I never noticed this before. We scrub the mast with rubbing compound, buff it down, wax it, and then buff the wax. Every evening we work on the mast to the sound of huge fans roaring continuously at the Georgia Pacific plant across the channel, their noise drowning out the other sounds here at the boatyard—seagulls, sanders and all sorts of sprayers.

One evening on the way to the boatyard Tom stops by West

Marine to pick up 600 feet of new rope for sheets, lines and halyards. The book I'm reading in the car this week is *Here We Are in Paradise*, a collection of short stories by Tony Earley. I especially enjoy the title, for at this particular chapter in my life, I am not in paradise. I spend all my time working on a mast in a boatyard so I can sail to the Graveyard of the Pacific. Nevertheless, as I work with Tom in the evenings it's fun to sigh and say, "Well...here we are in paradise."

The mast is finally ready, complete with new rigging. We motor THE SHOE back over to the boatyard to get re-masted, successfully dodging PELICAN and tying up at the dock without incident. The mast is quickly readied and the crane operator positions it over the boat while Tom and the rigger and a couple of other men guide the mast back into place. As the mast is being seated in the bilge, instructions are exchanged from above deck to below through an open hatch. Things don't go smoothly, of course, and the crane operator dings our Windex windvane, then a yard worker trips on the open hatch cover and bends it. The rigger attaches the new rigging from the mast to the deck. He says he'll coordinate with the boatyard on the hatch cover repair and he'll fix the Windex when he goes up our mast in his bosun's chair to tighten the rigging. After he finishes that, he says, he'll present us with his final bill. I can hardly wait.

Back at our slip, Tom attempts to sort out the tangle of electrical wires still hanging down from the ceiling in the head. Now that the mast is back up he needs to connect all the wires properly so the masthead lights and the radar unit will work. Things aren't going well with this task, and he becomes unusually irate.

"I'm about ready to ask you to cuss for me," he says.

"S...O...B," I say, enunciating each letter, happy to say out loud what I've been thinking for so long. "Will that take care of it for you?"

"Thanks. That's more than adequate for this job."

"If you want some more help with cussing, you just holler."

Tom arranges for our diesel fuel tank to be pumped out and inspected. We've heard of too many engines stalling out, just when they're needed most, because sediment at the bottom of the fuel tanks gets stirred up by wave action, plugging the fuel filter. Having our tank pumped out and inspected isn't cheap, of course, but it's less expensive than the consequences. Besides, no telling what size waves we'll encounter in the Graveyard.

A man with a pump arrives one afternoon, empties and cleans our fuel tank, pronounces it healthy and pours in a few gallons of fresh diesel. After he leaves, Tom changes the engine's oil and filter, then adjusts the packing nut. While he's draped over the engine he discovers several other items that need immediate attention—like corroded hose clamps that serve the critical function of keeping the ocean from flowing into the engine compartment and the boat. I've been hearing a lot about hose clamps, but I never truly appreciated them until now. We have dozens of hoses, all with at least one hose clamp securing them. Seems like hose clamps keep us afloat.

"Hand me two new hose clamps and the yellow-bellied nut driver so I can tighten them," Tom says, holding up a rusty clamp so I can judge the replacement size.

I hand him the requested items. Why don't they just make these things out of rust in the first place?

Later Tom says, "I read an article that makes me think we should replace all our hose clamps below waterline with some new Swedish-made ones that are especially corrosion-resistant."

"Are they expensive?"

"Sure they cost more," he admits, "but if they keep the ocean out of the boat they'll pay for themselves."

Next Tom stretches out on the floor the entire length of the galley and the saloon, cleaning the engine's water filter. This item filters the seawater before it's pumped in to cool the engine. While he does this, my job is to find a home for our new holding tank. I unscrew a panel underneath the port settee and another panel on the wall. What I find is dirt, goo, fuzz and mold, which I clean with a rag and my spray bottle of home-made mold-be-gone. Also located behind the fiberglass walls are recesses into the deep, dark bilge. I enlist Tom, with his long arms, to assist. He reaches into the bilge up to his armpit and brings forth a large pair of panties, even larger than mine.

"Oh, some hanky-panky last summer while I wasn't here?" I say.

"Very funny," says the captain.

Work continues, evenings and weekends. Tom brings home the

new 35-gallon water tank to replace the one we removed on Valentine's Day. After four months of measuring, cutting and fitting metal pieces together, welding at his friend's place, buying tubes and fittings, and after weeks of hearing the words "I sure hope it fits," a miracle happens. It fits. We're even able to draw water from the new tank.

Sometimes when I'm helping Tom on the boat, when I'd rather be doing almost anything else, he'll say, "I need you to...." I listen hard, my good ear cocked forward. I wait and wait for his instructions, while my time and my life slip away. I could be reading another story in *Here We Are in Paradise*. Other times he thinks it good and necessary to explain thoroughly why he's doing some little project a certain way, like exactly how the water tank is being installed, and why, and how all the hoses and valves work. At such times my eyes glaze over and I yawn—the same symptoms as the early stages of seasickness.

I'm none too sure of this lifestyle *without* all the incessant work on the boat, not to mention the expense of it. I feel like I'm being washed out to sea on a giant riptide. And, once again, the boat resembles the inside of one of the harbor Dumpsters. If we don't hurry up and finish these endless repairs and upgrades, our marriage is going to need more than a little laughter to hold it together—it's going to need some 5200.

For several days I'm too crabby to work with another person, especially Tom. We decide it would be best if I work alone, and I receive my very own list of tasks. One important errand is to locate just the right size cheek block, a pulley affair we need on the boom for the new third reef. I locate this item at half the price of a new one in the marine exchange store where used marine gear is sold. At the same store I also find a commercial gaff hook/club deal for killing the huge fish I'll catch on our vacation in Barkley Sound.

I wash our hard dinghy, SHOESTRING, first spraying off the garden of green grass and slime that has grown on it in the last six months while sitting in the water near our boat. Then I use a rag to scrub the dinghy with rubbing compound, back and forth, over and over, after which I polish it with a clean rag and a combination cleaner and wax, again rubbing back and forth, over and over. After a few hours of work the dinghy looks brand new. Tom hoists the thing onto his back and carries it up toward the main float. He doesn't want me to help, but the show is so good that I follow him—a dinghy-backed bird with dirty white deck shoes walking up the dock. Half way up to Gate 3 he stops and ties SHOESTRING onto the middle shelf of a three-tiered dinghy rack. Since seagulls roost and do their toilet on the top dinghies, and dogs lift their legs on the bottom dinghies, SHOESTRING will be safe during its stay in the middle. We'll use our inflatable dinghy while we're on vacation.

The morning after cleaning the dinghy I awake with severe pain in my left shoulder. I can't turn my head. I am disabled and it feels like a large animal, one with pliers for teeth, is trying to pick me up by my neck and shoulders. My local chiropractor is able to fix the problem.

Carol Hasse calls to say our sail is ready. After work on Friday, we head for Port Townsend via a ferry from Whidbey Island. We take our bikes on the ferry instead of our Bronco because ferries always have room for bikes. It's also cheaper. We pick up the sail in Port Townsend and purchase hanks and rings that Tom will sew onto the re-cut sail. He wants to practice the sail repair skills he learned at Carol's workshop in the spring. After writing a sizable check for the work on the sail and the additional materials, we head back to the ferry terminal with the huge orange sail bag tied on my bike rack.

During the week before we leave for our vacation, Tom spends the evenings sewing hanks on the jib. A hank is like a monster version of the eye hook on the end of a dog's leash, and our jib will have 10 or 12 hanks. When these hanks are clipped onto the forestay they will slide easily up the wire as the sail is hoisted. It takes Tom about 45 minutes to sew on a hank, during which time he drifts into some sort of alpha state. Sail work is like meditation for him. This is good, especially since we've been in such a frenzy trying to finish all the work on the boat before we leave, and before our funds run out.

The morning before we leave for our vacation the rigger comes by to do the final tightening on the new rigging. He also presents his bill—$280 over estimate, including an additional $70 to remove and re-install standing rigging. As I struggle to write out the six-figure amount on the check, including the cents, after we'd already paid $500 up front, I tell the rigger, "I guess I'd better learn to write big checks if we're going to have a sailboat."

"Well, you know what the letters B.O.A.T. stand for, don't you?" he says.

"No, please tell me."

"Bring On Another Thousand," he says, laughing.

"That's a funny one, all right," I say politely. When he leaves I hear him, still chuckling, as he makes his way up the dock with the last of my inheritance. At least now that the low-balance indicator light is blinking on our checkbook, I won't be writing any more six-digit checks.

It's time to get excited about our trip. Yet I feel apprehensive, as if I'm going into a hospital for surgery instead of on vacation. What am I afraid of? Just being cold, scared, and seasick. I'm also concerned that I'm not ready, that I won't know how to do some sailing task quickly enough, a task that could save our lives. That's all. I live such an ambivalent life—always going along with something, waiting for the big payoff. But I guess it will be good to leave, to finally go to Barkley Sound. I hope we survive this Graveyard of the Pacific so we can get back home to our slip, and I can kick back and read another good book.

25

SAILING THE GRAVEYARD

Finally, we're on our cruise shaking down. After one last trip to West Marine for more hose clamps, we leave our slip at 6:00 p.m. on the Thursday evening before the Fourth of July. We even remembered to untie all the lines from the dock before taking off. Things are looking good. After sailing for a couple of hours in a five-knot wind past the sailboat races in Bellingham Bay, where the crew of one boat points at our bumpers flying in the breeze, the wind deserts us and we turn on the diesel engine. Tom sets up our autohelm, good old Magellan, to steer the boat. Our goal is Spencer Spit on Lopez Island.

The engine drones on at six knots, not quite jogging speed. Motorsailing is about as exciting to me as plowing a field in a straight line on a quarter section, but soon I'm rescued by a glorious sunset. Oranges, fuchsias, lavenders, and pinks reflect off the top of each wavelet between the boat and the sunset. Off the other side of the boat, the water reflects the sky in all the colors of an oil slick—greasy lavenders, steel blues, hints of orange and pink like abalone shell. I gape at the water and the sunset. Slowly, slowly, the water rises up and swallows the sunset whole.

Finally, at midnight, we arrive at Spencer Spit. With the aid of a gibbous moon and our searchlight we weave our way through a maze of boats, some with no anchor lights. All the mooring buoys are taken. I don't see well at night and have zero depth perception, but Tom confidently snakes THE SHOE between two moored boats and heads for the spit. As instructed, I take the helm and proceed, while he poises himself near the anchor at the bow. Just before we crash into land, Tom drops anchor and the boat stops. After we smile up at the moon for a few minutes, it's time to go below to crawl into the V-berth.

Exhausted after our late night arrival and from weeks of preparing the boat for the trip, we sleep late the next morning. Tom charts our course for the day, and we leave at 11:45 a.m. for Port Angeles on the Olympic Peninsula, 50 nautical miles (nm) to the southwest, across the Strait of Juan de Fuca.

At the end of a cold day of little wind or incident, we arrive at the Port Angeles city dock. I'm wearing several layers of clothing, including an olive-green rain poncho and my safety harness/lifejacket. I leap without grace off the boat onto the dock. With so many clothes on, I discover I cannot bend over far enough to wrap the bowline on a cleat to stop the boat before it crashes into the pilings. My task is urgent. In order to do it in the timely manner called for by the captain, I ignore the onlookers and flop onto the wet dock in some seagull droppings next to the cleat, wrap the line, and bring the boat to a halt, like I'm roping a calf.

After removing our foul-weather gear and safety harnesses, Tom and I walk hand in hand up the dock past families catching squid. The squid are about five inches long, thick and round like slugs, like the way I felt a few minutes ago lying next to the cleat.

"Do you sell the squid to fishermen?" I ask two young boys.

"Oh, no. We just gut them and fry them. Taste like big fat French fries."

The city dock is not very protected from the wind and waves, and all night long our boat rolls wildly back and forth. In the morning we leave Port Angeles in light rain and almost no wind. The Olympic Mountains in Olympic National Park occupy the town's backyard, but we never see them because of low clouds. We motor out of the harbor and head toward Neah Bay, the north westernmost town in the continental U.S. We turn on both the Loran and the radar unit. Today we can expect to encounter our first ocean swells.

At about 10:30 Tom tries to raise the mainsail and discovers that the halyard is caught in something high up inside the mast. He decides that if he makes some adjustments to the lines we can use the spinnaker halyard to raise the mainsail. This requires that we relocate the spinnaker halyard to the other side of the spreader. We duct-tape and tie our two boat hooks together to make a long handle, then Tom climbs up onto the mast. As THE SHOE drifts aimlessly, out of gear, rolling in the huge sea ripples, he stands on the winches and cleats. This doesn't strike me as safe, yet I can tell he's enjoying himself. He has something to fix. He places the bundled end of the spinnaker halyard on top of the boat hook and lifts it up to the mast spreader. After several tries, he's able to nudge the halyard off the boathook and over to the aft side of the spreader.

Both sails are up now, mostly for show. As we regain our course and motorsail toward Neah Bay, the ocean rolls toward us like a giant green washboard. We can no longer see the shore of the Olympic Peninsula to port or the edge of Vancouver Island to starboard. Our view now is only water and low clouds. Magellan steers a course of 270 degrees, making his cricket noises, as we eat our lunch of beans, rice and muffins. When I made the muffins earlier I managed to spill honey, flour, and grated carrots all over the galley. The batter was too runny and flowed across the top of the muffin tin, then scorched, causing the smoke alarm to go off. Sometimes when you're sailing you have to make your own excitement.

"THE SHOE acts like Free Willy on her way to the ocean," Tom says.

I believe Tom is the one who feels like Free Willy. He strolls to the bow of the boat to watch the ripples roll toward him. In a few minutes two porpoises appear and leap along the bow wave, alternating sides, as they escort us into the Pacific.

"I like it out here," Tom keeps saying, glancing up from the navigation book he's now reading in the cockpit.

"It's not too bad," I say, yawning yet again.

It feels like we'll never reach Neah Bay, or anywhere. But at least we aren't seasick. We've been taking ginger pills for days, and we're each wearing acupressure wristbands and half a prescription patch behind an ear, like aliens.

At 7:00 p.m. we arrive at Neah Bay to a harbor bustling with fishing boats. No signs tell visitors where to moor so we tie up in a vacant slip near the busy fish-cleaning station. A small boat with two fishermen pulls in next to us.

"Looks like a lot of fishing going on around here, and catching, too," I say. "What were you guys fishing?"

"Halibut."

"Catch any?"

"Oh, a couple. We were just fishing for the fun of it. A few days ago a young woman caught a 62-pound halibut. She and her husband were here on their honeymoon. Husband didn't catch anything. He said she always outfishes him."

"Maybe that's why he married her," I say.

We walk to the office of Big Makah Moorage, off the main dock to the right, and pay $22.50 for the night (with no services). At that price we decide to move to a slip closer to shore, one that doesn't smell so fishy.

It's the Fourth of July, after all, even if it's cloudy, drippy, and 40° F. We take a walk along Main Street, the highway next to the waterfront, to see the sights of Neah Bay. On our walk we find low clouds, fog, drizzle, loose dogs (big, Montana-sized dogs), trailer houses, commercial fishing boats that have seen better days, and signs advertising bait for sale. Everywhere we go we smell fish. Fireworks pop and boom out over the bay and, thanks to the beans we ate for lunch, we contribute heartily to the fireworks.

Protected as the harbor is behind a high jetty, THE SHOE is so still in the night it's like we're up on blocks. No noises disturb us—not even the squawking of seagulls.

We leave Neah Bay at 8:45 a.m. on course to Bamfield, propelled forward once again by the iron spinnaker. After we clear the entrance we are greeted by our first *real* ocean swells, four to five feet waves rolling toward us. THE SHOE moves up and down, up and down, and sometimes side to side. Soon we'll be away from the sight of land. What will it be like out there?

A slight wind is now just off our bow, so Tom puts up the jib and the mainsail, with the third reef, to stabilize the boat and possibly increase our speed. What we're doing, of course, is called "slogging to windward," but you can't sail to Barkley Sound any other way but west into the prevailing winds. We could tack back and forth, not using the engine, and eventually get there. But we're on a tight schedule.

Magellan is steering while Tom cranks on lines using various winches to trim the sails just right, to gain another fraction of a knot. I'm reading in the cockpit. Every few minutes I survey the void of air and water to see if any manmade objects have ventured near. I look down through the open companionway to the green radar screen, then at the Loran to see if we're on course and how long it will take us to reach Bamfield. One time the Loran says five hours and one minute, and a while later it says five hours and thirty-six minutes. It does that. A huge rogue wave, maybe six feet high, just came and went, and THE SHOE shrugged it off. Good boat, good.

Tom heaves-to for practice, and so I can go below to the toilet without performing ride-em-cowboy on the toilet seat. While we're hove-to, the boat is as calm and quiet as our night at Neah Bay. On my return from the head I glance at the Loran. In the hove-to position it tells me Cape Beale is 99 hours and 26 minutes away.

Here we are on the Pacific Ocean, motorsailing along at three knots across the shipping lanes at the entrance to the Strait of Juan de Fuca, in thick fog. A ship or tanker as big as an island appears on our radar screen and I stare at the green blip until it passes safely behind us. Without the radar unit I'd be terrified. But it isn't raining, I'm not cold, and, so far, I'm all right about *being on the ocean*.

"Here we are on the Pacific Ocean," Tom says. "Isn't it wonderful?" He blabbers on about it several times, until I think about the big empty, the two-thirds of the globe that are blue, and the fact that I'm not on one of those other, more familiar, colors like green or brown. No, I haven't been kidnapped. I remind myself of this so I won't feel like the spoon the dish ran away with. In spite of these mental gymnastics, I begin to cry.

After my tears dry, Tom says again, "I sure like it out here."

"It's okay," I reply.

A cormorant flies past low, lost behind a wave, then visible again like a crop duster in the hills. We see hundreds of birds on the water, the size and shape of pigeon guillemots. What are they doing out here? A string of them appears off to starboard, like the twenty-mule team I watched on Death Valley Days in the fifties.

We are now officially in the Graveyard of the Pacific over Swiftsure Bank, a shallow underwater shelf (the chart shows 32 fathoms, or 192 feet). This is where waves can stack up, get mean and cause ships to sink. But the ocean is calm today. On these long passages of six to nine hours, food is my favorite diversion from the droning engine, the tedium and confinement. I search out snacks below deck and bring leftover marshmallows back up to the cockpit. Tom is reading. I put a marshmallow in each cheek, like a gopher. When Tom looks up at me I cross my eyes and smile. He is not surprised.

Where's a whale when you need one? They say thousands of gray whales migrate through here between late February and May, and about 40 remain year round. A couple of hundred orca whales are supposed to patrol the British Columbia coastline, too. I'd like to see one; right now would be a good time.

We finally pass Pachena Point and Seabird Rocks. The Graveyard is a peaceful place. At last we change course at Cape Beale and head north up Imperial Eagle Channel toward Bamfield.

At Bamfield we tie up to the dock in front of the general store on the west side of Bamfield Inlet. To check in with Canadian customs we are told to call an 888 number posted in a phone booth near the store. When Tom calls, a female customs agent answers and he reads her the boat's documentation number and name, our names and birth dates.

Then he says, "We're leaving Bamfield tomorrow for the Broken Group Islands."

"You know, we should rename them," she replies. "They sound like a 12-step group that didn't make it."

We leave the dock at the general store to find the government docks a little farther up the inlet. "You can't miss them," someone has assured us.

But no signs tell us where they are, and every single building has its own dock. I squat at the bow doing my hood ornament imitation,

ready to quickly affix the bowline to one cleat or the other. Tom motors toward a dock near shore, where I spot a small white sign.

"It says it's only one meter deep there," I yell over the engine
noise.

Tom nods, smiles, and continues to steer the boat, with its 5'6"
draft, toward shore and the dock where the water is only three feet
deep.

"Where are you going?" I shout.

Suddenly he notices the depth meter and guns the engine in reverse. Before he's able to turn back into the channel, the stern of our
boat comes within inches of a huge fishing boat. At times like these,
while I'm having a nervous breakdown, Tom acts mysteriously calm
and grins like a two-year old filling his pants.

"Didn't you hear me say one meter?" I yell in my worst fishwife
voice. "Why did you keep going?"

"Oh, no," he says calmly. "I didn't hear you say that." I know he's
made the decision not to add to my hysteria.

We're finally tied up among a dozen or so fishing boats at a government dock on the east side of the inlet. Bamfield is sometimes
called the Venice of Vancouver Island because Bamfield Inlet separates the west side of town from the east side, like a canal. We were
told at the general store that when residents or visitors want to cross
the inlet they use a dinghy, catch a water taxi, or bum a ride. Tom in-
flates our rubber dinghy. We row back across to the west shore to walk
on the boardwalk and poke our noses into the shops along the way.

Soon we're strolling along the boardwalk. We pass several cottages, each with its own boardwalk attached to the main walkway and
a wooden ramp extending down to a private dock. We pass a small
clapboard outpost hospital. The path continues over a trail of buttons
(yes, buttons), past a cappuccino stand to the Outport Art Gallery,
where area artists show their work. We continue on the trail through
dense forest, past wild roses pinker and sweeter-smelling than any
I've ever seen, then back to the boardwalk and the general store.
Geraniums, petunias, and lobelia bloom profusely in boxes along the
boardwalk.

In the morning all the fishing boats are gone. When we prepare to leave the dock for a marina to refuel before crossing the inlet, a distinguished-looking gentleman asks if he can catch a ride to the other side. At the marina, while Tom fills the diesel tank, buys ice for our icebox, and tops off the main water tank, our passenger helps me pick out a fishing lure and advises which of my three poles to use. On the ride across the inlet to the other side he tells me his name is Bristol Foster. He's a Canadian wildlife ecologist who films documentaries worldwide and is in Bamfield visiting his son, a salmon fishing guide. I ask if he goes fishing with his son and he tells me yes, often, and they always catch their limit.

While we're at the post office next to the general store, a huge Huey helicopter—thundering, exciting and bright red—lands nearby on the Coast Guard lawn. A young man tells me the Coast Guard works with Parks Canada and law enforcement agencies and that the Coast Guard also trains people to do rescues, which he says are frequent off Cape Beale.

"In the Graveyard of the Pacific?" I say, knowingly.

"That's what they call it. We lose a couple of people every year out there," he replies.

Today the weather is warm and sunny. Tom and I leave the boat tied up and hike to Brady's Beach, a 20-minute stroll through cedar, hemlock, ferns, alder, birch, salal and moss to a lovely sand beach covered with shells and driftwood logs. Rock pillars, stacks, and stunted trees jut from the beach into Barkley Sound. The trail to Brady's Beach is one of several trails in the Bamfield area, including the famous West Coast Trail.

That afternoon we leave for the Broken Group Islands. As we motor across Imperial Eagle Channel I troll, hoping to catch a salmon. Our 1:20,000-scale chart of the Broken Group shows our carefully drawn route through islands, islets and rocks to an anchorage at Nettle Island. As we approach the islands, however, we cannot see an opening where one is clearly indicated on the chart. In front of us we see only a wall of land. To make matters worse, fog begins to roll toward us from the ocean.

Tom slows the engine to a crawl and goes below to recalculate our course. Soon he's back up in the cockpit, says it looks right. While the boat is still going slowly I reel in the fishing line, cranking hard, wondering why it's so difficult and why I put out so much line. What I reel in is a shiny fish about 14" long with big bug eyes and a tiny tail. It's the biggest fish I've ever caught, but what is it? In the Sport Fishing Guide that came with my three-day fishing license, we find a picture that matches. It's a mackerel, not usually caught in these waters except for El Niño years.

We put the fish in a bucket of seawater and proceed to grope our way toward the mass of land, motoring slowly, hoping for a miracle. Our eyes are focused intently on the wall of trees. Finally we see the hint of an opening where one edge of trees appears to be slightly in front of the other. As we creep toward it, the channel opens up. Now we must stay carefully on course to avoid the submerged rocks shown on the chart. We really know how to have fun. After three days of motorsailing we finally enter the Broken Group, where a long passage is half a mile and where, if your chart work is sloppy, you can high-center on a rock or end up with tree branches in your cockpit.

We snake our way into the anchorage at Nettle Island, not far from a sailboat from Portland, THE ENTERPRISE, and the park ranger's float cabin. The three men on the other boat have a rubber dinghy with a small, quiet motor. They stop to say hello on their way to set out crab pots. We brought only oars with our rubber dinghy and Tom gets blisters when we row very far. With so many nooks and crannies to explore here it would be smart to have a canoe or sea kayak, or at least a motor for our dinghy.

I've read that native Indians inhabited these islands at least 4,000 years before the arrival of Europeans in the 1770s. They gathered shellfish, trapped herring and anchovies, and hunted whales and sea lions in the waters of Barkley Sound. Many islands, including Nettle, show remains of middens, fish traps, canoe runs, shellfish processing areas and defensive sites.

We're now snug in the quiet embrace of islets and trees. Instead of going ashore we dine on mackerel and enjoy a sunset of orange and pink, framed by rocky islets. The trees on shore at Nettle, mostly cedar and hemlock, appear to be pruned at a perfectly even height above waterline, like a browse line under leafy trees in a pasture. We hear a bird that sounds like a chickadee. Eagles wheel elegantly over-head repeating their singular echoing sound. According to our cruis-ing guide, Barkley Sound is blessed with one of the highest concentrations of bald eagles in North America. Tucked in as we are against Nettle Island with dozens of islands between us and the ocean, no winds touch us. THE SHOE is motionless all night.

In the morning we chart a course to the Pinkerton Islands, a small archipelago between the Broken Group and Vancouver Island, located outside the boundary of the Pacific Rim National Park. We retrace our route out of our anchorage, enter Peacock Channel, and motor toward the Pinkertons. Again, panic. As we approach the Pinkertons the rocks and trees present a solid wall with no entrance.

"Drive around in circles out here while I go below and recheck my figures," the captain says.

After I make several loops Tom comes back up to the cockpit. "I know where we are. Just a few degrees sure make a difference."

We motor toward the mass of land again. Only when we are practically on top of the opening do we find access. Careful maneu-vering brings us to a quiet anchorage in 10 meters of water. Although the Pinkerton Islands are privately owned, we see only two discreet cabins. It feels like we're in a secret hiding place, a wilderness among dozens of tiny islands. In every direction, trees lean, reach, arch and dip—their image reflected in the calm surface. We're surrounded by views of sunlight shimmering on water, yellow algae on exposed rocks at low tide, the nearby mountain peaks of Vancouver Island. We hear only the chittering of eagles.

From the Pinkertons we weave a circuitous route through the Broken Group Islands to Clarke Island. Trusting our navigation skills more, we pass within spitting distance of dozens of islands. These is-lands in the Outer Broken Group are dramatic, with their sea caves, seabird rookeries, wave-battered bluffs, and trees shaped by ocean winds.

I troll the entire way between the Pinkertons and Clarke Island, catching only kelp. At Clarke we anchor in a cove about 50 feet off-shore in five meters, not far from a rock bluff archeologists call a de-fensive site. Villagers on the island once found refuge behind these sites when other natives attacked them. Since leaving Bamfield we've seen only a few other boats, mostly off in the distance. Now a sleek Canadian sailboat arrives in the anchorage, drops anchor and rows to shore to tie a stern line to a tree.

We row to shore, too. As the nose of our dinghy touches land, a sudden growl like the MGM lion close up startles me. The sound comes from a blow hole in the rocks where air is trapped when water surges in, then growls when it's released. We secure the dinghy to a log and follow the trail through a rain forest of giant cedars, hemlocks and spruce trees. The evening sun slants through drooping, moss-covered branches as we walk past several kayakers, resting and talking. At the northwest shore of Clarke Island are dozens of islets with wind-sculpted, cloud-pruned vegetation in grotesque, even humorous, shapes. A knob of vegetation on one islet is a fat chick. Other trees are slender and straggly, in a permanent lean away from the prevailing wind. We climb over drift logs, pick up shells, take too many pictures. Back at the boat the full moon rises in a sky streaked with peach.

The next morning I set the fishing pole up in its holder with a blue squiggly lure for catching bottom fish. The boat is rocking gently side to side, jigging the line for me. Later, with no fish to clean, I lay the course that will take us safely to Effingham Island, the largest island in the Broken Group. I route us around to the east of the island near Meares Bluff, where salmon are supposed to run. We'll arrive there at the exact time the Tide and Bite Guide says is optimum for catching fish. I'll troll back and forth. With any luck, we'll have barbecued salmon steaks for dinner.

This evening we're anchored in Effingham Bay, dining on spaghetti with pasta sauce and tofu. Fishing didn't pan out. Seven other boats are anchored here, including THE ENTERPRISE from Portland. We haven't seen this many boats all week.

The weather in Barkley Sound has been sunny and warm; our last day in the Broken Group is no exception. We spend the afternoon ashore on Effingham, hiking under drooping, tuberous limbs through old growth rain forest. We crawl over mossy logs on the trail that leads to a former Indian village site and a protected cove with a sand and shell beach. We follow along the beach, climbing over granite boulders and drift logs as we make our way south toward Meares Bluff in search of a sea cave we've read about. When we reach the cave the receding tide is still too high to enter it.

Tom, wearing his rubber boots, makes it into the cave first and calls me to join him. I step over sea stars, orange starfish, and other curious creatures in the wet cavities of the rocks. After removing my tennis shoes I wade up to my knees through the icy water to the higher, drier sandy floor of the cave, and we walk about 75 feet into the cool, dark, dripping cavern to a row of drift logs. We turn around in time to see two kayakers paddle past the cave entrance. They do not see the cave or us as we snap their picture.

All too soon we must leave Effingham Bay for home and reality. At 4:15 a.m. the next morning, we pull up our anchor under a perfectly full moon. Several carefully navigated courses and 45 minutes later we clear the entrance to the bay and head toward Cape Beale. A few minutes later, when I'm at the helm and Tom is below deck in the galley making oatmeal, he hears the engine change its tune. The V-belt has broken. It couldn't have happened at a better time—now while we're safely clear of all obstacles, in very little wind. In thirty minutes Tom has a new belt installed and we ghost slowly along, sails up, as I steer us toward Cape Beale, the Graveyard of the Pacific, and home.

26

SHOE REPAIRS

We return from Barkley Sound to a mailbox overflowing with bills and a notice from our bank of $64.50 in overdraft charges. I immediately call the bank to discuss the problem. I eat dirt, but I stop short of telling the truth: our boat ate all our money.

The vacation has ended and we'll be living on a diet of beans and rice until our funds recover. And now Tom reminds me that summer is nearly over. I've always found that anticipating summer is a lot like waiting at the station to catch a train. You stand and wait, checking your watch off and on, and then the train, a streamliner, roars past without stopping.

"This nice weather isn't going to last," Tom says. "We have to remove the toerails and the stanchions so we can re-bed them and stop all that rainwater from leaking into the lockers."

Three long strips of gray, weathered teak toerail trim each side of THE SHOE. We must remove them, scrape their undersides, sand them down to raw teak and apply Cetol before re-bedding them. Tom assembles screwdrivers, chisels, hammers and a small crowbar. First he'll remove the front starboard rail.

"I'm afraid that when I lift off these rails I'll find we need a whole new boat," he says as he begins to unscrew the first rail. "No telling what's under here."

What he discovers is that the hull and deck joint are separated in the areas where the boat leaks. We investigate below deck in the V-berth behind the wall panels and find several dislodged wooden supports on both sides of the bow.

"The bow flexes," Tom says. "It's been flexed enough to knock out these supports. I'd say someone slammed into a dock pretty hard."

"This would have happened before we purchased the boat, right?" I say.

"Of course."

"Does this mean we need a new boat?" I ask hopefully.

"Oh, no. It's just a good thing we're re-bedding the toerails. It'll take some time but we can fix the problem."

Using a scraper, I remove the dried adhesive—the adhesive of choice during the geologic era that was 1972, the year THE SHOE was assembled. The stuff has formed a metamorphic layer on the underside of the rail. I scrape for hours, then find Band-Aids to stop the flow of blood on my cut, bleeding hands. Next I sand the teak rail with our macho, noisy orbital sander while Tom attempts to remove the mid-section starboard toerail. This rail has a metal track on it with dozens of screws and bolts holding it to the deck. The nuts securing the bolts are down inside the boat, of course, in the pilot berth, the cupboards and lockers. After removing all the fasteners, it takes both of us to wrench this section of rail and track off the boat.

I resume sanding. Our middle-aged bachelor neighbor brings a young woman aboard his boat. He does not introduce her as they walk past, step over the orange electrical cord on the dock, and disappear into his boat. She's possibly old enough for college. For the next two hours I wonder what the bachelor and his guest are doing, and whether the sound of the sander just inches away affects the quality of their experience. The workings of my imagination and the activities of seagulls entertain me while I work.

G-east dock, where we're located, has only one row of outside slips parallel to the jetty. A hulking boathouse the size of an airplane hangar abuts the inside edge of the dock, and because its roof is relatively flat the seagulls use it as a rookery. Today fluffy brown baby seagulls cheep loudly and incessantly at their mothers for food. The adult seagulls launch off the top of the boathouse to find food, bombing my hat, the teak rail, and the rickety old steps I'm using as a workbench. When their droppings hit the water between me and the bow of our neighbor's boat, I feel especially lucky.

Seagull foraging goes like this: once a seagull finds a piece of food, all the other seagulls chase it and try to take it away. In the aerial chase and squabble above the boats, the seagull with the food usually ends up dropping it. No one gets a bite. I've noticed, however, that when one of them scores a starfish, all the other seagulls sit around watching and laughing.

During the second week after returning from our vacation Tom asks me to stop at the harbor office to request an inside slip on another dock. While we've enjoyed the relative privacy and small amount of foot traffic past our boat, Tom wants an easier slip to exit and enter when it's windy. We also want a slip farther away from the boathouses and the seagulls that live on top of them. Because THE SHOE is narrower in the beam than most sailboats, we're offered several choices. We move to a slip next to our friend, Jeff, on G-west.

At our new location we can still hear seagulls squawking, but the noise level is greatly reduced since the rookeries are farther away. We now hear strange and mysterious new harbor noises. One of the sounds seems to be the dock rubbing against a piling as the tide changes. Tom says the noise reminds him of the sound in his head when he used to grind his teeth. Another sound made by a nasal female from the fish processing plant on shore drifts out across this end of the harbor.

"Don Riley, please report to the crab house. Don Riley, please report to the crab house." These and other messages sing out across the boats and into Bellingham Bay from early morning until late at night.

Hundreds of boats line both sides of G-west and a steady stream of foot traffic flows past our boat. Neither are we lonely as we resume work on the toerail refinishing/re-bedding project. 'Tis the season for boating in the harbor. Sanders hum, teak dust flies, people caulk and stain and wash their boats. It takes a village.

At our new location we're fortunate enough to have the only bench right in front of our slip. This gives me a solid surface for the sanding that makes my hands numb and the scraping that keeps them bloody. A person who suffers a repetitive stress injury from eating popcorn should not be doing this kind of work. She should be hiking. We have an unobstructed view of Mount Baker from our cockpit. Sometimes I stare at this crystal white volcanic peak for long periods, and think about leaving. We never go hiking any more. All we do is work on the boat.

"You have such a good attitude," Tom says at such times. "I really appreciate your help."

I wish he wouldn't watch me work.

For weeks it doesn't rain. Thanks to a high pressure system, the weather is perfect for working outdoors. One Sunday it's downright scorching hot. We borrow a huge blue tarp from Mark and Lisa and string it up between Jeff's boat and ours for some shade. We're toiling away under our makeshift awning when Jeff arrives home from church with a family. We try to put them all to work, without success. Instead we untie our tarp and help cast them off for a Sunday afternoon sail, then we take a needed break and drive to the supermarket parking lot to hide from the boat.

One week night, in spite of the fact that Tom has to get up at 4:00 a.m., we stay up until after 11:00 p.m. caulking and re-bedding a mid-section toerail and its track. During this time the temperature drops nearly 30 degrees. We bundle up and keep working, though, because once you apply caulk you have to finish what you start. First we caulk both the teak rail and the receiving deck surface, which Tom has sanded smooth. Then we screw the teak rail down with dozens of screws as white caulk oozes out the sides. The rail is straight and the boat is curved, of course, which requires that I push the rail in toward the boat a fraction of an inch at a time as Tom screws it down. Then we affix the metal track onto the toerail in much the same way.

Our social life has picked up since moving over to G-west. We receive lots of advice and encouragement from neighbors and passers-by. Steve, a liveaboard bachelor from the sailboat across the dock, comes over this evening carrying a sandwich. He sits down on the edge of our dock to eat and talk and watch us work.

"First thing I did when I got my boat was to rip off all the teak and slap down some aluminum strips," Steve says, chewing a mouthful of sandwich. "Didn't want to spend all *my* time sanding teak."

He's sitting on the dock a little too close and slightly in the way. Tom's bent figure hovers over our guest as he slowly moves along glueing and screwing the rail and metal track onto our boat, while I hold each rail and nudge it into place.

"That teak rail isn't seated properly there," Steve says, his mouth full. He points to a spot Tom just screwed down.

"Thanks," Tom says, re-tightening the screws in that area.

Steve takes another bite of his sandwich and says, "Which end of the track are you planning to put the slides on?"

After a long silence Tom says, "I'm going to put them on up here at the bow end."

Steve finally leaves to sit in the cockpit of his own boat.

Mark and Lisa come by with a baby seagull in a box, looking for someone to adopt it. They've been feeding it with a turkey baster. Seagulls are clumsy when they first learn to fly, and this one had fallen from the sky into the water where it wasn't welcome. Some grownup seagulls had attacked it. Mark rescued the pathetic youth from a grisly death.

Before proceeding with the next step of our chore, Tom admits to me that he had forgotten all about the slides on the track. He now removes the bolt at the bow end of the track so he can put on the slides, glancing over at Steve's boat to make sure he isn't watching. Next Tom cleans out the cockpit lazarettes and crawls into them one at a time. While I grip a monster screwdriver and hold the head of each bolt securely, Tom tightens the nuts on the bolts underneath with a ratchet. Afterwards he helps me pry my fingers off the screwdriver.

For several weeks we continue to work on the boat. Another project needing attention is our main halyard, which is still stuck on something inside the top of the mast, the same line that became caught on the second day of our vacation. A friend Tom works with, a former rock climber, comes to help him levitate up the mast in the bosun's chair using climbing gear. He and Tom take turns going up the mast, even though they joke about how this activity is threatening their manhood. After determining that the steel cable portion of the halyard is lodged between its pulley and the mast, they tinker and pound on it for a couple hours, without success. A few days later another neighbor, Wayne, goes up the mast to see what he can do. He pounds on the problem for a couple of hours and the pinched cable finally breaks free. Now we'll be able to use the main halyard to raise the mainsail instead of the spinnaker halyard. A few days later, however, Tom tests the main halyard and it jams again. The pulley must be replaced—an expensive, special-order item for our boat. Installing the new pulley will also require that we have the boat dismasted again, to the tune of several hundred dollars. We'll continue to use the spinnaker halyard to hoist the mainsail.

Now that the toerails have all been scraped, sanded, Cetoled and re-installed Tom decides to remove all the stanchions and lifelines. With drill in hand, he then prepares to drill out the old screw holes that held the stanchions in place. I scrunch myself into the stuffy, dank sauna of a chain locker and hold a yogurt container under the stanchion base holes to catch waste while Tom, up on the deck, drills out the old holes.

"My wife's in the chain locker," I hear him say to someone.

"Now is not a good time for you to brag," I yell through the fiberglass deck in my mean and ugly voice. "It's hotter than hell in here."

After he drills out the holes I sand the under surface of each one, as instructed, then wipe it down with acetone, apply duct tape and seal each hole carefully. This way when Tom fills the holes with epoxy from above, the stuff won't run down and leak all over everything. My job is important, because if the epoxy leaks into the chain locker it might glue the anchor rode into a rock-hard glop. Tom wouldn't be able to pull it out of the chain locker the next time he tries to anchor the boat. When the epoxy dries Tom will drill out smaller holes so that when the stanchions are re-bedded these important deck features will be more secure.

After I finish my assignment in the chain locker I leave Tom to pour his epoxy and I return to the bench on the dock to sand some trim blocks. A woman in her early sixties stops to talk to me and tells me that she and her husband, a retired airline pilot, recently sailed straight through from New Zealand.

"It's too cold here," she says. "We sailed naked most of the way from New Zealand. It was great. Finally had to put some clothes on as we got closer to Washington. I've been cold ever since." I'm jealous. I'd enjoy being cold right now myself.

"Didn't you get scared out there?" I ask.

"Well, when there's reason to be afraid you don't have *time*. At other times there's simply no need to be afraid."

"I'll think about that," I reply.

A few minutes later when I climb down the companionway, I manage to step onto the pump handle of the epoxy container. In my surprise I kick over a nearby yogurt-container of screws, nuts, washers and small backing plates. Some items end up in the spilled epoxy; others simply vanish. I clean up the mess and leave for West Marine with the Visa card to buy replacements for the items that disappeared into the bilge.

When I return from my errand Tom reports that in my absence he heard someone on the other side of the jetty cry "Help! Help!"

"Another guy down the dock heard it, too," Tom says. "He dropped his paintbrush, hopped in his dinghy and rowed like crazy to the other side of the jetty. I called the Coast Guard on Channel 16 and they put out a radio call to anyone boating in the vicinity who could help. After that I monitored the radio and heard that a man had fallen overboard, but someone rescued him and saved his boat from crashing into the jetty."

Overnight the epoxy cures rock-hard in the stanchion base holes. Using a grinding wheel on the drill, I smooth both the stanchion bases and the receiving deck surfaces. Tom drills new holes and installs the stanchion bases, then repositions the stanchions and lifelines.

Slumped on the bench in front of the boat, we gaze at our floating home. The teak now looks loved and cared for instead of old and gray, even though white caulk still oozes out all along the teak rails and tracks. But I've had about all of this boat I can stand for a while. It's time to celebrate with a night at a bed and breakfast, somewhere way out in the woods, where I can drink champagne while immersed in the only water around—a huge claw-foot bathtub filled with bubbles.

"Finished at last," Tom says. "Now let's go sailing."

27

AS *THE SHOE* SAILS

We leave the harbor in the evening. At 1.8 knots we sail along even more slowly than we walk on the docks, but we don't care. This evening of Labor Day weekend is a warm one, and we aren't working on the boat. I raise the head sail, pulling the jib sheet instead of the halyard. Nothing happens, of course, until I pull the halyard. Later when we tack I pull one of the two jib sheets again. This is the correct sheet to pull, except that first you have to uncleat and loosen the jib sheet on the other side of the cockpit. Since we haven't sailed for a few weeks I'll probably have to relearn everything.

As THE SHOE drifts along in Bellingham Bay in the growing darkness, an evening star appears. Then the full moon begins to rise—at first just a hint of light through the tall firs on Chuckanut Ridge. For the next few minutes the bright gold ball hovers behind the trees. While I stare at the moon it does not appear to move. When I glance away and then look back, though, I can see that the moon has risen slightly. Finally, ever so reluctantly, the tallest fir tree on the ridge lets go of the moon and it floats free of the horizon.

We ghost into Inati Bay under the starry sky and drop our hook. Even more dazzling than the stars overhead are their reflections shimmering on the water's surface.

"Come with me to the bow," Tom whispers. "I want to show you something."

Holding onto the grabrail, I move forward on deck, mesmerized by all the star galaxies flashing in the water. At the bow Tom lifts some slack in the anchor rode and drops it back into the water. The rode shines like a giant glowworm all the way down to the bottom.

The stars in the water are actually glitters of tiny phosphorescent plankton.

After a quiet night we awake to a stunning sunrise. A loon keens the quiet morning stillness. The bird's resonating echo is more refined than a squeal—more like the bugling of a timid elk. The loon is now about seventy-five feet away, and I watch through my binoculars as she rolls over on her side about ninety degrees, like a knockdown. She sticks her port leg straight out of the water to aft, spreading her webbed toes, and preens her belly with her bill. She rolls back upright, rises up on her tail, and vigorously flaps her wings and shakes her head. This shimmy lasts several seconds. She then sits quietly in the water and takes a drink. Following a roll onto her other side, she sticks out her starboard foot and repeats the preening ritual. Watching the loon reminds me of one reason I'm still living on a sailboat. Someday, when most of the repairs on THE SHOE are done, we'll have more time to contemplate moonrises, watch phosphorescent plankton, and attend loon performances.

Tom loves to sail away from an anchorage. In the past I haven't been much help, but it's time to learn. While still at anchor, Tom loosens the main sheet so the boom can swing free while he hoists the mainsail. We each keep track of the swinging boom, so it won't bean either of us in the head. As soon as the wind or the current nudges the boat into a position to tack, Tom weighs anchor. I center the boom by pulling the main sheet, then secure the sheet to a cleat. The mainsail catches the wind and propels us forward toward one of the rock cliffs.

"Let the boat gather some speed before you turn," Tom yells. "Otherwise we won't have enough momentum to keep going after we tack."

I give him the thumbs up signal. We pick up speed.

"Turn now!" he shouts. "What are you trying to do?"

Just before we hit the rocks, I turn the boat smartly through the wind. The second the bow is on the other side of the wind, Tom quickly raises the jib. Now, with both sails up, we're picking up speed toward the rock cliff on the other side of the tiny bay. Another tack, a little sooner this time, and we head out into Bellingham Channel.

Just when I begin to relax and feel pleased with myself, a small powerboat putters across in front of us.

"What should I do?" I yell.

"Don't worry about it. We're the stand on vessel," Tom replies calmly.

Miraculously we miss the powerboat, after the driver throttles up and scoots out of our path. As I sail proudly out into Bellingham Bay, feeling a bit haughty, the wind dies completely. Tom takes the helm and we motor home at six knots with the warm sunshine at our backs. I mend a sleeve on my black turtleneck, push back my cuticles, and suddenly we're approaching the harbor entrance. A huge powerboat roars toward us out of the entrance, veers and misses us by about fifteen feet. Tom turns into the monster wake to take it head on.

After surviving that foolishness, we enter the harbor and Tom asks me to take the helm. Motoring along at our slowest speed always feels a little fast to me, with all those other boats so close.

"I think you're ready to dock the boat," Tom says. "I'll talk you through it."

I've never been able to dock the boat, but today I think I can. Following Tom's directions, I aim toward the bow of SHAWMANEE, across the channel from the back end of our slip. Two or three slips before ours, I must shift into neutral to slow the boat. This requires that I duck down in the cockpit so I can push the gearshift lever. When I do this, of course, I cannot see where the boat is going. When we're within a few feet of SHAWMANEE, Tom tells me to turn right into our slip and aim for the inside corner.

"You're doing fine," he says.

"If I keep going like this, we'll climb up on top of the dock."

"Just keep going. Otherwise, the boat won't end up close enough."

When we're part way into the slip Tom yells "reverse!" and I squat down quickly to move the gearshift. When I stand up again at the helm, Tom says, "Okay. Now give it some throttle and back all the way out."

When I do this the boat backs out shockingly fast toward SHAW-

MANEE. I crank the wheel just like I'm backing a car out of a parking space, but the boat doesn't turn. As soon as we clear the stern of the boat in the slip next door, I drop down again and push the gearshift forward. We miss SHAWMANEE by several feet and roar toward the harbor entrance. Then I slow and turn the boat in a complete circle in front of several large trawlers tied up at the fish plant, comforted to see they have vehicle tires dangling from all sides for bumpers. I head back toward our slip, repeating my previous performance. This time I don't get close enough to the dock and must back out to try again. By now I don't mind; I'm having fun. On the third try I get the boat close enough for Tom to step off the boat onto the dock with the lines. A perfect docking.

28

TO BE ROOTED IS THE PROPERTY OF VEGETABLES
—AN EPILOGUE

Some mornings when I wake up early and lie in bed I decide, with absolute certainty, that I do not want to live on a sailboat here or anywhere. At such times I know for sure I don't want to go sailing around on a fluid piece of nothing solid that can swallow me whole. Instead, I want to be safely rooted on land. Early in the morning I feel these things with great conviction. I lie in bed thinking back over the past two years, how I escaped my disenchanted life and liquidated my assets to launch off into a romantic new life with my husband on a sailboat. It was a gamble. Yes, the lifestyle has proven to be exotic and stimulating. Then I wonder, how much excitement is too much?

Soon Tom wakes up. We drink coffee and talk about the Caribbean or what to fix next on the boat. It's as if I don't own my ambivalent feelings, as if some fictional character I invented is the one who's confused.

These inner contradictions make me crazy. I've sunk all my savings and my inheritance from Uncle Sam into this boat. And I've worked on the boat so many evenings and weekends that the idea of sailing somewhere exotic has a hold on me. I can't turn back now, I want the payoff. I want to see what the big promise really holds. To learn to sail, to travel by sailboat to the Caribbean, to live in warm sunshine while anchored in bays—is that asking too much of myself?

In an interview, one of my favorite authors, Jamaica Kincaid, talked about life and family and leaving home. "To me," she said, "the truth is that things mean many things at once, all of them opposed to each other, and all of them true." I like this kind of talk; it makes perfectly good sense to me.

It's a good time for me to visit Montana. Maybe I'll think more clearly about my new life after visiting my old life on land.

Finally, after making plans to return to Montana and canceling them twice—in June and again in July—here I am in September on a Greyhound bus between Missoula and Helena. The windows are hazy and bug-spattered and the bus shakes like it's out of alignment, but it feels good to be moving through the sagebrush flats, past grazing cattle, along rivers, and now into the mountains.

During my ten-day trip I stay mostly with Jeff and Lee, who recently moved into a house in East Helena. It's fun to see my son in his first real home. I help cook and clean a little and spend a lot of time reading in the bathtub. On the weekends Jeff and I ride bikes to the store. We also go for a drive in his truck, a 1971 International named *Cornbinder*. The three of us drive up to Rimini, where we see that the brothel sports a new metal roof—bright red, of all colors. On the way home we hike up Lazyman Gulch past yellow aspen trees. At night we watch videos on their large-screen TV.

During the week I take Lee's car and run errands around town. I get a permanent at the beauty college, and visit the Forest Service offices. Everyone is surprised and happy to see me.

"You look ten years younger," Fred says.

"Hi, cutie," someone else says. "How's it going with sailing?"

"Don't ask."

Everyone within earshot guffaws. People seem much happier than when I left a year ago. It feels good to slip back into town and find I haven't been forgotten.

After a week of warm welcomes, big smiles and many hugs I take the bus from Helena to Laurel, Montana, where my sister, Marian, and her son, John, pick me up and take me to Lander, Wyoming. My visit coincides with the one-year anniversary of Marian's brain tumor surgery. Her recovery is nearly 100 per cent. She works full time again, paying off medical bills, and is thankful to be alive. We celebrate the special day by driving the Loop Road over the Wind River Mountains to South Pass City, stopping along the way to hike to Popo Agie Falls (pronounced poh-poh-zha). The weather is perfect as we hike among rock outcrops, past sagebrush and junipers. We sit on boulders in the stream, then hike the rest of the way to view the falls. I can hardly keep up with Marian on the hike, and neither of us can keep up with John, who is Jeff's age. At the end of our day together in the mountains, we arrive home to the smell and taste of fresh bread. Marian had planned this surprise, setting the timer on her bread machine before we left.

All too soon it's time to return to Helena, where I'll spend another day with Jeff and Lee before leaving for Bellingham. Somehow, I've found resolution about my leaving Montana last year—tied up loose ends, put my old life out to pasture. Even though it's hard to leave my family again I'm ready to go home now, to return to Tom and our future on the boat.

As I fly from Missoula to Seattle, watching the clouds scud past the scratched little window, I think about speed. Einstein said *time slows down as speed increases.* I wonder what that means for people sailing along on the ocean at hardly more than a brisk walking pace. And I hope there isn't a reciprocal to what he said, like *time goes faster as speed slows down.*

Back aboard THE SHOE the first thing I do is to conk my head on the hatch cover.

It's cool on the boat. Tom fires up Dick for the first time this fall. He wants to take the chill off the air and reduce the condensation that's beginning to bead up on the walls and ceiling, now that fall is here. Dick's pacemaker groans. After a few minutes, Tom lights a wadded up piece of paper and tosses it into the stove. In about thirty seconds the stove begins to roar. Tom turns on the stove's fan to help move the smoke up the chimney but Dick goes "poof," the cabin smokes up, and the smoke alarm goes off. Tom reaches around the corner and deactivates the shrill, squealing noise.

"Welcome to the 1998-99 heating season," he says.

Soon the excess fuel burns out of Dick and everything quietens down except for the pacemaker, groaning away under the floor panel. Tom lifts the panel, picks up the nearby monster wrench, and whacks the fuel pump. For a few seconds the boat is gloriously quiet, with only Dick purring along, warming the cabin. We step out onto the deck to watch a Technicolor sunset. A great blue heron flies slowly, elegantly, past in front of us, silhouetted against an orange and pink sky until he is lost to view in front of Lummi Island's dark profile.

I'm glad to be home; however, I wake up in the middle of the night feeling convinced, once again, that I do not want to pursue this sailboat lifestyle. I lie awake mentally packing my bags, making preparations to head for higher ground where I can smell wet bark and sagebrush. But I also think about my brave Grandma Meta. During her last visit, in the fall of 1959 when I was in the ninth grade, she told us that Oscar (her son, my uncle) had taken her canasta club for a speedboat ride that summer.

"Oscar drove us around that lake close to shore, slow and pretty," she said. "We're all getting up in years, you know, and he didn't want to scare us. But it was boring as hell. When he brought us back to shore, I stayed on the boat while he helped the old ladies climb out of the boat. He offered me his hand, too, but I said, 'Now Oscar, let's open this thing up and see how fast she'll go.' We roared around that lake spraying water off both sides. I grinned so hard I had to clean the bugs off my teeth when I got home."

One day I had Grandma all to myself for a few minutes in the kitchen on a Sunday afternoon.

"Grandma," I said, "I think I want to be a ballet dancer."

"I believe you could," she said, as she reached into the wood-box for a piece of wood and poked it into the kitchen stove.

"Mom thinks I'm weird because I play classical music on the record player."

Grandma said nothing, so I continued. "And she's mad at me because I bite my fingernails. But I tried and I can't stop."

"Yes you can," she said, looking at me. "Ballet dancers don't bite their nails."

The next day while my sisters and I were at school, Mom and Grandma went to town. After dinner Grandma said to me, "Go look under your pillow."

When I first saw the little flat, black purse I didn't know what it was until I unzipped it and found a manicure set. I never did become a ballet dancer, although I believe I could have, but I never again bit my fingernails. Grandma was killed a few weeks later when the car she was riding in slid off the icy, washboard road on Shingle Mill Hill. It was late at night. When the people she was visiting decided to drive into town to eat, she didn't want to be left behind.

Even though my Grandma Meta lived on farms nearly all her life, had she been offered the opportunity to sail on the ocean she surely would have leaped at the challenge. She loved people and adventure and she didn't want to be left out of the action, not ever. I will continue to seek the unexpected and the contradictory, even if there is only 1/4-inch of fiberglass between me and the ocean. At least we won't be moving so fast that I'll have to scrape bugs off my teeth.

Throughout history women travelers have deliberately courted danger in unconventional and unfamiliar situations. From what I can gather, they had in common the belief that to travel was to be free.

At a reading here in Bellingham, Barbara Hodgson, author of *The Sensualist*, talked about the value of travel. "So it makes you uncomfortable. Sometimes you lose your way and it shakes you up. Travel is good for the senses," she said, then asked us, "Why *not* get lost?"

To be rooted is the property of vegetables. I read that somewhere once, and what it means to me is that it's better to go to sea than to seed.

One sunny fall day as I walk along the main dock I meet a woman on the deck of a large sailboat recently sold by San Juan Sailing.

"You have a nice boat there," I say to her.

"Thank you. They say it's been around the world."

"Well, then it knows the way."

"Maybe so, but I wish I felt more certain about this whole idea," the woman says, shaking her head.

"Let me buy you a cup of coffee," I offer. "We have some things to talk about."